Catering
Start and Run
a Money-Making Business

Judy Richards

D1567684

TAB Books
Division of McGraw-Hill, Inc.
New York   San Francisco   Washington, D.C.   Auckland   Bogotá
Caracas   Lisbon   London   Madrid   Mexico City   Milan
Montreal   New Delhi   San Juan   Singapore
Sydney   Tokyo   Toronto

2 3 4 5 6 7 8 9 0 DOH/DOH 9 9 8 7 6 5 4

Library of Congress Cataloging-in-Publication Data

Richards, Judy.
    Catering : start and run a money-making business / by Judy
Richards.
        p.   cm.
    Includes index.
    ISBN 0-07-052272-3
    1. Caterers and catering. 2. Home-based businesses. I. Title.
TX911.2.R5   1994
642'.4—dc20   94-3959
                                                                CIP

Acquisitions editor: April Nolan
Editorial team: Joanne Slike, Executive Editor
                Susan W. Kagey, Managing Editor
                Marianne Krcma, Book Editor
Production team: Katherine G. Brown, Director
                Tina M. Sourbier, Coding
                Wanda S. Ditch, Desktop Operator
                Kelly S. Christman, Proofreading
                Brenda Wilhide, Computer Illustrator
                Joann Woy, Indexer
Design team: Jaclyn J. Boone, Designer   0522723
                Brian Allison, Associate Designer   TAB1
Cover photograph: Brent Blair, Harrisburg, Pa.

Contents

Acknowledgments

Many leaders in the catering industry have contributed to the completeness of this book. They include Karen Borgan and Jim Bannister of the National Caterers Roundtable Association; Mary Martin and Iris Muckle of the National Restaurant Association; Mindy Schwartz and Traci Osborne of the National Association of Catering Executives; the Society for Foodservice Management; Jim Frost of the Health Division, Oregon Department of Human Resources; Bill Wasserman of the Office of Consumer Advisor, U.S. Department of Agriculture; Scott Vigil of At-Your-Service Software, Inc.; and Don Cozzetti of CEO Software, Inc.

Also helping with the conception and development of this book are Kimberly Tabor, April Nolan, and Stephen Moore of TAB Books/McGraw-Hill, Inc.; Roy L. Fietz and Lori Capps of the Business Development Center at Southwest Oregon Community College; Jim Jackson, George Lord, J. C. Mascari, and Beatrice Dare of the Service Corps of Retired Executives, Portland, Oregon, District Office; Steve Herman, Sandra Thompson, and Ron Hoyt of the Oregon Technology Access Program; Irene Vawter of the Bureau of Consumer Protection, Federal Trade Commission. In addition, the author thanks the U.S. Small Business Administration, Office of Business Development; U.S. Department of Commerce, Office of Business Liaison and Minority Business Development Agency; U.S. Treasury, Internal Revenue Service; and NEBS, Inc.

Business forms in this book were created using PerFORM Forms Designer from Delrina Technology, Inc.

Foreword

Catering: Start and Run a Money-Making Business is "must" reading for anyone seriously considering opening his or her own catering business. Ms. Richards' work is more than a comprehensive "how-to" book; it causes readers to question whether or not they should attempt a start-up business, teaches them how to analyze the market before making the plunge . . . and even warns them why other new catering businesses fail. Once the decision is made, the book is both an excellent guide and a checklist to help new business owners along the way.

I also recommend this book as valuable reading for established caterers. What catering business couldn't stand improvement? The chapters on pricing, getting and keeping good customers, finding and keeping good employees, keeping costs down, reducing risks, solving business problems, and ensuring long-term success contain sound business advice for any caterer . . . regardless of how long they have been in business.

—James R. Bannister, CEM
Executive Vice President
National Caterers Roundtable Association

Introduction

The catering industry is the fastest-growing segment of the expanding food-service industry. Sales in 1993 are estimated at $2.7 billion—up 7 percent from the previous year. Why?

People obviously love food. People also love to be catered to. In the era of fast and frozen foods, people want fresh food, served conveniently. They want to invite guests over and not have to cook and clean all day and night. They want to plan a luncheon business meeting without having to plan the lunch. They want to celebrate marriages without making a career of the wedding. They want to call the caterer and not worry about it.

That's where you come in. If you have experience in the food-service industry, you can share in its future. You can start and run your own money-making catering service, with the help of this book. It adds vital information about operating a successful catering business to your knowledge of food service. It even gives you resources for expanding your food-service knowledge. Most important, you'll get the advice and specific help of dozens of successful caterers on how to make your new business profitable and fun.

This idea-packed book can also help current catering service owners become more successful. It includes extensive information on how to reduce costs, reduce risks, and increase profits through proven management tools and techniques.

This book is illustrated with numerous charts, tables, and forms that you will use to learn the secrets of other successful catering services. The appendix includes nearly 50 forms to profitably manage your business: journals, work orders, employment applications, credit applications, cash flow statements, and more. They can be personalized in minutes and reproduced on any copy machine.

As you consider starting and running your own money-making catering service, a dozen important questions will pop up:

- Should I start a catering service?
- How can I start my own catering service?
- How do I set up my catering business?
- What are the financial requirements?
- How do I price my catering services?
- How do I get and keep customers?
- How do I find good employees?
- How do I keep accurate records?
- How can I keep costs down?
- How can I reduce risks?
- How do I solve business problems?
- How can I ensure long-term success?

The answers to these questions are so important that each is developed in a complete chapter. Within these chapters, related questions are answered based on the experiences of women and men working in the catering industry today.

But knowledge is only part of the solution; action is also vital. At the end of each chapter in this book you'll find a "Success Action Plan." This list gives you step-by-step activities for making your dream a reality. It helps you apply what you've learned toward starting and running your catering business.

This book also shows you how to use electronics and computer technology for greater profits from your catering business. You'll learn how to find computer programs that reduce your costs, increase your profitability, and expand your knowledge of the catering business.

1

Should I start a catering service?

Making decisions is one of the most difficult aspects of living. On the other hand, making *good* decisions can be one of the most enjoyable ingredients of living.

This first chapter helps you make that important decision: Should I start a catering service? It presents the information you need to make the right decision, and tells you how others have made this decision and what they learned from it. Use it to guide you from an idea to a plan.

THE WORLD OF CATERING

There are now about 20 million small businesses in the United States—up 54 percent from 1980. Small business is really big business, adding about $370 *billion* to the U.S. economy and employing more than half of the private work force. Why so many new small businesses?

A recent study of successful business owners said that 54 percent began their venture because they wanted independence, 33 percent identified a need or market opportunity, 8 percent wanted to make more money, and the rest had other personal reasons. The study also indicated that those who simply wanted to use their knowledge or experience were less successful than those who wanted their freedom. Both are necessary, but the desire to "be your own boss" is a powerful incentive to these successful entrepreneurs.

How about catering? *Catering* means preparing food in an approved food service facility and transporting this food for service and consumption at some other site. (That's a broad definition that will be further defined in a moment.) To start your own catering service, you need a number of resources. First, you need to have extensive knowledge, skill, and experience in the field of catering or food service. You should have worked in the trade for at least five years. More is better. You'll be paid very well for what you know; the more you know, the more you'll be paid.

If you don't have such experience, or wish to have even more, considering serving an apprenticeship with a local caterer. That is, with the understanding that you want to go out on your own in a year or two, get hired as an assistant manager or assistant caterer. You'll work long hours at low pay, but you'll gain a valuable education. Of course, first make sure that the caterer to which you apprentice yourself has something valuable to teach.

You can also go back to school to get the necessary skills. Many community colleges offer food-service and catering courses. *College Blue Book: Occupational Education* (MacMillan Publishing, 212-702-2000) lists them by state, city, and curriculum. There are also many culinary arts colleges throughout the country. *The Guide to Cooking Schools* (Shaw Guides, 305-446-8888) covers approximately 300 cooking schools in the U.S. Both books are available through larger public libraries or interlibrary loans.

Should you start your own catering service business? Ask yourself the questions in Fig. 1-1—then get a friend or relative to answer them for you as well. Of course, you won't have the answers to all of these questions yet. The intent of this book is to help you get the right answers to these and other questions important to your success.

In addition to knowledge and experience, you'll need some physical assets in order to succeed as a catering service. Most are obvious: food preparation and service equipment, delivery equipment, and office equipment. (Chapter 3 covers the selection of these assets.) You'll also need another very important asset: cash. Many new businesses fail within a couple of years because they run out of money. You don't have to be rich to go into business for yourself, but you do need some cash and at least a few assets (such as home equity, cars, and investments) that can be quickly turned into cash if necessary.

Another vital part of building your business is building your credit. Even if you lack some of the cash you need, your credit can make start-up easier. Chapter 4, explains how to profitably use your credit and save your cash for emergencies. If your credit is poor or nonexistent, use this information to build it up to a valuable asset to your business and your success.

One of your most important assets is your time. You will spend lots of time starting and building your new business. Make sure that you're ready to work 50, 60, or even more hours each week with your new business. Later, you'll be able to cut back and enjoy the benefits of owning your own business. But for now, you'll be living, eating, sleeping, and breathing your catering service.

Another essential asset that doesn't always get discussed in business books is work ethics. Ethics are rules of conduct. So work ethics are the rules you set for yourself for performing the work that you do. If you set—and stick to—the "golden rule" in your business dealings, you will find, as thousands of others have, that gold comes to those who follow the rules. It's just good business to treat your customers they way you want to be treated; you'll be so far ahead of the "anything for a buck" catering services that you can't help but prosper. More important, you will feel good about yourself and what you do. Your customers will also be your friends and they will help you to prosper.

Your relatives can be another vital asset to your business success. That is, if you have family and close friends who will help you and support you, you have already succeeded. If your family is not supportive of your business ideas, start searching for common ground where you and they can be comfortable with this new adventure. Maybe they are concerned about your health, about the possibility of failure, or about your being away from home so much. Or maybe they are simply jealous of your success. Take time to talk with them and get them to share their real feelings about your ideas.

You might find that you have relatives or friends who want very much to see you succeed and have skills or assets they will share with you. Make them a part of

Questionnaire: Should I start my own business?

* Do I sincerely like people? ✓Yes __No
* Do others turn to me for help in making decisions? ✓Yes __No
* Do I get along well with others, even those with whom I don't agree? ✓Yes __No
* Do I like to make decisions? ✓Yes __No
* Do I enjoy competition? ✓Yes __No
* Do I have self-discipline? ✓Yes __No
* Do I plan ahead? ✓Yes __No
* Am I a leader? ✓Yes __No
* Am I willing to work long hours? ✓Yes __No
* Do I have the physical stamina to handle a busy schedule and heavy workload if
    necessary? ✓Yes __No
* Am I willing and able to temporarily lower my standard of living in order to firmly
    establish my business? ✓Yes __No
* Is my family or others close to me willing and able to go along with the struggle for
    business success? ✓Yes __No
* How much money am I willing to gamble on this venture, knowing that I may be risking
    all of it? ✓Yes __No
* Do I have sufficient experience in this field to know what's required to be successful?
    ✓Yes __No
* Have I had any training in the basics of business? If not, am I willing to take some
    time learn them? __Yes ✓No
* Is there a need for this service in my area? ✓Yes __No
* Is my goal of becoming a caterer in my area realistic and attainable?
    ✓Yes __No
* Who else is offering such a service in this area? _____
* How busy are these competitors? _____
* Why will my service be of greater value to customers? _Service_____
* How can I let prospects know the value of my service? _ADV._____
* Who will my customers be? _____
* What do they want? _____
* How much will they pay? ___50/50_____
* How will I keep these customers happy? ___Service_____
    _____
* Where will I set up my business? _____
    _____
* How will I keep my business going when the economy changes? _____
    _____
    _____
* How can I make my business more profitable without diminishing the quality of my
    work? _____
    _____

1-1 There are many questions you should ask yourself before starting your own catering business.

your journey and your success. Maybe your spouse or a parent has business skills you need, can help with office duties, or has other resources that will help you build your business. Ask for participation, ideas, and suggestions. You certainly don't have to accept all of them, but you might find just the right pieces to make the puzzle become a complete picture.

As you can see, you need many assets to start your own catering service business. But don't let the lack of any of them discourage you from starting. In the pages that follow, you'll learn how to make the most of what you do have and how to increase these assets until they are sufficient for success.

WHY SOME CATERING SERVICES DON'T MAKE IT

The statistics about business failure are enough to make you quit before you start. Many businesses close their doors within the first year, and most close within five years. Why?

Not all businesses that close their doors have failed. Some actually merge with other firms, or sell off their assets at a profit. Unfortunately, however, too many do fail, losing money in the process.

So why do people continue to open businesses? Because most people feel that they can beat the odds. If this weren't so, Atlantic City would be a small beach town. The ones who win at Atlantic City or in business are those who know the odds, learn how to master them, and know when to quit.

Many business experts say that businesses fail because of *undercapitalization*. That is, they don't have enough money to survive. More specifically, if they're in the business of making—not spending—money, the actual problem is that they didn't *make* enough money. And how does a business—any business—make money? By supplying a product or service to those who need it. So the real reason businesses fail is that they fail to communicate the benefits that customers will receive by using their product or service. Or they fail to successfully communicate their business philosophy and ethics to all employees.

Communication is the distribution of information. That information might be fact, opinion, or emotions. This book communicates information to you through black marks on paper that your mind recognizes and translates into ideas. Of course, information can also be communicated in many other ways—some direct, some more subtle.

So what does communication have to do with a catering service business? In any business, there must be a source, a communicator, and a receiver in order to make things happen. You're the source of knowledge about catering. In a way, your hands and tools communicate this knowledge to the job you're performing. If you want to get prospects to know about your skills and use them, you must communicate with prospects. If you want employees to perform their jobs accurately and efficiently, you must communicate with your employees. If you want bankers to lend you money—and be glad to do so—you must communicate with these bankers. If you want your friends and family to be proud and supportive of what you do, you must communicate with them.

Communicate what? Communicate accurate information that you want them to know in terms that they want to hear. That is, communicate *benefits*. A benefit is simply an advantage or a reward that one product or action has over another or over not doing anything.

The benefit of this book to you is that, if you invest time, effort, and money, you will learn what you need to know to own a successful catering business. That's the clear and understood reward you can receive for applying what you learn here.

What benefits does your catering business offer that you can communicate to prospects, customers, employees, bankers, family, and others? Start thinking about them, writing them down as they occur to you. They are discussed throughout this book as you design your business, market your services, and communicate with others.

HOW CATERING SERVICES SUCCEED

Maybe you've been in your line of catering or food-service work for many years and want your own business to specialize in it. Or maybe you want to move into a closely related field that better fits your interests. Or maybe you want to transport your food service knowledge and skills into an entirely new field such as serving ethnic foods at bazaars.

The next few pages summarize many fields of catering that have proved successful for others. This list might confirm to you that your chosen specialty is the right one for you, or it might give you new ideas about a specialty that will be more enjoyable and more profitable for you.

There are dozens of types of catering services: reception dinners, brown-bag lunches, business luncheons, social buffets, hors d'oeuvres, street-cart fare, and much more. Which one will bring you success?

Caterers are often categorized as *on-premise*, meaning they cater food at the restaurant (banquets), and *off-premise*, meaning they prepare food for off-site service (dinner parties). An easier way to categorize catering services is "cold service" and "hot service." *Cold-service* catering obviously serves most food cold or at room temperature. *Hot-service* catering serves most food hot or at least warm. Beyond these two general categories of catering services are many specialties. Let's consider these opportunities to help you decide which is best for you.

Cold-service catering

Cold-service catering is the easiest and least expensive for the new entrepreneur. Cold-service catering offers brunches, lunches, sandwiches, snacks, deli foods, hors d'oeuvres, and related food that is usually served cold or cool. A recent study by the National Restaurant Association indicates that lunches are the preference of 54 percent of those surveyed for catered events outside the home.

Convenience is more important than service to the clients of cold-service caterers. The foods might be served prepackaged (as sandwiches on an industrial catering truck), on a tray (as hors d'oeuvres at a party), in a bag (as from a lunch service), on paper plates (as at a catered picnic), or other convenience. The food might be delivered to the job site, client's home, or business meeting, picked up at a retail outlet, or selected from a push cart. Customers might be either individuals or groups. Food is usually prepared off-site.

The business day for a cold-service caterer can begin as early as 7 a.m., but rarely goes past 7 p.m. Of course, preparation and clean-up time can extend these hours.

Hot-service catering

Hot-service catering is what most people think of when they consider catering. In hot-service catering, food is served hot or warm. Service is as important as convenience, sometimes more so. The food is typically served as a dinner or supper: formal dinners, wedding or reception dinners, banquets, gourmet dinners, etc. Food is often served at or from a table. The food might be prepared on-site in the client's kitchen (for smaller dinners) or off-site in the caterer's commissary (for larger dinners and events outside the home). The food is usually prepared for a group on behalf of the host/client. The study by the National Restaurant Association notes that dinner is the preferred meal (70 percent) for catered events inside the home.

The hot-service caterer might also provide linen, serving wear, tables, and even bar service. The business day for a hot-service caterer is typically from 6 p.m. to midnight, with cooking, setup, service, and clean-up extending this time.

Specialized catering

Within the two broad categories of catering, hot service and cold service, are many variations. Some specializations are based on food, others on service. For example, a hot- or cold-service caterer can specialize in such categories as kosher, regional, Mexican, European, Asian, other ethnic meals, desserts and pastries, fast food for workers, home cooking, gourmet foods, society events, weddings and receptions, picnics and barbecues, adult's or children's birthday parties, business meetings, and church events.

IS THERE A NEED FOR MY CATERING SERVICE?

By now you might have chosen one or two specialties where your knowledge, skills, experience, and interests come together. But you still might not be sure which would offer you the best chance for success. After all, the success ratio for a high-society catering service in Miles City, Montana, or a Cajun food catering service in Nome, Alaska, is small. You're either going to have to change specialties or move. No matter which specialties you're considering, the next step is to evaluate the local need for your service.

First, check the local telephone book's yellow pages under "Catering Services" and related headings. Count the number of listings under each heading. Then count the number of listings that indicate by name or wording that they would be a competitor. If you're in a large metropolitan area, you could mark the location of each potential competitor on a map to determine if a geographic area is unserved. Maybe there's a good reason for an area with no catering services, but maybe it's a gold mine waiting to be worked. It's worth further investigation.

Contact your local or state health authority to determine what food-service permits have been issued in your area and to whom. This information helps you determine who is now serving your market.

Also, talk with people who would become your customers, such as influential local people, businesses, and social groups. Ask them what catering services they use, what they like and don't like about them, and what their future needs might be. You'll not only learn your market, you'll be building your prospect list.

If you know any catering services in other regions, or know someone who could introduce you to them, interview them as well. These noncompeting catering services might give you additional information that will help you build your new business. Although any information can be useful, be aware that conditions in their market might be different from yours.

WHO WOULD USE MY CATERING SERVICE?

Okay, you've done some research to find out if there is a local need for your service. You've studied area telephone books, reviewed health permits issued for the last year or two, and interviewed catering business owners for information and opportunities. Now, look at the market itself—who are your customers?

To clearly define who your customers are, you first need to define who you are to them. That is, you have to understand what it is you offer them. At this point, you only have to express it in broad terms:

"I want to own a catering service business specializing in one-person jobs that can be performed in just a few hours a day."

"I plan to offer a catering service that manages awards dinners and banquets for large corporations."

"I'm a businessperson who uses my knowledge of the field to hire independent caterers for almost any type of catering job there is."

"I am a caterer who prefers to spend my time working rather than marketing, so I want larger jobs from long-term clients, even if they aren't as profitable."

"I am a well-known caterer with extensive experience who would prefer to find a young, energetic partner who will do much of the work so I can spend time with my family and hobbies."

Get the point? By defining your own skills and interests, you can better define those who might hire you—your market. (Finding customers for your catering service is discussed in greater detail in chapter 6.)

WHAT WILL I SELL?

A *process* is a series of actions performed to get a specific result. An automotive assembly line is a process in which a series of actions are performed—bodies attached to frames, doors and dashboards installed—to get a specific result: a car. Makes sense.

But did you ever think about what *you* do as a process? It is. Your process might be preparing and serving unique desserts to the after-theater crowd. Like the automobile assembly process, it requires specific tools, materials, procedures, and knowledge. And it has a specific result. No one gets paid unless they perform a needed process for someone else. A tailor makes a suit, a McDonald's makes a hamburger, Boeing makes a commercial aircraft.

By now you've selected one or two catering ideas that appeal to you most. To define the process you will perform, first define the end products or service you will sell to your customers. For example, you might offer complete homemade dinners for large groups. Clearly defining this end product helps you and the client maintain clear expectations of the result. It also helps ensure that your business stays focused.

For your particular catering service, the process might be simple or complex, but it has many things in common with other tasks performed by catering services—and by other service firms:

- A process has tools. These might be basic or complex tools, or simply your hands. What are the tools you need in your process?
- A process also has raw materials. You might be supplying bag lunches to office workers or vegetarian meals at parties. What are the raw materials you need in your process?
- A process requires skill or the application of certain knowledge. It might be the skill of planning ethnic meals or setting up appetizing buffets for large groups. It's probably a combination of many skills and extensive specialized knowledge. What are the skills and the knowledge you need in your process?
- A process produces a benefit for others. Is your process a convenience for them, or do they actually make money from it (such as making sandwiches for someone else's catering trucks)? How much money? The more someone else profits from your process, the more you will profit.

Knowing the answer to these questions helps you become more efficient—and more profitable—at what you do. You will know exactly what tools and materials you need, understand what you do to these materials, and what the result is for your customer. This might sound pretty basic, but understanding your process helps you become more successful at it. Defining your process also helps you from getting sidetracked on jobs that really don't fit your goals and won't be as profitable for you.

WHAT CAN I EXPECT TO MAKE?

One of the primary motives for your catering service is monetary. You want to make a profit. It's the American way!

How much money should you expect to make with your catering service business? Of course, much depends on your local market, specialty, capital, time in business, management skills, and many other factors. According to the Internal Revenue Service's records, a "typical" breakdown of costs as a percentage of sales for a typical catering service is shown in Fig. 1-2. As you can see in Fig. 1-2, you'll typically only receive a 3 percent profit.

That's it? Yes, and be happy with it—because it is 3 percent of total sales. That is, if your firm sells $1 million in services in the coming year, your profit is $30,000. That's after paying a salary to yourself and any partners. Obviously, as your sales grow and you learn more about your business, your profits increase. But expecting a net profit of more than 5 percent isn't realistic. In fact, most large, successful catering services earn a net profit of much less.

Most catering businesses sell at least five times as much per year as their net worth, so your capital is actually earning 15 percent or more (5 × 3%). If annual sales become 7 times your firm's net worth, you're now earning 21 percent!

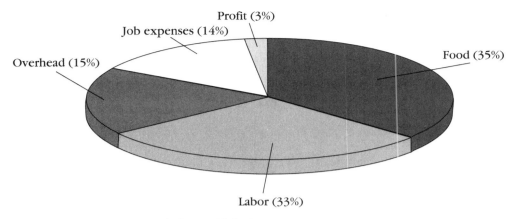

Profit (3%)
Job expenses (14%)
Overhead (15%)
Food (35%)
Labor (33%)

1-2 Typical expenses and profit for established catering services.

HOW CAN I GET THERE FROM HERE?

Every business has a goal of being successful. But what's success to you? Here are some goals set by catering service owners. Select any that seem to apply, and make them yours:

- Become a well-respected businessperson in my community.
- Build a catering business that will furnish me with a comfortable living and an ample retirement.
- Establish a successful catering business that I can sell for at least $500,000 within 10 years.
- Build a successful catering business that I can pass to one or more of my children when they reach adulthood.
- See my name on the side of a dozen billboards.
- Build a large catering business by offering good service and eventually taking over unprofitable catering businesses in the area.
- Take on a partner with more marketing knowledge who can help me build this business.

These are just a few of the goals that catering services set for themselves as they start their business. Of course, your goals might change along the way, but they give you a target to aim for.

Your business goals, your process, and your assets all come together in a single document called a *business plan*. For large corporations, a business plan might be as large as a metropolitan telephone book. But for your new enterprise, a business plan is simply a few pages of ideas and numbers that help you focus on the future. Your business plan should include at least the following:

- A definition of your process, describing what you do, how you do it, and what tools and materials you require to produce an end product.
- A description of potential customers who would be most likely to purchase this service from you, including their background, location, typical annual sales, association memberships, and other precise information.

- Information on the name of your business, location, required licenses and bonds, form of ownership, names and qualifications of members or partners, and related structural information.
- A list of the assets (what you own) and liabilities (what you owe) you bring to the business, including a list of the professional skills, certifications, and training you have.

Of course, you're not going to be able to complete this business plan today. However, you can start it today with a spiral-bound or loose-leaf notebook. Call it your "business notebook." Start by defining your process and business goals as just discussed. Then make a section for each of the other categories: prospects, business structure, and assets. As you read through this book and come up with new ideas, write them down in your business notebook and you'll soon have the first draft of your business plan.

WHO ARE MY CUSTOMERS?

Who would ever want to hire you? Hopefully, lots of people. You're skilled, ambitious, knowledgeable, honest, brave, thrifty, etc. The more you know about those who will hire you, the more they will.

Demographics is a study of statistics about people: where they live, how much they make, how they buy, their favorite foods, etc. Retailers use census information to build demographics that help them decide where to build a store. Catering services can use demographics to learn who would use their services and where to find them.

For example, a catering service specializing in serving Cajun and southern foods in Denver, Colorado needs to know how many people enjoy such foods and where they are now getting it, if at all. This and additional information is available from a number of sources. You might know of some of these sources yourself. (If not, I'll tell you later where to find this information at low cost.)

Psychographics is learning *why* people buy. You would think that most people buy from logical reasons. However, in many cases, even in the business world, people buy for emotional reasons and justify their decision with logical reasons. Knowing why your clients buy helps you sell to them more effectively.

For example, if you specialize in hot-service catering on short notice, clients will use your service because you're efficient and can get a quality job done in the least amount of time. Price, while certainly important, is a secondary consideration.

If you've built a solid reputation in your area as a catering service whose name means quality, you can sell that name. People want to go with a winner, so you will get some jobs just because people know you were involved. Learn what makes your customers buy, and help them to buy from you.

Prospecting for clients

A *prospect* is someone who might become a customer. Why "might"? Because they don't know you, your services, or the benefits of becoming your customer. Turning prospects into customers is covered later. For now, let's start looking for prospects.

If you've defined who your customers will be, you have a pretty good idea of who your prospects are. If you know that your customers will be large businesses in your area that need luncheons with important clients catered, these businesses are your prospects. Many successful catering services start prospecting for clients by building a list of those who might someday purchase their services. In this example, you would build a list of large businesses in your area, augmented with data from telephone calls to these prospects.

The same process can be applied to building up a list of prospects for your specialty catering business.

Business planning

Your business notebook helps you plan and start your catering service. Bankers, investors, and potential partners, however, typically want a more formal business plan. Your business plan might be the most important document you ever write. It includes specific information on the structure and direction of your catering firm. It not only tells others what your business is about, it also helps you think about and focus your business ideas.

A business plan compiles the answers to the following basic business questions:
- Why am I in business?
- What business am I in?
- What's my market?
- How will I make a profit?
- How much do I need to start and operate this business?
- How will I find customers?
- Who is my competition?
- How will I sell my service?
- How will I plan my work?
- Who will do the actual work?
- What tools and materials do I need?
- Will I have employees, use subcontractors, or do all of the work myself?

Take out your business notebook and record your answers to these and related business questions. You might need additional information from other sources to answer some of these questions. Once this information is gathered, you can develop your business plan.

A successful business plan includes the following information, as appropriate to your business:
- Description of your business and a statement of its purpose.
- Table of contents of your business plan.
- Description of the services or products your business will provide.
- Information on the location of your business and, if necessary, plans for expansion of the physical plant.
- Definition of the management of the business, their job descriptions and qualifications.
- List of personnel who will initially be employed.
- Description of your business' marketing plan.
- Information on your competition and market share.
- Outline of your price structure and the philosophy behind it.
- Facts on short- and long-term trends in the market.
- Discussion of quality and how you expect to obtain and retain it in your business.

- Description of the sources and requirements of funds, including inside and outside investors, and their participation in your business.
- A capital equipment and capital improvement list.
- An opening balance sheet for your business.
- A break-even analysis for your business.
- Monthly income projections for the first three years of business.
- A list of the accountants, attorneys, and other independent professionals hired to assist you in the establishment and management of your business.

Market planning

A *marketing plan* is a description of how you plan to market or develop customers for your catering business. You can incorporate your marketing plan into your business plan or you can make it a separate document; it depends on how you will use your marketing plan. If you will implement your own marketing plan, incorporate it into your business plan. If you will hire a marketing consultant or an advertising agency to implement your marketing plan, make it a separate document that doesn't require a copy of your business plan to be understood. In some cases, your banker or potential investors will want to see your marketing plan as well as your business plan.

A typical marketing plan includes the following:

- *Executive summary*: Overview of the plan, short description of your service and how it differs from services offered by other catering services, the required investment, and a summary of anticipated sales and profits.
- *Introduction*: A full description of your service and how it fits into the marketplace.
- *Situation*: An analysis of local demand and trends for your service, laws and regulations, financial requirements, competitors, and structure of your company including key employees.
- *Market*: More specifics on your target market, its size and requirements, its needs, and the problems that your catering service will solve for this market.
- *Strategy*: Details on how you will reach this target market, the promotional tools you will need, the image you will present, and how you will react (or not react) to competitors.
- *Control*: How you expect to manage your catering firm to improve your services and increase your share of the customers.

A marketing plan can be as long or as short as required by its purpose. If you're planning to bring on a big-bucks investor, you will want to develop a detailed marketing plan. If you're both the writer and the implementer of the marketing plan, a few pages might suffice. In either case, the act of writing helps you clarify your intentions and visualize the outcome.

SUCCESS ACTION PLAN

There is no "road to success." Success is the road rather than the destination. How you travel this road and how you help others along the road is the best way to measure your success. Here are some things you can do right now to succeed *today* as an independent caterer:

❏ Complete the worksheet in Fig. 1-1.

❏ In your new business notebook, list the assets you have that will help you if you decide to start a catering business: experience, tools, equipment, contacts, and finances.

❏ Make a list of the ways a catering service can fail.

❏ Make a corresponding list of ways a catering service can turn failure into success through good communications.

❏ Describe five cold-service catering opportunities that appeal to you.

❏ Describe five hot-service catering opportunities that appeal to you.

❏ Place a *1* by the catering opportunity that most appeals to you, a *2* by your second choice, etc.

❏ Check regional telephone books for a listing of catering services that serve your area and note their specialties. How would you improve on what they are doing?

❏ Define your process for the top three or four catering opportunities you listed.

❏ Start making notes on your business plan in your business notebook.

❏ Begin a section of your business notebook for your marketing plan.

2
How can I start my own catering service?

Chapter 1 got you thinking; this chapter gets you moving. In it you learn how to name your business for success, decide where to locate your business, review licensing requirements, and set up a business checking account. You also learn about the many resources available to you: franchises, trade associations, conventions, trade journals, advanced training, and government resources.

WHAT SHOULD I NAME MY BUSINESS?

Naming a business is like naming a baby. In some ways, it gives direction to its growth. A well-named business seems more successful to prospects and will then become so.

A business name should make it clear to prospects what the firm does, or at least the industry the firm is in. If the owner or a partner is well-known in the area or in catering, his or her name could be incorporated into the business name. Here are some examples of possible catering business names:

- *Midwest Catering Services* denotes the region and the industry.
- *Betty's Catering* identifies the industry, but is personalized at the expense of sounding like a small business.
- *Peterson Catering Services, Inc.* sounds bigger; surnames are better than first names, and "Inc." implies that it is a larger firm. (Note, however, that to use "Inc." in your name you must, in fact, be incorporated. More on this later.)
- *Acme Catering Service* specifically identifies the service, although "Acme" isn't a modern business name.
- *Smithtown Foods* is unclear about what service is involved.
- *Quality Catering Services* clearly identifies the industry and, hopefully, the owner's attitude.

In selecting a business name, many firms write a defining motto or slogan that's used in all stationery and advertisements to further clarify what the firm does. Consider the following:

- "Specializing in bar mitzvahs and kosher meals"
- "Specializing in elegant parties for intimate groups"
- "Commercial and industrial catering services"
- "Good food on short notice"
- "On-call 24 hours a day"

- "Since 1984"
- "Your one-stop catering service"

In your business notebook, write out a few possible business names and slogans. Of course, check the local telephone book to make sure someone else doesn't already use the name or the slogan. You might also need to do a national check, perhaps with the help of a professional researcher or attorney, to make sure the name or slogan hasn't been copyrighted.

An *assumed business name* is a name other than the *real and true name* of each person operating a business. A real and true name becomes an assumed business name with the addition of any words that imply the existence of additional owners. For example, "Bob Smith" is a real and true name, while "Bob Smith Company" is an assumed name.

In most states and counties, you must register an assumed business name to let the public know who is transacting business under that name. Without the registration you can be fined or, worse, not be able to defend a legal action because your assumed business name wasn't properly registered.

In many states, an assumed business name is registered with the state's corporate division. Some states also register your assumed business name with counties in which you do business, while other states require that you do so. In some locations, you must publish a public notice in an area newspaper telling everyone that you (and any other business principals) are operating under a specific business name. The typical assumed business name registration requires the following information:
- The business name you wish to assume
- The principal place of business
- The name of an authorized representative
- Your SIC (standard industrial classification) code (5812-12 for a catering service)
- A list of all owners with their signatures
- A list of all counties in which your firm will transact business (sell, lease, or purchase goods or services; receive funding or credit)

WHERE SHOULD I LOCATE MY CATERING BUSINESS?

The next question is where to locate your business: at home, in a portable commissary, from a catering truck, in a shared commissary, or in a retail storefront? The answer depends on how much business you expect to initially contract, what your space requirements are, your budget, and whether you plan to have clients visit your place of business.

Here are some factors you should consider as you determine the location of your business:
- Electrical requirements and available service
- Parking space for employees and customers
- Lighting, heating, air conditioning, and ventilation
- Restroom requirement
- Site alterations
- Shipping and delivery docks
- Insurability of site
- Water and sewage requirements

- Fire safety requirements
- Availability of transportation
- Quality and quantity of employees in the area
- Tax burden
- Opportunities for signage
- Quality of police and fire services
- Environmental factors
- Physical suitability of building
- Opportunities for future expansion
- Personal convenience
- Cost of operation

Considering these factors, let's look at your options.

Home commissary

In many locations, a commercial commissary cannot be located in a private residence for various reasons. If your health department allows it, a home commissary can be a low-cost site for your catering business until it grows because you have little or no additional rent expense. It is also more convenient for you to have all your records at home where you can review them at any time. In addition, you could have a family member or roommate help by answering the telephone while you're away on jobs. Finally, you might be able to deduct some of your household costs as legitimate expenses and reduce your tax obligation.

However, many states have health laws that discourage or prevent the use of a home kitchen for commercial cooking. The health department might require special floor finishes and drainage systems, lead-free wall paints, stainless steel appliances and equipment, and other requirements that are not easily met in the typical residential kitchen. Even if you do meet health codes, many health departments will not license commercial kitchens in a home. Some locations allow the preparation of candies and baked goods in commercial kitchens in a home, but not other products. To find out, call your state or county health department.

Some new caterers set up an office in their home and use the client's kitchen as their commissary. This is legal in many areas.

If you're considering using a portion of your home as a business office or commissary, order "Business Use of Your Home" (Publication 587) from the Internal Revenue Service (Washington, DC 20224). It will help you determine if your business qualifies for this option, as well as how to take advantage of it to lower your taxes.

Portable commissary

A portable commissary is a practical work site that you can use instead of or in addition to your home office. It is typically a travel trailer converted into a self-contained commissary or a trailer specially designed and manufactured for food preparation and service. In addition to the portability, it also offers two large side panels where your business's name can be painted to advertise wherever you go.

In most cases, you will need a catering vehicle that can easily and safely transport food and equipment between your commissary and the client's serving site. A standard or a step-in van is best. It gives you the room you need, serves as a moving billboard for your business, and can also be your tow vehicle if you have a portable commissary.

Your catering vehicle can either be purchased or leased. Depending on how much you use your catering vehicle and portable commissary for personal use, you can either list all costs of operating the vehicle as an expense or you can deduct a standard mileage rate as an expense when you file income taxes. For more information, request "Business Use of a Car" (Publication 917) from the Internal Revenue Service.

Catering truck
Mobile caterers or industrial caterers use specially built trucks to sell foods to workers at the work site. A typical mobile catering truck costs $20,000 to $40,000 and is manned by an employee on salary or salary-plus-commission, or by a subcontractor. To be profitable, a mobile caterer must make between 15 and 25 stops and sell at least $400 in food per day. A good two-person route in a large city will sell up to $1000 per day.

Shared commissary
You might have friends or relatives who own a restaurant or other food-service business. You could share a kitchen with them, reducing your costs and bringing them some rental income. Of course, don't share a site with anyone who might be a competitor or be associated with a competitor. Prospects calling for you could be diverted. If you're specializing in a single aspect of catering, look for an office-mate who might be able to bring you prospects, and vice versa. You might even decide to strike up a partnership and join forces.

Your own catering office and commissary
Depending on local health and business codes, your own office and commissary might be the minimum entry level for your catering business. The biggest disadvantage of such a location is the cost. There are many advantages, however. First, your own catering office gives you an image of being a large, successful, and permanent firm. Second, if your business requires that prospects, clients, suppliers, or contractors visit your office, a catering office and commissary of your own gives them a better first impression of your business. Finally, you have control over your own space that you cannot have if you're working out of a shared or portable commissary.

Retail storefront
Some catering businesses choose to set up in a retail storefront because they want to open a retail outlet for their foods and, thus, get double service from their investment in equipment. A catering service can operate out of the back of a sandwich shop or a deli.

The most important factor in selecting a retail location is *retail compatibility*. Locating your store near a traffic-generator in its first years of operation, with limited funds for advertising and promotion, can help you survive. You'll often find restaurants grouped together.

As the old saying goes, the three most important factors in selecting a retail site are location, location, and location.

The next most important factor in selecting your retail site is the availability of a local merchants association. A strong merchants association can accomplish through group strength what an individual store owner couldn't dream of. For example, a merchants association can speak as a booming voice to city planners and bulk-buy advertising at lower rates to promote their own events. Make sure, though, that you understand your responsibilities to the association before you sign up. If the site you select doesn't have a merchants association, consider starting one.

Other factors to consider when selecting a site include the responsiveness of the landlord and the opportunities for negotiating a favorable lease. Make sure your new landlord is continuing an investment in the property, including regular maintenance and quick repairs. Talk with other commercial landlords in your area to ensure that your lease is the best you can negotiate.

You can often get assistance on selecting a retail site by talking with local and regional chambers of commerce about your needs. They might be able to give you an educated guess on what you will probably have to pay for a property that will help your business become successful.

Zoning laws

Your choices for a business location might be limited by local zoning laws. Before deciding where you will set up your catering business, even in your truck, talk to the local zoning office about restrictions. You might find that so-called "cottage" or home businesses are allowed in your neighborhood as long as no client comes to your home and no equipment or job trucks are parked on the street overnight. Or such businesses might not be allowed at all.

Certain zoning classifications allow you to set up a catering office at home, but not prepare hot food there. Ask questions about zoning and restrictions *before* you set up your commissary.

Americans with Disabilities Act

The Americans with Disabilities Act offers employees and customers in many firms access to business locations without physical barriers. The ADA requires business owners to offer easy access to their location that does not restrict people with disabilities. This act applies to all businesses with 15 or more employees. To learn more about ADA requirements, contact the Small Business Research and Education Council (800-947-4646).

Clients and suppliers

One last, but important, question you should ask as you decide where to locate your business is, where are your jobs and your suppliers located? To ask the question more specifically, is your office close enough to typical jobs that you won't be wasting time and gas getting to and from them each day? And, if your catering business requires frequent runs for groceries, is your office close to your primary wholesale grocer? If you're not close to them, consider the cost of fuel and time in your estimate of costs for the site.

HOW DO I LICENSE MY CATERING BUSINESS?

Unfortunately, the licensing requirements for catering businesses are not universal. In some communities, all you need is a local business license and a health permit.

In other locations, you must apply for state, county, and local business licenses; pass professional requirements; and furnish bond and insurance certificates.

The best way to learn the requirements for your area is to contact your state government. Some states have a "one-stop" business telephone number where you can find out what the requirements are, or at least the telephone numbers of governing offices. You might be required to include a state license number on all correspondence, bids, estimates, advertisements, and vehicles.

Commercial food preparation requires permits from your local or state health department. In most localities, both the kitchen or commissary and the food handlers must be licensed. Health department rules dictate how food is to be prepared, stored, and served. Figure 2-1 shows a typical application form for a health unit license for caterers.

HOW DO I SET UP A BUSINESS BANK ACCOUNT?

Some new small businesses set up a commercial account at the bank where they have their personal account. If you have a good relationship with the bank, this is a sound idea. However, some long-time catering businesses complain of bankers suddenly changing policy and withdrawing credit from otherwise trustworthy customers. They then begin to shop around for a new banker. The best time to shop for a second banker is when you begin your business. As your business becomes more successful, you might even want to have business accounts at two or more banks because both will probably solicit your complete business, making you offers you would not get from a single "suitor."

One more reason for separate banks for personal and business accounts is fewer errors. Small businesses with both types of accounts at a single bank might find that checks are deposited to the wrong account, especially deposits made to a cash machine. Doing business with two banks gives you twice as many options.

To start a business account, you'll have to have some "seed" money, typically a hundred dollars or more. Also, most banks require a copy of your Registration of Assumed Business Name form approved by the appropriate government office. If you make large night deposits, you'll want a night-deposit bag and key. With the proliferation of cash machines, your deposits can be made anytime and almost anywhere. You'll also need to furnish a federal ID number (discussed later) or your social security insurance number.

HOW SHOULD I LEGALLY STRUCTURE MY BUSINESS?

One of the most important decisions you will make as you start your catering business is what legal form it takes. Why so important? Because how you record expenses, how you build your business, how you pay taxes, how you treat profits, and how you manage liability all depend on the structure you give your business.

Of course, as your business grows you'll be able to move from one type of structure to another, but sometimes there is a cost. This cost usually is to the IRS as it decides whether you changed structure to avoid paying your "fair share" of taxes. One of the reasons you might change your business structure is because you want to legally reduce tax liability—and that's okay. It's the *abuse* of tax laws that brings the wrath of the IRS.

OREGON STATE HEALTH DIVISION
Department of Human Resources

APPLICATION FOR LICENSE
COMMISSARY, VENDING MACHINE, MOBILE FOOD AND BEVERAGE UNITS

NAME OF COMPANY _____ ESTABLISHMENT NO. _____

EXACT LOCATION OF BUSINESS _____
   STREET AND NUMBER   CITY   TELEPHONE

MAILING ADDRESS (IF DIFFERENT THAN ABOVE) _____

NAME OF OPERATOR _____

COMMENCED BUSINESS (MONTH and YEAR) _____ HAS COMPANY NAME OR MANAGEMENT CHANGED IN PAST YEAR ☐ ☐

COMPANY IS OWNED BY _____   YES   NO

N O T E

OAR 32-100 (2) REQUIRES EITHER A COMMISSARY

OR WAREHOUSE FEE TO BE PAID BY EVERY VEND-

ING OPERATOR DEPENDING ON THE TYPE OF OPER-

ATION.

NUMBER OF LICENSED UNITS *

COMMISSARIES	
WAREHOUSES	
MOBILE UNITS	
* FOOD MERCHANDISERS (SANDWICHES, ETC.)	
* SOFT DRINK MACHINES	
* HOT DRINK MACHINES (COFFEE, COCOA, ETC.)	
* MILK MACHINES (TYPE VENDING MILK ONLY)	

* ALL OTHER VENDING MACHINES ARE LICENSE EXEMPT,
EXCEPT THE ABOVE TYPES.

FEE SCHEDULE INFORMATION

LICENSE FEE FOR EACH COMMISSARY.............................
LICENSE FEE FOR EACH WAREHOUSE.............................

LICENSE FEE ENCLOSED:

AMOUNT: _____

CHECK ☐   MONEY ORDER ☐

MAKE CHECK OR MONEY ORDER PAYABLE TO:

NO. UNITS	FEE	NO. UNITS	FEE	NO. UNITS	FEE
1 to 10		41 - 50		251 - 500	
11 to 20		51 - 75		501 - 750	
21 to 30		76 - 100		751 - 1000	
31 to 40		101 - 250		1001 - 1500	
				1501 - 2000	

FACILITIES SERVING OTHER AREAS OF OREGON

LOCATION OF EACH COMMISSARY _____
   NUMBER   STREET   CITY

LOCATION OF EACH WAREHOUSE _____
   NUMBER   STREET   CITY

LOCATION OF EACH GARAGE, SHOP, ETC. _____
   NUMBER   STREET   CITY

(IF MORE SPACE IS REQUIRED, PLEASE COMPLETE THE ABOVE INFORMATION ON THE REVERSE SIDE)

ALL LICENSES ISSUED UNDER THIS ACT SHALL TERMINATE AND BE RENEWABLE ON DECEMBER 31, OF EACH YEAR. IT IS AGREED THAT I WILL COMPLY WITH THE PROVISIONS OF CHAPTER 624 , OREGON REVISED STATUTES, AND THE ADMINISTRATIVE RULES OF THE OREGON STATE HEALTH DIVISION PERTAINING THERETO.

_____
SIGNATURE OF APPLICANT AND TITLE

_____
ADDRESS

DATE _____

DO NOT WRITE IN THIS SPACE

DATE APPLICATION RECEIVED _____ DATE LICENSE ISSUED _____

APPROVED _____ NOT APPROVED _____

REMARKS: _____

COUNTY COPY

SAN-43 (Rev. 11-77)

2-1 Typical application for a state health license.

There are three common types of business structures: proprietorship, partnership, and corporation. Each has specific advantages and disadvantages, but they must all be considered against your individual circumstances, goals, and needs. Consider each of them as they relate to the following questions:

- What's the ultimate goal and purpose of my enterprise, and which legal structure can best serve its purposes?
- What's the investors' liability for damages, injuries, debts, and taxes?
- What would the life of the business be if something happened to one or more of the owners?
- What legal structure would insure the greatest flexibility in managing the business?
- What are the possibilities for soliciting additional capital?
- Would one type of business structure attract additional expertise over another?
- What are the costs and procedures in starting?

Sole proprietorship

The *sole proprietorship* is usually defined as a business that is owned and operated by one person. However, in many states, a business owned jointly by a husband and wife is considered a proprietorship rather than a partnership. A sole proprietorship is the easiest form of business to establish; you only need to obtain required licenses and begin operation. For its simplicity, the proprietorship is the most widespread form of small business organization and is especially popular with new catering services.

Advantages of sole proprietorship

The first and most obvious advantage of a proprietorship is its ease of formation. Less formality and fewer legal restrictions are associated with establishing a sole proprietorship than with a partnership or corporation. A proprietorship needs little or no governmental approval and is usually the least expensive form of business to start.

Another advantage of a proprietorship is that it doesn't require you to share profits with anyone. Whatever is left over after you pay the bills (including taxes) is yours to keep. You report income, expenses, and profit to the IRS using Schedule C and your standard 1040 form, and make quarterly instead of annual estimated tax payments to the IRS so you don't get behind.

Control is important to the successful catering service. A proprietorship gives that control and decision-making power to a single person: you. Proprietorships also give you flexibility that other forms of business do not. A partner must usually get agreement from other partners. In larger matters, a corporation must get agreement from members of the board of directors or corporate officers. A proprietor simply makes up her or his mind and acts.

One more plus: The sole proprietor has relative freedom from government control and special taxation. Sure, the government has some say in how you operate and what taxes you pay. But the government has *less* to say to the sole proprietor.

Disadvantages of sole proprietorship

There's a downside to being the only boss. The most important disadvantage is unlimited liability. That is, the individual proprietor is responsible for the full amount of business debts, which might exceed the proprietor's total investment. With some exceptions, this liability extends to all the proprietor's assets, such as a house or car. One way around this is for the proprietor to obtain sufficient insurance coverage to reduce the risk of physical loss and personal injury. If your suppliers aren't getting paid, however, they can come after your personal assets. Also, when the business is a single individual, the serious illness or death of that person can end the business.

Individuals typically cannot get the credit and capital that partnerships and corporations can. Fortunately, most catering services don't require extensive capital. But when they do, they seriously consider the advantages of taking on a partner or becoming a corporation.

Finally, as a sole proprietorship, you have a relatively limited viewpoint and experience because you're only one person. You're more subject to "tunnel vision," seeing things in a narrow way based on your necessarily limited experiences. You don't have someone with a commitment to your business who can give you a fresh viewpoint or new ideas.

Partnership

The Uniform Partnership Act (UPA) adopted by many states defines a partnership as "an association of two or more persons to carry on as co-owners of a business for profit." How the partnership is structured, the powers and limitations of each partner, and their participation in the business are written into a document called the "Articles of Partnership." The articles or descriptions can either be written by the partners, found in a legal form from a stationery store, or written by an attorney. Using an attorney is the best option, since it ensures that the document is binding and reduces disputes that typically come up once the business is growing.

Your firm's Articles of Partnership should include the following:
- The name, location, length, and purpose of the partnership
- The type of partnership
- A definition of the partners' individual contributions
- An agreement on how business expenses will be handled
- An outline of the authority of each partner
- A summary of the accounting methods that will be used
- Definition of how profits and losses will be distributed among the partners
- The salaries and capital draws for each partner
- An agreement of how the partnership will be modified or terminated, including dissolution of the partnership by death, by disability of a member, or by the decision of partners to disband
- A description of how the members will arbitrate and settle disputes as well as change terms of the partnership agreement

There are many types of partners within a partnership. An *active partner* is one who actively participates in the day-to-day operation of the business and is openly identified as a partner in the business. A *secret partner* is an active partner who is *not* openly identified as a partner for whatever reason. A *dormant partner* is one who is inactive and not known as a partner; he or she usually participates by furnishing money or advice. A *silent partner* is one who doesn't actively participate in the business, but might have their name on the partnership—such as a retired owner or figurehead. The silent partner who only lends his or her name to the business is not actually a true partner, but is a *nominal partner*. Finally, a *limited* or *special partner* is one who agrees to furnish financial assistance but does not participate in the ongoing business decisions. Limited partners can only lose their investment in the business; creditors cannot go after other assets because their liability is limited.

Advantages of a partnership

Partnerships are easier and less costly to form than corporations. All that's really needed is the Articles of Partnership just discussed. In fact, that isn't always a legal requirement. If you want to form a partnership with a handshake, you can in many states.

Partners are naturally more motivated to apply their best abilities to the job than the same people working for an employer. An active partner is more directly rewarded.

A partnership can typically raise capital more easily than a proprietorship because it has more people whose assets can be combined as equity for the loan. Also, lenders look at the credit ratings of each partner, so make sure that your business partners have good credit.

Partnerships are frequently more flexible in the decision-making process than corporations, although less flexible than proprietorships. Like proprietorships, partnerships offer relative freedom from government control and special taxation. A partnership doesn't pay income tax. Rather, all profits and losses flow through the partnership to the individual partners, who pay income and other taxes as if they were sole proprietors.

Disadvantages of a partnership

Of course, partnerships do have some minuses. Like sole proprietorships, at least one partner (the "general" partner) assumes unlimited liability for the business. You can obtain sufficient insurance coverage to reduce the risk of loss from physical loss or personal injury, but as the general partner, you're still liable.

A partnership is as stable or as unstable as its members. Elimination of any partner often means automatic dissolution of the partnership. However, the business can continue to operate if the agreement includes provisions for the right of survivorship and possible creation of a new partnership. Partnership insurance can assist surviving partners in purchasing the equity of a deceased partner.

Though a partnership has less difficulty in getting financing than a sole proprietorship, the fragile nature of partnerships sometimes makes it difficult to get long-term financing. The best source of financing is using the combined equity of the partners from assets they own as individuals. In fact, many partnerships are started because an active partner needs equity or financing that he or she cannot get without a partner with more assets or better credit.

Depending on how the partnership agreement is drawn up, *any* partner may be able to bind all of the partners to financial obligations. Make sure your Articles of Partnership accurately reflect your intent regarding how partners can or cannot obligate the partnership.

A major drawback to partnerships is the difficulty faced when a partner leaves. Buying out the partner's interest might be difficult unless terms have been specifically worked out in the partnership agreement.

As you can see, partnerships have numerous pluses and minuses. Many of the disadvantages can be taken care of in your Articles of Partnership. That is why you should use an attorney experienced in such agreements as you construct your partnership; the value is usually worth the cost.

Corporation

We've been moving from the simplest to the more complex forms of business: proprietorship, partnership, and now the corporation. As businesses grow, they often become corporations, identified by an extension to their name: "Corp.," "Inc.," or, in Canada, "Ltd."

Over 150 years ago, the U.S. Supreme Court defined a corporation as "an artificial being, invisible, intangible, and existing only in contemplation of the law." In other words, a corporation is a distinct legal entity, distinct from the individuals who own it. It is a legal being.

A corporation is usually formed by the authority of a state government. Corporations that do business in more than one state must comply with the federal laws regarding interstate commerce as well as with the individual state laws. The steps to forming a corporation begin with writing incorporation papers and issuing capital stock. Then, approval must be obtained from the Secretary of State in the state in which the corporation is being formed. Only then can the corporation act as a legal entity separate from those who own its stock.

Advantages of the corporation

The primary advantage to incorporation is that it limits the stockholder's liability to their investment. If you buy $1000 of stock in a corporation and it fails, you can only lose up to the $1000 investment. The corporation's creditors cannot come back to you demanding more money. The exception is when you put up some of your own assets up as collateral for the corporation.

Ownership of a corporation is a transferable asset. In fact, the New York Stock Exchange and other exchanges make a big business out of transferring stock, or partial ownership in corporations, from one investor to another. If your catering business is a corporation, you can sell partial ownership or stock in it (within certain limits). In fact, this is how many corporations get money to grow. A corporation can also issue long-term bonds to gain cash required to purchase assets or build the business.

Your corporation has a separate and legal existence. It is not you or anybody else; it is itself. Therefore, in the case of illness, death, or other cause for loss of a corporate officer or owner, the corporation continues to exist and do business.

The corporation can also delegate authority to hired managers, although they and the owners are often one and the same. Thus, you become an employee of the corporation. And the corporation can draw on the expertise and skills of more than one individual.

Disadvantages of the corporation

The corporation's state charter might limit the type of business it does to a specific industry or service while other states allow broad charters that permit corporations to operate in any legal enterprise.

Corporations face more governmental regulations on all levels: local, state, and federal. That means your business will spend more time and money fulfilling these requirements as a corporation than it would as a proprietorship or a partnership.

If your corporate manager is not also a stockholder, he or she will have less incentive to be efficient than someone with a share in your business.

As you can imagine, a corporation is more expensive to form than other types of businesses. Even if you don't use an attorney, forms and fees quickly add up. However, an attorney is a good investment when incorporating your catering business.

Finally, the federal and some state governments tax a corporation's income twice: once on the corporate net income, and once as it's received by the individual stockholders in the form of salary or dividends. One way to avoid this double taxation is with a subchapter-S corporation, which allows a small business to pay taxes as if it were a partnership (no income tax) and pass the tax liability on to the individual stockholders. Talk with your attorney about this option.

SHOULD I INVEST IN A FRANCHISE?

Franchising is a form of licensing in which the owner (the *franchisor*) of a product or service distributes through affiliated dealers (the *franchisees*). The franchise license is typically for a specific geographical area.

The product or service being marketed has a brand name, and the franchisor controls the way it is marketed. The franchisor requires consistency among the franchisees: standardized products or services, catering marks, uniform symbols, equipment, and storefronts. The franchisor typically offers assistance in organizing, training, merchandising, and management. In exchange, the franchisor receives initial franchise fees and an ongoing fee based on sales levels.

Why consider a franchise for your catering business? A successful franchise can reduce your risks, increase initial sales through name recognition, and help you make more money.

Numerous opportunities are available if you want to start your own catering service franchise. An excellent source of information is the *Franchise Opportunities Handbook*, produced and published by the United States Department of Commerce and available through the Superintendent of Documents (U.S. Government Printing Office, Washington, DC 20402) or your regional federal bookstore. This handbook lists basic information on franchises available in 44 categories, including "Foods." Information includes the name and address of the franchisor, a description of the operation, number of franchises, how long the franchise has been in business, how much equity capital is needed, how much financial assistance is available, what training is provided, and what managerial assistance is available.

Another source of information on franchises is

International Franchise Association
1350 New York Ave., NW, Suite 900
Washington, DC 20005

The IFA's *Franchise Opportunities Guide* is a comprehensive listing of franchisors by industry and business category. *Franchising Opportunities* is their bimonthly magazine. Their newsletter, *Franchising World*, includes information on developing trends in franchising. Other sources include *Entrepreneur, Income Opportunities*, and other magazines available on most newsstands.

Catering franchises include

Augies, Inc.
1900 West County Rd. C
St. Paul, MN 55113
612-633-5308

O! Deli
65 Battery St.
San Francisco, CA 94111
415-765-1500

Wee-Bag-It
2200 Corporate Blvd., NW, Suite 317
Boca Raton, FL 33231
800-533-7161

How do you know if the franchise you're considering is reputable? Many laws regulate franchising. Trade regulations issued by the Federal Trade Commission offer you important legal rights. For example, you have the right to receive a disclosure statement and standard franchise agreement at your first personal meeting with a franchisor. You must also receive documentation on how the franchisor arrived at any earnings claims. If you have questions about your rights or think they have been violated by a franchisor, you can contact the Franchise and Business Opportunities Program (Federal Trade Commission, Washington DC 20580). In addition, your state might have a franchise monitoring office.

Once you've done your homework, purchasing a franchise license can be less risky than starting a business by yourself—but more expensive.

WHAT TRADE ASSOCIATIONS CAN HELP ME?

As the owner of a catering business, you're a professional. National and regional associations of professionals just like you can help your business grow through knowledge. Obviously, they are not going to share their catering secrets, but most will help your business become more professional and more profitable.

Trade associations serving the catering service business include the following:

International Food Service Executive's Association
1100 S. State Rd. 7, Suite 103
Margate, FL 33068
305-977-0767

Mobile Industrial Caterers' Association
7300 Artesia Blvd.
Buena Park, CA 90621
714-521-6000

National Association of Catering Executives
304 W. Liberty St., #201
Louisville, KY 40202
502-583-3783

National Caterers Roundtable Association
Blendonview Office Park
5008-25 Pine Creek Dr.
Westerville, OH 43081
614-891-7989

National Restaurant Association
1200 17th St., NW
Washington, DC 20036
800-424-5156

Society for Foodservice Management
304 W. Liberty St., Suite 201
Louisville, KY 40202
502-583-3783

HOW CAN I MEET OTHER CATERERS?

Catering trade shows and conventions offer much more than an opportunity to get out of the kitchen. They update you on the latest tools, methods, and opportunities, inspire and entertain you, and train you.

The three primary annual conventions in the catering industry are

- The National Caterers Roundtable Association's Annual Meeting and CaterEXPO
- The Mobile Industrial Caterers' Association Convention and Exhibition
- The National Association of Catering Executives Convention and Exhibition

Contact the trade associations listed in the previous section for additional information on the dates, locations, and requirements for attending these trade shows and conventions.

WHAT TRADE JOURNALS ARE AVAILABLE?

Many magazines are written specifically for those in the catering and food-service trade. They offer you an opportunity to keep up on the latest production and marketing ideas in the business as well as gather information on new products and services.

A few of the magazines and trade journals in the catering industry are

A La Carte
7300 Artesia Blvd.
Buena Park, CA 90621
714-521-6000

Catering Today
2070 South Monaco, C-305
Denver, CO 80224
303-758-8022

Kosher Outlook
201-837-0500

Modern Food Service News
15 Emerald St.
Hackensack, NY 07601
201-488-1800

NCRA CommuniCATER
Blendonview Office Park
5008-25 Pine Creek Dr.
Westerville, OH 43081
614-891-7989

Restaurants USA
1200 17th St., NW
Washington, DC 20036
800-424-5156

HOW CAN I GET ADVANCED TRAINING?

There are also many resources for expanding your food-service and catering skills. Videocassettes on banquet service, buffet layout and service, courtesy and service, and related topics are available from

National Educational Media
21601 Devonshire St.
Chattsworth CA 91311
818-709-6009

Videocassettes on buffet catering and cookery and kosher catering created by Culinary Institute of America are available from

The Learning Resources Center
Hyde Park, NY 12538
914-452-9600

Numerous videocassettes on food preparation, merchandising, and service can also be ordered from

RMI Media Productions
2807 W. 47th St.
Shawnee Mission, KS 66205

Finally, the National Association of Catering Executives offers a Certified Catering Executive certification program and other services to the catering industry. Contact them at the address listed earlier in this chapter.

HOW WILL THE GOVERNMENT HELP ME?

Several branches of federal and state governments can also help you start your catering business. The most widely known and used government resource is the Small Business Administration, or SBA. Founded more than 40 years ago, the SBA has offices in 100 cities across the United States with a charter to help small businesses start and grow. Its main address is

Small Business Administration
1441 L St., NW
Washington, DC 20416

The SBA offers counseling (requested through the form in Fig. 2-2) and booklets on business topics, and administers a small-business loan guarantee program. In addition, it sponsors the 13,000-member Service Corps of Retired Executives (SCORE) and Active Corps of Executives (ACE), Business Development Centers, and Technology Access Centers.

To find your area's SBA office, check the white pages of metropolitan telephone books in your region under "United States Government, Small Business Administration."

Publications

The SBA offers a number of valuable publications and videotapes for starting and managing small business. VHS videotapes on business plans, marketing, and promotions can be purchased from the SBA or borrowed through many public libraries. Publications are available on products/ideas/inventions, financial management, management and planning, marketing, crime prevention, personnel management, and other topics. The booklets can be purchased for one or two dollars each at SBA offices or from

SBA Publications
P.O. Box 30
Denver, CO 80201

Ask first for SBA Form 115A, *The Small Business Directory*, which lists available publications and includes an order form.

The SBA recently added a computer bulletin-board service, cosponsored by SPRINT, for businesspeople who want to retrieve business information over a computer modem. You can also talk with other small business owners and catering professionals around the country. If you have communications software and a modem (300, 1200, or 2400 baud) on your computer, you can call it at 800-859-4636. For 9600 baud modems, the number is 800-697-4636.

To use this and many other bulletin boards, your communications software should be set for full duplex, no parity, 8 data bits, and 1 stop bit (written "full-N-8-1"). (Chapter 3 covers computers and technology for caterers in more detail.)

In addition, the SBA offers low-cost videos on business plans, marketing, promotion, and home-based businesses in the Small Business Video Library. Your SBA office will have more information, or you can write to

SBA/Success Videos
P.O. Box 30
Denver, CO 80202-0030

The SBA also funds small business "incubators" throughout the country. Incubators are facilities in which a number of new and growing businesses operate under one roof with affordable rents, sharing services and equipment, and with access to a variety of business services. For more information, contact your regional SBA office or

The Office of Private Sector Initiatives
1441 L St., NW, Room 317
Washington, DC 20416

OMB Approval No. 3245-0091

U.S. SMALL BUSINESS ADMINISTRATION

REQUEST FOR COUNSELING

A. NAME OF COMPANY	B. YOUR NAME (Last, First, Middle)	C. TELEPHONE (H) (B)

D. STREET	E. CITY	F. STATE	G. COUNTY	H. ZIP

I. TYPE OF BUSINESS (Check one)
1. ☐ Retail   4. ☐ Manufacturing
2. ☐ Service   5. ☐ Construction
3. ☐ Wholesale 6. ☐ Not in Business

J. BUS. OWNSHP./GENDER
1. ☐ Male
2. ☐ Female
3. ☐ Male/Female

K. VETERAN STATUS
1. ☐ Veteran
2. ☐ Vietnam-Era Veteran
3. ☐ Disabled Veteran

L.
- INDICATE PREFERRED DATE AND TIME FOR APPOINTMENT
  DATE _____ TIME _____
- ARE YOU CURRENTLY IN BUSINESS?   YES _____ NO _____
- IF YES, HOW LONG? _____
- TYPE OF BUSINESS (USE THREE TO FIVE WORDS)
  _____

M. ETHNIC BACKGROUND

Race:
1. ☐ American Indian or Alaskan Native
2. ☐ Asian or Pacific Islander
3. ☐ Black
4. ☐ White

b. *Ethnicity:*
1. ☐ Hispanic Origin
2. ☐ Not of Hispanic Origin

N. INDICATE, BRIEFLY, THE NATURE OF SERVICE AND/OR COUNSELING YOUR ARE SEEKING

_____
_____

O.
- IT HAS BEEN EXPLAINED TO ME THAT I MAY USE FURTHER SERVICES SPONSORED BY THE U.S. SMALL BUSINESS ADMINISTRATION   YES _____ NO _____
- I HAVE ATTENDED A SMALL BUSINESS WORKSHOP   YES _____ NO _____
- CONDUCTED BY _____

P. HOW DID YOU LEARN OF THESE COUNSELING SERVICES?
1. ☐ Yellow Pages   3. ☐ Radio   5. ☐ Bank   7. ☐ Word-of-Mouth
2. ☐ Television   4. ☐ Newspapers   6. ☐ Chamber of Commerce   8. ☐ Other _____

Q. SBA CLIENT (To Be Filled Out By Counselor)
1. ☐ Borrower   2. ☐ Applicant   3. ☐ 8(a) Client   4. ☐ COC   5. ☐ Surety Bond

R. AREA OF COUNSELING PROVIDED (To Be Filled Out By Counselor)
1. Bus. Start-Up/Acquisition   5. Accounting & Records   9. Personnel
2. Source of Capital   6. Finan. Analysis/Cost Control 10. Computer Systems
3. Marketing/Sales   7. Inventory Control   11. Internat'l Trade
4. Government Procurement   8. Engineering R&D   12. Business Liq./Sale

I request business management counseling from the Small Business Administration. I agree to cooperate should I be selected to participate in surveys designed to evaluate SBA assistance services. I authorize SBA to furnish relevant information to the assigned management counselor(s) although I expect that information to be held in strict confidence by him/her.

I further understand that any counselor has agreed not to: (1) recommend goods or services from sources in which he/she has an interest and (2) accept fees or commissions developing from this counseling relationship. In consideration of SBA's furnishing management or technical assistance, I waive all claims against SBA personnel, SCORE, SBDC and its host organizations, SBI, and other SBA Resource Counselors arising from this assistance.

SIGNATURE AND TITLE OF REQUESTER	DATE

FOR USE OF THE SMALL BUSINESS ADMINISTRATION

RESOURCE	DISTRICT	REGION

SBA FORM 641 (2-91) PREVIOUS EDITION IS OBSOLETE

WHITE   COUNSELOR
YELLOW: SBI OR SCORE OR SBDC SUB.
PINK   DO OR NSO OR SBDC LEAD

2-2 Individualized business counseling can be requested through SCORE.

SBA loans

The volume of business loans guaranteed by the SBA has increased from $3 billion in 1989 to a projected $7.5 billion in 1993. According to the SBA, the average loan was for $250,626 over a term of 11.5 years. About one-fifth of these loans went to companies less than two years old. Here is a summary of current SBA loan opportunities:

SBA 7(a) guaranteed loans These loans are made by private lenders and can be guaranteed up to 80 percent by the SBA. Most SBA loans are made under this guaranty program. The maximum guaranty of loans exceeding $155,000 is 85 percent. SBA has no minimum size loan amount and can guarantee up to $750,000 of a private sector loan. SBA provides special inducements to lenders providing guaranteed loans of $50,000 or less. The lender must be a financial institution who "participates" with the SBA. The small business submits a loan application to the lender, which makes the initial review. If the lender cannot provide the loan directly, it may request an SBA guaranty. The lender then forwards the application and its analysis to the local SBA office. If approved by the SBA, the lender closes the loan and disburses the funds.

SBA direct loans Loans of up to $150,000 are available under this program only to applicants unable to secure an SBA-guaranteed loan. Direct loan funds are available only to certain types of borrowers, such as handicapped individuals, nonprofit sheltered workshops, Vietnam-era veterans, disabled veterans, businesses in high-unemployment areas owned by low-income individuals, or businesses located in low-income neighborhoods. The applicant must first seek financing from at least two banks in their area.

SBA micro-loans The newest SBA loan opportunity is intended for smaller businesses who want to get started or grow and only need a few thousand dollars. The typical SBA micro-loan is for about $10,000. Contact your regional SBA office for additional information and requirements.

SBA loans generally have maturities of five to seven years unless they are used to finance a fixed asset, such as the purchase or major renovation of business real estate. The SBA requires that available assets, such as your home, be pledged to adequately secure the loan. Personal guaranties are required from all principles owning 20% or more of the business, and from the chief executive officer with any share in the business.

If you're interested in applying for an SBA guaranteed or direct loan, call your regional office of the Small Business Administration. Even better, ask for the name of an SBA-certified lender in your area. The SBA loan program, notorious for its paperwork requirements, can be expedited by a banker who knows how to work within the system. You'll get your loan faster. In fact, those bankers that have "preferred-lender" status can handle your SBA loan without the SBA even being involved.

SCORE

The Service Corps of Retired Executives is a national nonprofit association with a goal of helping small businesses. SCORE members include retired men and women, as well as those who are still active in their own business (ACE), who donate their time and experience to counsel individuals regarding small business. SCORE is sponsored by the U.S. Small Business Administration. Your local office is probably in or near that of the local SBA office. You can contact the main office at

SCORE
1441 L St., NW, Room 100
Washington, DC 20416

To take advantage of the services of a SCORE counselor, complete a SCORE Request for Counseling worksheet and return it to the local office in person or by mail. The interview will be in person at a mutually agreed time. The worksheet asks about the type of business; whether you're starting, buying, or currently operating the business; how much experience you have in this business; and how much knowledge you have of accounting. It also asks you to categorize your questions into one or more of the following areas:

- Accounting/taxes
- Patents/copyrights
- Construction
- Insurance
- Marketing
- Distribution
- Legal matters
- Manufacture
- Importing/exporting
- Business plans
- Home industry
- Sales projections
- Customer service
- Other (specify)

SCORE counselors are typically highly experienced businesspeople; some might have direct experience in the catering business. They do not charge for their time and assistance, nor are you required to follow their advice. The more counselors you have, the greater the opportunity for success as a catering service.

Business Development Centers

Business Development Centers (BDCs) are regional centers funded by the Small Business Administration and managed in conjunction with regional colleges. A BDC offers free and confidential counseling for small business owners and managers, new businesses, home-based businesses, and people with business ideas related to retail, service, wholesale, manufacturing, and farming.

BDCs sponsor seminars on various business topics, assist in developing business and marketing plans, inform entrepreneurs of employer requirements, and teach cash-flow budgeting and management. They also gather information sources, assist in locating business resources, and make referrals.

Call your local SBA office or college campus to determine if there is a Business Development Center near you and, if so, what services they can provide as you build your catering business.

Technology Access Centers

Technology Access Centers (TACs) are a new and little-known service provided by the Small Business Administration and the National Institute of Standards and Technology (NIST), a division of the U.S. Department of Commerce. In fact, there are currently just six Technology Access Centers in the country. Your SBA can tell you whether there is one near you and, if so, how to contact it.

TACs use the power of the computer to access information from large computer libraries called *databases*. You pick the topic, and the TAC searches these computerized libraries for information about the topic. You can ask for articles and data on catering, information on your competitors, information about codes and regulations in your region, and related topics. (Some of the information for this book was located through a regional TAC.) Depending on the databases they have access to, TACs can find data that will help improve your business or marketing plan, and better identify profitable catering opportunities.

The process is simple. A TAC representative interviews you to determine what information you need, and then writes it into terms that can be searched in computer databases. If the search is successful, you get a printed report of the results mailed to you. There is often a charge, but it is only a fraction of the cost charged by the database firm. The TAC sponsors pay the rest to encourage small business development.

NIST has another service to business owners and other professionals called *FedWorld*. FedWorld is an online computer system that allows you access to information from over 100 federal bulletin boards. It offers census information, small business resources, other government resources, and the opportunity to talk with other people starting or operating a catering service. Computers and BBSs (bulletin board systems) are covered in the next chapter. If you already know about them, you can call FedWorld by modem at 703-321-8020.

Other government resources

One more valuable federal resource is the U.S. Department of Commerce (Washington, DC 20230). It's Office of Business Liaison is the initial contact point for questions about the department's business assistance. The Bureau of the Census is part of the Commerce Department, and has detailed statistics on people and businesses in the U.S. compiled from many sources.

Some of the publications available through the Department of Commerce include
- *Census of Business: Retail-Area Statistics—U.S. Summary*
- *County Business Patterns*
- *County and City Data Book*
- *Directory of Federal Statistics for Local Areas: A Guide to Sources*
- *Standard Metropolitan Statistical Areas*

These publications are available from the Department of Commerce or at federal GPO bookstores in most major cities. You can also get them by contacting the Government Printing Office at

GPO
Superintendent of Documents
Washington, DC 20402-9328

The Commerce Department's Economic Development Administration provides financial and technical assistance to businesses willing to locate in economically distressed areas of the nation. Its address is

EDA
Room 7800B
Washington, DC 20230

The department's Minority Business Development Agency (MBDA; Room 5053 at the same address) encourages the development of minority-owned businesses. It provides management, marketing, financial, and technical assistance through business development centers, minority business catering organizations, and MBDA field offices.

The U.S. Treasury Department's Internal Revenue Service offers many Small-Business Tax Education Program videos through their regional offices. Topics include depreciation, business use of your home, employment taxes, excise taxes, starting a business, sole proprietorships, partnerships, self-employed retirement plans, sub-chapter-S corporations, and federal tax deposits.

States, too, want to encourage small businesses. Check with your state corporation division, your state legislator, or similar sources to find out what resources are available to you. After all, government is a partner in your business. In fact, they will take their profit (taxes) before you get yours.

SUCCESS ACTION PLAN

Many people dream of managing their own catering service. You only succeed if you take action on this dream. Here are some things you can do right now to move down the road of success as an independent caterer:

- ❏ List five business names for your catering business and describe why each was chosen.
- ❏ Find out how an assumed business name is registered in your area.
- ❏ List at least three choices for locating your catering business and describe why each was chosen. Include estimated costs for each location.
- ❏ Determine which business and health licenses you will need to start and operate your catering service.
- ❏ Decide whether your catering service will be a proprietorship, partnership, or corporation, and set it up per instructions in this chapter.
- ❏ When ready, open a business checking account under your new business name. Apply for a bank card at the same time.
- ❏ Check into franchise opportunities for your catering business.
- ❏ Contact catering service trade associations to determine what benefits they offer your new business.
- ❏ Write for sample copies of appropriate magazines and trade journals for potential subscriptions.
- ❏ Contact your regional SBA office for resources and loan information.
- ❏ Contact your regional SCORE office for a SCORE Request for Counseling

worksheet and an appointment to discuss your new business with a SCORE counselor.

❏ Contact your regional Business Development Center for additional resources. Ask about a regional Technology Access Center.

❏ Contact other government resources for additional marketing and management information. You've paid for it!

3

How do I set up my catering business?

Once you've decided about the form and location of your catering service, the next important step is to determine the equipment and supplies you need. This chapter helps you make these decisions. Use it as a reminder or a checklist, depending on what type of catering service you're setting up, where, how large it is to be, and what you already have available.

The three categories of equipment and services you need are catering service equipment, wholesale services, and office equipment. As part of your office, experienced caterers strongly recommend using technology to leap ahead of the competition. So this chapter also covers computers, advanced communications equipment, and specialized computer software written for catering services.

WHAT CATERING EQUIPMENT DO I NEED?

I will not presume to tell you all of the culinary tools and equipment you should have in your commissary for two reasons. First, you probably have already built up a supply of functional tools based on your unique experience. Second, your specialty might require unusual equipment found in few catering kitchens.

Nevertheless, let's review the basic tools as a starting point for the newer caterer and as a reminder to the more experienced:

- *Commissary equipment*: Ovens, microwaves, refrigerator, freezer, coffee maker, dishwasher, sinks, garbage disposal, mixer, scale, steam kettle, food slicer, food chopper, prep tables, warming lamps, transport racks, dolly
- *Utensils*: Carving knives, cleaver, bread knives, cutting boards, carving boards, kitchen spoons, measuring spoons, measuring cups, ladles, tongs, spatulas, whisks, colander, egg slicer
- *Cooking pots and pans*: One-through five-quart pots, baking pans, pie pans, oval cake pans, rectangular cake pans, angel food cake pan, muffin pans, cookie sheets, frying pans, roasting pans, omelette pan, pizza pans
- *Servers*: Chinaware, glassware, chafing dishes, bread baskets, food warmers, serving trays, coffee urn, warmers

Obviously, a hot-service caterer needs more equipment than a cold-service caterer, and a caterer who specializes in Mexican food buffets requires different equipment than a street-cart caterer. Begin listing the equipment and tools you will need in your business notebook and identify which ones you must purchase or lease.

Many directories and buyer's guides list sources of catering equipment. They include the *ICA Caterers' Buyers Guide* (312-922-0966), *Catering Today's Buyers Guide Issue* (published each spring; 800-937-4464), *Directory of Food Service Distributors* (212-371-9400), *Foodservice Equipment and Supplies Specialist Buyer's Guide* (708-635-8800), and the *National Food Brokers Association Directory of Members* (202-789-2844). Call them for current pricing information.

In addition, new and used food preparation equipment can be purchased through restaurant suppliers in your area. Check your local telephone books under "Restaurant Equipment & Supplies" for coolers, freezers, grills, ovens, ranges, fryers, exhaust systems, mixers, slicers, dishwashers, food warmers, and other equipment.

WHERE DO I BUY WHOLESALE GROCERIES AND SUPPLIES?

Purchase all of your food—except maybe last-minute items—from wholesale grocers in your area. To find the best supplier, check your local yellow pages under "Grocers-Whsle," then make a few telephone calls. Explain your business, what foods you require, and expected quantities, and ask how to establish an account. You'll find some wholesale grocers will discourage you from using them and others will be very helpful. Within larger cities, wholesale grocers often specialize. Some work primarily with large supermarkets, while others handle "mom-and-pop" restaurants and catering firms. A few specialize in ethnic foods. Find one or two that you can work with and set up an account with each.

Since you'll probably be on a cash basis for the first few orders, ask about discounts allowed for cash. Also ask for *dock pricing* (picking up the food yourself) as well as delivered prices. Learn how the wholesaler takes orders, how quickly they are filled, when deliveries are made, and how they handle returns. This information will help in selecting a primary and a secondary wholesaler for your catering business.

Fruits and vegetables are often ordered separately through wholesalers listed in the telephone book under "Fruits & Vegetables-Whsle." Prepared foods are sometimes ordered from firms listed under "Frozen Foods-Whsle" or "Food Products." Fresh meats are purchased through businesses listed under "Meat-Whsle." Alcoholic beverages and spirits can be ordered from wholesalers listed in the telephone book under "Wines-Whsle," "Beer & Ale-Whsle," and "Liquor-Whsle."

HOW DO I FURNISH MY CATERING OFFICE?

Let's assume that you've selected the type of office most appropriate to your needs—and budget. Now it's time to start gathering the office tools and equipment you will need to manage your business efficiently.

Office equipment

Depending on your catering specialty and the initial size of your business, you might consider many pieces of office equipment. Stick with the basics, however, until your business is profitable.

One of your most vital office tools is your briefcase—your "portable office." Purchase one that will stand up to the rigors of daily use as well as protect its contents. Look for hard plastic cases rather than leather. Make sure the hinges will hold up well.

What goes in your portable office? Your daily planner, calculator, order forms, workbooks, file folders on current jobs (if they'll fit), and anything else that will help you be continually productive.

All offices, even in a vehicle, require some type of desk or flat surface where you can gather your telephone, records, and other business tools. If in your car, a briefcase can serve as your desk. In fact, many successful small catering services never grow beyond the briefcase stage, managing all their jobs out of manila folders carried around in the briefcase. They usually have a secondary storage area, such as a file cabinet, for inactive jobs and other records.

The next step up is simply a hollow-core door laid horizontally across two file cabinets. It's practical, inexpensive, and can withstand abuse. It's just not very pretty. A 30-inch door fits well over standard two-drawer file cabinets. If your budget won't allow two cabinets, buy one and add a couple of legs to the other side.

Depending on how much time you'll be spending in your office, you can then graduate to a desk from a business supply store for $250 and up. If you plan to keep a telephone, fax machine, computer, files, and trays all on top of your desk, you'll want a larger unit. If your partner, secretary, or office assistant will share some of the duties, you should consider two smaller desks. Many small businesspeople place their desk facing a wall or in a corner so they can attach shelves or mount notes that can be easily read while on the telephone.

Most office workers soon learn the value of a good-quality chair, especially if they sit in it more than a few hours a day. If you're out of the office most of the time, you can buy an inexpensive chair. Even a folding chair can serve until your catering business is built up. Once your business is successful and you're spending more time in the office, invest in a good-quality chair to keep you comfortable all day and reduce stress.

Depending on your specialty, you might want shelves on or near your desk so you can refer to recipe books, telephone books, directories, and other reference materials. If cost is a greater concern than attractiveness, consider setting bricks or building blocks a few feet apart on the floor, then laying 1-by-10-inch boards across the top, followed by more blocks and 1-bys. However, don't build your block shelves higher than 32 inches unless they are securely anchored.

If you have clients coming to your office and feel that they need to be impressed, consider renting office equipment that will "show" better than what's described here. This is especially important if you're working on larger jobs with clients who aren't familiar with the typical look of an entrepreneur's office: dislocated clutter.

Office supplies

You will also need a variety of office supplies to help you gather, record, correspond, and track your business. These supplies include paper clips, a stapler, pens and pencils, a pencil sharpener, file folders and labels, rubber bands, typing paper, calculator tape, stationery (letterhead and envelopes), and postage.

If your office won't include a computer, you should have a typewriter. Look for a good used electric typewriter and make sure that replacement ribbons are readily available.

Telephones

The most important tool for your catering service's office is the telephone. With it, you can talk directly to dozens of prospects or clients each day without leaving your office. Without it, you must drive all over town and hope that your contacts are available when you are.

Depending on local telephone company requirements, you might need to order a separate business telephone line for your catering business. The criteria is if you answer with a business name rather than a personal name, you need a business telephone line. For example, if your name is Betty Jones and your firm is "Betty Jones Catering Service," you can answer "Betty Jones" and not confuse your prospects and clients. But if you're "ABC Catering Service" and you answer "Betty Jones," callers might think that they have the wrong number.

The cost of a business line has decreased over the last few years because of the competition among telephone companies. This competition can also make the selection of the *best* telephone service more difficult. However, for the small, fledgling catering business, telephone bills will not be so large that the typical discount structure will make much difference. Go with you favorite until you've built up your business and better know what your telephone service needs will be. Then you can review the "small business packages" offered by competing telephone companies to see which will save you the most money.

Discount stores, drug stores, and many other retail outlets offer standard telephones that can support basic services offered by many telephone companies: call forwarding, call waiting, redial, speed dial, etc. The cost is typically under $50 per telephone. You don't want anything fancy, you want something sturdy with standard features. Go with brands you know, and buy from someone who will take it back within a reasonable time if it doesn't work.

Cordless telephones

Cordless telephones are more expensive than regular ones, but also more convenient. Today, you can buy a good-quality cordless telephone for $100 or less (full-featured models are a little more). The greatest advantage to the cordless phone is its portability. You can carry it throughout your office, wherever you're working, to avoid the quick dash to your desk to catch it before the third ring.

With every plus, there's a minus or two. In the case of cordless telephones, the minus is that it runs on batteries that need to be recharged. If you keep it with the main unit, it will charge, but then it won't be handy. So look for a cordless telephone that can run the longest time away from the main set. Many can operate up to a week off the base unit. Another minus can be overcome: You might forget where you put the gadget. However, many new cordless phones have a "paging" button that can be pressed on the main set and will beep at the handset (if the battery isn't dead!) to tell you where it is.

As with other tools, buy the best quality phone that you can reasonably afford and purchase it from someone who knows the product. Their phone might cost a couple of dollars more than the discount house, but you get added value because you bought the most appropriate tool for your budget.

Cellular telephones

Mobile or cellular telephones offer the ultimate portability. You can take them in your car, in a briefcase, to a job site, to your home, and still answer calls from your prospects and clients.

How do they work? Cellular telephones are battery-operated and require long-life batteries. Your car battery can support a cellular phone, or you can carry a rechargeable battery pack with you. The signal is carried by wire or satellite link to a transmitter or repeater that covers a wide area, so your conversation is being broadcast much like the signal of an FM radio station. The difference is that anyone with a radio can listen to the FM station, while only you and the person you're talking to (hopefully) can hear your telephone conversation. I say "hopefully" because, with the right equipment, a competitor can listen in on your conversation unless you have special scrambling equipment.

Rather than get into the specifics of cellular phone technology, which change almost daily, I recommend that you call a local cellular telephone service and find out what's new. Prices, too, are changing. To get more customers, cellular services are offering telephones at low initial costs, but you must sign up for at least six months of their service. Because of air-time charges, this service is much more expensive than standard-line telephone service. It might still be a bargain, though, if you're a one-person office who has no one else to answer your calls.

And, if you're brave, ask for a demonstration of a portable cellular workstation. Housed in a briefcase, it's a cellular telephone, laptop computer, modem, fax, and other goodies. The complete set weighs as much as a bowling ball: 16 pounds. But it's a whole office for those on the go.

Pagers

A pager is one of the most valuable—and most annoying—tools a catering service can have. A pager allows other people (office employees, customers, suppliers, and field employees) to contact you wherever you are.

The type of pager you should select depends on your budget and how you will use your pager. A *tone pager* simply alerts you to call an agreed-upon telephone number, usually that of your office. A *voice pager* delivers a message recorded on your office telephone directly to you, wherever you are. A *digital display pager* pages you and then displays the telephone number you should call. An *alphanumeric display pager* can give you a written message.

Many catering services start by renting a tone pager, then, as business requires, move up to a voice or display pager. Check your local telephone book's yellow pages under "Paging & Signaling Equipment & Systems" or similar headings for local suppliers.

Answering machines

Not long ago, an answering machine was an annoying and misused tape recorder that attempted to drive off the people who called you. Today's answering machine is much more accepted, especially in business. It's also easier to buy and use.

Tape answering machines use either mini- or standard-sized audiotapes to record an outgoing and any incoming message. The good ones have a separate tape for each. The better ones don't have time limits for incoming messages. The best ones have features that allow you to hear your messages from any other telephone, let you know if you have any messages at all, and allow you to easily change your message from a remote location.

Digital answering machines use computer chips to record outgoing messages and, in some cases, incoming calls. The sound quality is often better, but the length of the message might be limited. However, advances in digital sound technology will make next year's models even more useful. Be certain that the system you purchase announces the date and time of the call on the incoming message.

Unfortunately, many businesses misuse their answering system by putting cryptic announcements and background music on the system that confuse or intimidate callers. An effective message should be something like this, "Hello, this is ABC Catering Service's answering system. Your call is important to us. Please leave your name and telephone number after the beep and someone will get back to you as soon as possible. Or, if you'd prefer, please call again later. Thank you."

Actually, once you and your clients get comfortable with using an answering machine, you'll find them even more effective than taking live calls. You call a client and leave a list of questions on their machine, then make some other calls. They call your answering machine and leave the answers while your regular telephone is busy. "Telephone tag" becomes obsolete. And, if necessary, you can review the recorded conversation to ensure that you understand the information. You can even leave important or confidential messages in private "mailboxes" on your system that can only be accessed with a code by your manager, your best client, or another important person. It's how business will be conducted in the future.

Fax machines

The digital facsimile (fax) machine is actually over 100 years old in concept. But it wasn't practical until about a decade ago. Today, there are more than 25 million fax machines in the world, with most of them installed in businesses.

The concept of the fax machine is simple: It "reads" a sheet of paper for light and dark spots much like a copy machine does. It then converts these spots into a code that's sent across a telephone line at a speed of nearly 10,000 bits of information per second. Based on some international standards, the fax machine on the other end knows how to read these signals and convert them into light and dark spots that conform to the image that was sent. This image is printed on a piece of paper, and you have a fax.

The smart caterer can now send menus, recipes, proposals, sales letters, copies of invoices, and other printed material to prospects, clients, and others in just seconds. She can also quickly get a written quote from a wholesale grocer anywhere in the country, and almost immediately fax a quote to a client. A typical one-page fax, like the one in Fig. 3-1, takes less than 30 seconds to transmit on a Group 3 fax machine. Depending on the distance and time of day, this page costs about as much to fax as to mail.

A facsimile machine looks like a small printer with a tray to hold outgoing paper and a telephone set either attached or nearby. How does it work? When you call the number you're faxing to, your fax machine sends out a tone that tells the other machine it would like to transmit a facsimile. The receiving machine sends your machine a high-pitched tone, then you might need to manually press your machine's "start" button and hang up the telephone. The fax is being transmitted. Some machines automate the process; you simply put the copy into the machine and press a button that calls a specific telephone in memory and sends the fax without any help.

123 Main Street, Yourtown

FAX COVER

To: Frank Simpson

Company Name: Yourtown Wholesale Foods

Fax Number: 234-8888

From: Judy Richards

Description:

Attached is our food order for this week.

We also need a quote on 24 fresh Maine lobsters delivered July 3. Thanks. See you at Kiwanis tomorrow!

Number of pages (including cover): 3

Date sent: June 30, 19XX   Time sent: 11:20 am

If there are any problems receiving this transmission please call: 234-6754

3-1 Fax machines have made written communications instantaneous.

There are dozens of things to know about buying a fax machine for your business. However, many are frills. Most important is that your fax machine is Group 3 compatible. Beyond that, explain to the salesperson what you need your fax machine for, and let him or her show you the newest features. You can get a basic fax machine for $300 or $400, a better one for $400 to $800, and your heart's desire for a thousand dollars or more. You can also rent or lease a fax machine. Leasing is an especially good idea with equipment like fax machines that quickly become obsolete.

Some fax machines combine functions of other office equipment. It might, for example, have a standard telephone handset that you can use for your primary or secondary business line, as well as a tape or digital answering machine. In some ways, this makes sense because you have the business telephone line feeding into one machine that can serve three purposes: let you answer, take messages, or take faxes. But, like any machine that combines functions, if one goes out or becomes obsolete, they might all go. Compare the cost of a combined unit against the cost of individual units. If there is little difference, go for the separate components.

You should also consider PC fax boards, if you decide to purchase a computer for your catering business. These printed circuit boards fit inside your computer—even a small one—and allow you to plug in a telephone and use it as a fax. Some models can also serve as your answering machine. Fax boards are typically purchased through computer stores.

DO I NEED A COPIER?

Copy machines can be very useful to your catering business, especially if you don't have a PC and a printer. You will want to conveniently copy outgoing correspondence, recipes, menus, proposals, contracts, agreements, drawings, procedures, and other business documents. A good copier can be purchased for under $500. If you're producing a client newsletter, your own brochures, direct mail pieces, or other marketing documents, your copy machine can be more cost-effective than running down to the copy shop or printer for a few copies every day.

Features to look for in a copier include enlargement and reduction, paper trays, collating of multiple copies, and reproduction of photos. You won't need a copier the first day you open your doors; wait until you have a genuine need before you buy. By then you'll know what features you require.

If you purchase a medium-to-large copier, you should consider a service contract, especially if routine maintenance calls are included at a nominal charge. In your busy office you might forget to perform such maintenance and it can eventually add up to a major repair. Be careful of costs, however; some maintenance programs are more profitable for the copy machine representative than are the machines themselves.

DO I NEED A COMPUTER?

Many people are still intimidated by computers. Maybe that's because they haven't discovered how friendly and helpful computers can be. If you do choose to add a computer to your catering business' office, you'll soon find dozens of ways to profitably put it to work. You can write letters, keep track of your income and outgo, manage your accounts receivables and make collections easier, keep track of your customers and your prospects, schedule jobs, order supplies, learn about your competitors, and much more.

People are often frightened by computers because of all the new terminology that they must decipher: CPUs, bits, bytes, bauds, networks, boards, hard disks, RAM, monitor interlacing, and on and on. Don't worry about it. You'll quickly pick up what the terms mean. Here's a simplified introduction to computers—or perhaps a review, depending on your experience. Most business computers are "IBM-compatible," so that's what I'll discuss. Apple's Macintosh computers use a different operating system, but the basics are the same.

CPUs

A CPU is a *central processing unit*. The name gives it away; it is an electronic machine built around a small "chip" called the microprocessor that processes information for you. You could loosely compare it to the engine in your car.

A particular CPU is typically referred to by the same name as the microprocessor chip that is its brain. For example, early PCs (personal computers) used a microprocessor chip called the 8088 (eighty eighty-eight), so they were called "88s" (or by the IBM brand name for the model, the "XT"). The next-generation microprocessor and CPU was the 80286, referred to as the "286" (two eighty-six) or by the IBM brand model, the "AT." Then came the "386," the "486," and, just recently, the "586" or "Pentium." These different classes of CPUs could be relatively compared to the two-cylinder, four-cylinder, six-cylinder, V8, fuel-injected V8, and other engines. It's not a one-to-one comparison, though, because each CPU is at least five times faster than the previous model.

In between chips like the 386 and 486 are incremental steps identified by letters like "SX" (similar to a half-step) and "DX" (a full step). Don't worry about them for now.

The other number to understand in looking at CPUs is the "clock speed." In our simplified automotive comparison, the clock speed would be like the transmission—it makes the engine (CPU) go faster. XT chips started out with clock speeds of about 5 MHz (mega—or million—hertz). Today's newer 486 and Pentium CPUs have clock speeds of 50 MHz and more!

So all you really need to know about the CPU of a PC is that a 486 is faster than a 286 or 386, and a clock speed of 66 MHz is faster than one that's 33 MHz. If you're going to do some drafting or have pictures (graphics) in your system, you'll want the newest and fastest CPU that you can afford. Fortunately, there's not more than a few hundred dollars difference between darn good and great.

Hard disks

So where do you keep all the information that the CPU processes? Believe it or not, the hard disk (or hard drive) in your PC can hold thousands of pages of information on several stacked disks that look something like miniature LP records stacked on a turntable. It knows where to look for any information you've put into it and can give you the information in a small fraction of a second.

A hard disk is measured by the number of *bytes*—or computer (not English) words—that it can store. Actually, capacity is normally measured in megabytes (abbreviated M). Older PCs were equipped with hard disk of 10M, 20M, or 40M. Newer

PCs typically store 120M, 200M, or even a gigabyte (G)—one billion bytes—or more. A 1G hard disk could theoretically store about a half-million typed pages—quite a large library!

Why would you need so much storage space? Graphics or picture files often require a lot of storage space on the hard disk; some need a megabyte or more per picture. Also, the software (programs) that you will use to write letters, keep your books, and so on usually take up a considerable amount of space. It's not unusual for a modern program to require 20M of storage—and that's before you do anything with it!

RAM

A hard disk is a storage area much like a library where millions of pieces of information can be kept. But a computer also needs a work area—like library tables—where books can be opened and used. This place is called the *random access memory* or RAM.

Just like disk storage, RAM storage is measured in megabytes. Depending on the size of the programs you will be using, your PC's RAM should be at least 2M. Older PCs offered 1M or less of RAM, but today's PCs typically come with 4M to 16M. The larger this work area is, the more work you can do simultaneously. Some programs like Microsoft Windows and Novell Netware require at least 2M and really work better if you have 4M of RAM or more.

Disk drives

So how does all this information get into your PC in the first place? It usually enters on small, portable disks (or diskettes) that are slipped into your PC's disk drive and copied to your computer's hard disk. Each one of these disks, sometimes called "floppies," can store from a third of a megabyte up to nearly three megabytes of information.

In the past ten years since PCs have become popular, a number of disk *formats* have evolved. A format tells the diskette how much information it can store on its surface. Early disks were 5¼ inches square, and were made of a thin, round, bendable Mylar disk (hence "floppy") placed in a sleeve and sealed. As programmers and engineers learned more about storing information on diskettes, a greater amount of information would fit on the diskette. It started with 360K (kilo—thousand—bytes), and quickly multiplied to 1200K, or 1.2 M. Many PCs still use this format.

Another format soon emerged, the 3½ inch disk, with a thin, round plastic disk housed in a hard plastic case. The first popular format stored 720K, or twice that of the physically larger 5¼ disk of the time. But soon, technology doubled storage on the same-size diskette to 1.44M. And the newest format can store up to 2.88M of information on a diskette that will fit into a shirt pocket. Amazing!

Ports and peripherals

As you consider and shop for a PC for your catering business, you will also want to know about *ports* in your PC where you can plug in printers and other equipment. Most PCs today have sufficient ports for most applications. Just let your PC store know what you want to do and they will help you select the appropriate PC and *peripherals*, or related equipment.

One peripheral you'll certainly need is a *monitor*, a device similar to a TV screen where the information you're working on is displayed. A monochrome (black and white) monitor is least expensive, but color monitors are easier to read—and more attractive. It's not necessary here to get into a boring description of interlacing and pixels; just look for a good-quality monitor that's easy to read. If you can't see the difference between a $300 monitor and one that costs $1000, don't buy the expensive one.

Later in this chapter, you'll learn how to use a computer to bring years of business experience to your catering business with computer programs.

Selecting a printer

Computers are great, but you want a printed copy of your information to share with others: business letters, work schedules, plans, income statements, and so on. That's where the printer comes in. You can attach a printer to one of your PC's ports and transfer computer data into a readable form.

There are many types of printers to select from. We'll just cover the three basic types here so you'll know which ones to look for as you go shopping:

- The *dot matrix* printer forms letters from a bunch of dots. A 9-pin printer uses nine tiny pins—three rows of three—to form each letter. A 24-pin printer does the same job but uses 24 pins—four rows of six. So the letters formed by a 24-pin printer are easier to read than those of a 9-pin printer. Today, most dot matrix printers use 24 pins. Some will even run over each line twice to make the letters easier to read.
- A *laser* is simply a beam of light that's focused by a mirror. A small laser in your printer actually writes the characters on a piece of paper, some black dust called *toner* is passed over it and it sticks to the places the laser light touched, then the sheet travels through a heater that fuses the black toner to the paper. Magic! Your words are printed. Some so-called laser printers use *LEDs*, or light-emitting diodes, instead of laser beams to achieve the same results.
- Similar to the laser, the *ink jet* printer sprays special ink onto the page in patterns cut by heat. Ink jet printers are typically less expensive than laser printers, and provide relatively inexpensive color output. They don't provide quite as high-quality printing as lasers, though, and the inks might smear when wet.

The type of printer you should buy depends on the type of work you need to do on your computer. Review your needs—and your budget—with your local computer shop. They can help you make a good choice.

HOW WILL COMPUTER SOFTWARE HELP MY BUSINESS GROW?

Now that you understand the basics of computers, you can better see how computer programs work for you. And, even though computer hardware is discussed first in this chapter, you will probably select the computer programs or software before you choose the computer to run it on. The majority of business computers are IBM-compatible, but a growing number of businesses use Macintosh computers (or "Macs") if they find software they prefer in that format.

A *computer program* is a set of instructions written in a language that your computer understands. The program can be as simple as putting your words onto paper or as complex as planning every aspect of an elegant dinner for 200.

Types of software

Computer software can be grouped by application: *horizontal* or *vertical*. Horizontal programs are those that can be used by nearly all businesses, such as word processors, spreadsheets, and databases. Vertical software, on the other hand, helps a specific type of business or industry, such as catering services.

Word processors

Word processors let you type words into the computer, move them around, insert and remove them, and make any changes you want before you print them. You can use word processors to write letters or other documents to suppliers, clients, prospects, employees, regulatory boards, or anyone else. I've been using word processors for ten years and would never go back to manual or even electric typewriters. Word processors let you change your mind.

You don't need a fancy word processing program. If one comes with your computer, use it. If not, you can buy a good one for less than $200 and a great one for less than $500. Even many of the budget word processors include built-in tools that help you check your spelling, add fancy characters, and otherwise enhance your documents. You only need a great word processor if you're publishing what you write as brochures or other sales documents.

Spreadsheets

A spreadsheet is to numbers what a word processor is to words: It puts them into readable form. It's roughly named after the wide multi-columnar sheets that accountants used to make journal entries.

You'll soon find yourself using a spreadsheet software program in many ways. For example, you can purchase a basic spreadsheet program for about a hundred dollars that lets you enter horizontal rows, or lines, of job expense names (Food, Labor, etc.) and vertical columns of numbers ($428.52, $3200, etc.). Most important, the program can perform most mathematical functions on any or all of the columns or rows in less than a second. If you update a number, it automatically recalculates any equations that use that number for you.

Fancier and more costly spreadsheets can follow instructions you write, called *macros*, to do special calculations automatically. For example, you might want to write a macro that selects all of the invoices over 60 days old and totals them up. Better spreadsheets also do fancy graphs and pie charts that impress bankers and other financial types.

Databases

A database program is much like an index-card file. You can write thousands or even millions of pieces of information and store them. A database program is much better than a file box, though, because it finds information in the files in a fraction of a second.

The most common application of a database program for catering services is a client file. If you only have a few clients, a database might not be necessary. But as you add clients, prospects, suppliers, and other business contacts, you'll soon need at least a simple database program to keep track of them.

Use your prospect/client database to keep information about company names, addresses, telephone and fax numbers, contact names, annual budget information, lists of events you've completed for them, even information about contacts' hobbies. Then, if you want to find out how many of your clients are located in a specific city and did more than $1000 in business with you last year, you simply tell your database program to search its files for you. It's that easy.

One note on selecting a database program: There are *relational* databases and *flat file* databases. Unless you're going to catalog all of your inventory, raw materials, and every bit of information in your business, you probably won't need to spend the extra money for a relational database. Buy a flat file version at a lower price.

Integrated programs

Speaking of relational, you can purchase integrated software that combines the three primary programs: word processor, spreadsheet, and database. Ask your local computer store to recommend a good integrated program. Some also include other related programs such as communications software that lets your PC talk to other PCs over the telephone using a modem. The cost of a good-quality integrated system is usually much less than the total price for the individual components.

Another plus to integrated programs is that their elements can easily "talk" to each other. That is, your word processor can include financial figures from your spreadsheet in your correspondence, and send it by modem to someone listed in your database. Just as important, an integrated group of programs developed by a single software firm has similar commands in each component program. You won't have to learn three separate programs, you'll learn one larger program.

Integrated programs are especially recommended for those who don't want to spend a lot of time selecting and learning numerous software programs. Your local computer shop can show you the latest in integrated business software.

Other helpful programs

Once you're hooked on computers, you'll buy a PC magazine or two, get on someone's mailing list, and soon be saturated with information about new software programs. The following is designed to help you sort them out.

DOS stands for *disk operating system*. It comes with your PC and translates commands like "COPY A:*.* C:*.*" into a language that your PC understands.

Shell programs make your PC easier to use and perform a number of important maintenance functions. They're called shells because they "wrap around" the less-friendly DOS program to make it easier to copy, delete, and manage files. Some shell programs also include *utilities*, special programs that help you keep your data organized and safe.

Windows is a program developed by Microsoft that lets you open a number of overlapping boxes, or windows, on your computer screen, each with different programs in it. You can be writing a letter when a client calls and quickly switch to a window with information about the client and your current project.

Backup programs let you copy all the information on your hard disk onto disks or tapes as a backup of your system. Backups ensure that, if something happens to your hard disk and you lose your data, you still haven't lost everything. Of course, you must back up your hard disk regularly, a process that takes only a few minutes every day and is well worth the time.

Vertical software

The programs discussed up to this point are horizontal software; they are used by most businesses, not just catering services. There are also vertical programs written specifically for caterers. Some are advertised in catering-service magazines and trade journals. Others are found by talking with noncompeting catering services or local association members. Vertical software is typically available in the "IBM-compatible" format, but some also have Macintosh versions.

Some of the features you can expect to find in programs written for catering services and related businesses include the following:

- *Estimating*: Event scheduling, recipe development and cost reports, price sheets, proposals, and event worksheets
- *Billing*: Invoices, customer information, account balances, credit management
- *Inventory*: Food inventory tracking and management, ingredient costs, and procurement

Some vertical programs include their own word processor, spreadsheet, or database elements. Others allow you to integrate their data into your favorite programs. A few will do both.

One vertical software program written specifically for off-premises caterers is The Recipe Writer Pro, from

At-Your-Service Software
450 Bronxville Rd.
Bronxville, NY 10708
800-433-8368

It tracks food costs, helps plan menus, modifies recipes, and provides pricing. The reports it produces include a food list, recipe pricing report, inventory pricing report, and cross-reference reports. It also interfaces to event management software. Inventory Pro, from the same company, manages food-service inventory, while Sales Analysis Pro tracks and reports sales.

Another software program useful for the catering industry is Scheduler Plus, from

CEO Software, Inc.
2231 Indian Ruins Rd.
Tucson, AZ 85715
800-441-2581

Scheduler Plus manages all kinds of events, including catering events, meetings, and seminars. Scheduler Plus offers an optional module for independent catering services that assigns predefined menus, catered service, and beverage services to any location.

MicroBiz also offers a software program for catering services. Contact them at

500 Airport Executive Park
Spring Valley, NY 10977
800-637-8268

As a catering service owner, you have a world of tools and equipment available to you. On the one side, they are expensive. On the other, they can be very profitable to own. The difference is your knowledge of what you need and what will do the job profitably. You might not need all of the tools that technology offers, but knowing what they are and what they can do for you helps you keep ahead of the pack. You'll be successful longer.

SUCCESS ACTION PLAN

Your plan to start a catering service is moving into action. Your dream is becoming a reality. Here are some things you can do right now to realize your dream of becoming an independent caterer:

❏ List the commissary and serving equipment your catering service requires, then check off every component that you already have.

❏ Contact restaurant equipment suppliers in your area as well as national catering equipment buyer's directories for pricing on equipment you need.

❏ Depending on your catering specialty, contact wholesale food suppliers in your area to learn about their products, delivery, and terms, and to set up an account.

❏ Start furnishing your catering office with furniture, telephones, and fax and answering machines.

❏ Contact firms offering catering service software to determine price and value.

❏ If appropriate, consider purchasing a computer and vertical software to help you profitably manage your catering service.

❏ Take time to learn your computer system. It is a tool that can make you money or waste your time; your choice.

4
What are
the financial
requirements?

Singer Ray Charles said it best: "You gotta have money in order to get money. How you get it in the first place is still a mystery to me!"

This adage might seem true as you start adding up all of the expenses you'll have in order to operate a—hopefully—profitable catering service. This chapter will help you determine your business' financial requirements as well as your resources. Don't be discouraged. Thousands of women and men have successfully funded their catering business; you're simply following in their well-worn footsteps.

HOW MUCH MONEY DO I NEED?

You've decided to start your own catering business. But you're not sure how much capital you'll need. Let's develop a capital requirements worksheet for your new business venture, as shown in Fig. 4-1.

Estimating start-up costs

The first step in estimating capital requirements is determining how much it will cost to start up your business. You'll determine the costs to:

- Prepare your selected business site as a catering office and commissary
- Add the equipment you need to start your business
- Equip your office with desks, chairs, shelves, and other equipment
- Purchase initial office supplies
- Purchase a start-up inventory of required food and supplies
- Equip your office with the necessary telephone, answering machine, fax, computer, printer, and software
- Make the necessary utility deposits
- Obtain the required licenses, permits, and certifications
- Purchase initial insurance coverage and surety bonds
- Hire legal and financial professionals to help you set your business up properly

Capital Requirements Worksheet

Estimated Start-Up Costs:

Site preparation	$_____
Catering equipment	$_____
Office equipment	$_____
Initial office supplies	$_____
Initial food inventory	$_____
Telephone, computer, etc.	$_____
Utility deposits	$_____
Licenses & permits	$_____
Insurance	$_____
Professionals	$_____
Signs	$_____
Initial advertising	$_____
Miscellaneous expenses	$_____
Total Estimated Start-Up Costs	$_____

Estimated Operating Costs:

Living expenses	$_____
Employee salaries	$_____
Rent	$_____
Utilities	$_____
Advertising	$_____
Insurance	$_____
Office supplies	$_____
Replacement food inventory	$_____
Taxes	$_____
Equipment maintenance	$_____
Total Estimated Operating Costs	$_____

Estimated Financial Resources:

Assets

Checking and savings	$_____
CDs and securities	$_____
Owed to you	$_____
Real estate	$_____
Autos and vehicles	$_____
Insurance cash value	$_____
Other assets	$_____
Total assets	$_____

Liabilities

Credit cards	$_____
Household credit	$_____
Auto loans	$_____
Taxes	$_____
Education loans	$_____
Mortgages	$_____
Other liabilities	$_____
Total liabilities	$_____
Total net worth	$_____

4-1 This capital requirements worksheet helps you estimate start-up and operating costs as well as financial resources for your catering business.

- Purchase initial signs
- Advertise the opening of your business
- Cover unanticipated expenses

What's the total of the above start-up costs?

Estimating operating costs

Once your catering operation is set up and initial start-up costs are covered, you will be in business. You will have income and expenses. Your next step in determining capital requirements for your business is to estimate your expenses for an average month. Determine how much you will need to do each of the following:
- Live comfortably without a significant change in your current lifestyle
- Pay employees you plan to hire
- Pay the rent on your home office, commissary, or storefront, or make payments on your mobile catering truck or portable commissary
- Pay the utilities (including telephone service) for your office and commissary
- Maintain a minimum amount of advertising (such as yellow pages contracts and service directory listings)
- Continue insurance premiums for your business
- Replace office supplies used in your business
- Replace food and supplies used during the month
- Pay required local, state, and federal taxes
- Maintain your business equipment and vehicles

What's the total of your estimating operating expenses for an average month?

Estimating total capital requirements

Many small businesses fail each year—some of them established by otherwise qualified professionals. There are a number of reasons for these failures, but one of the main reasons is insufficient funds. Too many entrepreneurs try to start up and operate a business without sufficient capital.

So how much is enough? Obviously, the more the better. But a reasonable amount to have is enough to cover your start-up expenses and three months' of operating expenses. So add the total of the start-up expenses you've calculated to a total of three months' of estimated operating expenses. That's the minimum amount of capital or money you should have before you start your catering business. If you have the resources, a six-month reserve of estimated operating expenses is much better.

Of course, there are some exceptions to this guideline. If you have a working spouse with sufficient income to cover household expenses while your business gets on its feet, your capital requirements will be much less than that of a "sole breadwinner" with eight kids. In addition, if you have a number of regular clients lined up who have already made firm commitments to you for work, you won't need as much operating reserves. However, keep in mind that even if you start work for these clients tomorrow, you might not get paid for 60 or even 90 days.

The best advice from those who have been there is to build up your reserves before you start and keep your operating expenses at a bare minimum until your business is established.

WHERE CAN I GET THIS MONEY?

Few people know their true financial *net worth*, which is how much they own minus how much they owe. Before you decide to start your catering business you must first determine your financial net worth.

Your assets

Assets are simply what you own. You might have more financial assets than you are aware of. First, there are two types of assets: *short term* and *long term*. A short-term asset is one that can be quickly liquidated or turned into cash. If someone owes you $1000 and promises to pay you next month, that's a short-term asset. If you won't get paid for another five years, that's a long-term asset. A short-term asset is one that can be turned into cash within one year. So an asset is important, but also important is its *liquidity*, or how quickly it can be turned into cash if necessary.

To determine your total assets, answer the following questions:

- How much cash do you have in your checking accounts, savings accounts, in a safe deposit box, or other resources?
- How much money do you have in certificates of deposit, savings certificates, stocks, bonds, securities, and other easily sold short-term assets?
- How much money is owed to you (accounts receivable)?
- What's the market value of real estate that you own (how much could you sell it for)?
- What's the book value of automobiles and other vehicles that you own—even if you have a loan against them?
- What's the cash value of insurance policies in your name?
- What's the value of other assets you own (such as furniture, jewelry, tools, and equipment)?
- What's the total value of all short-term assets (those you could turn into cash within one year)?
- What's the total value of all long-term assets (those that require more than one year to turn into cash)?
- What's the total value of all short- and long-term assets?

Your liabilities

A liability is money that you owe to others. Some liabilities are secured by assets; others are secured by your "signature" or personal pledge to pay. As with assets, there are short-term liabilities and long-term liabilities. A short-term liability is one that will be paid off within a year, such as a credit card. A long-term liability is one that will take more than a year to pay off, such as a car loan.

To determine your liabilities, answer the following questions:

- How much do you owe on credit cards?
- How much do you owe on installment payments for furniture, appliances, or other household items?
- How much do you owe on your vehicles?
- How much do you owe in local, state, and federal taxes?
- How much do you owe in education loans?

- How much do you owe on a mortgage or note against your home or other real estate?
- Do you have any second mortgages on any real estate?
- How much do you owe on other liabilities?
- What's the total value of all short-term liabilities (those that must be paid off within one year)?
- What's the total value of all long-term liabilities (those that won't be paid off within the next year)?
- What's the total value of all short- and long-term liabilities?

Estimating total net worth

The purpose of this exercise is to discover your total financial net worth: your assets minus your liabilities. In other words, if you sold everything you owned and paid off everything you owed, how much would you have left?

Don't be discouraged by the results of this exercise. You can do a number of things to improve your financial net worth. In fact, once your business becomes successful, your total net worth will grow. You'll own more and more assets while owing fewer and fewer people. Even if the total is in negative numbers—you actually owe more than you own—this chapter helps you learn what to do about it.

WHAT OTHER FINANCIAL RESOURCES ARE AVAILABLE?

You now know how much you have and how much you need to start your catering business. But maybe you've discovered that you don't have enough assets to start your business with sufficient funds. Or maybe you're determined to put six months' expense reserve in the bank before you start. There are several sources for additional assets.

Who you know

By now, you've probably met hundreds, maybe thousands, of people in your lifetime: relatives and friends; current and former employers; your suppliers, banker, accountant, attorney, and doctor; prospective clients; fellow members of associations, clubs, and churches; friends of friends of friends. Each is a potential source of assets. You're not begging from them. You're simply asking them if they wish to invest money in a potentially profitable enterprise and reap some reward for their investment.

Some of these contacts will not be interested, others might want to invest only a few hundred dollars, still others will become your primary resources because they expect a return on their investment. Develop a business plan that helps investors understand what you're doing, how much it will cost, what you need, and what they will get for their risk. You probably won't be looking for general partners who advise you on how to run your business. You want investors or limited partners who will invest money but stay out of the day-to-day management.

Commercial bankers

A banker is much like you, someone who has a product received from others—money—who sells it at a profit to someone who needs it. This, too, is not charity. It is good business. But bankers are notoriously not risk-takers. The caricature that bankers carry umbrellas year-round is not true, but is based on truth. They are "stewardly."

Your approach to bankers, therefore, will be conservative. If you want to borrow from them, have a complete written description of what you want to do, how you plan to do it, how much it will cost, and what you expect to profit from it. Most importantly, explain in detail how you will pay the loan off.

Venture capitalists

Venture capitalists are people who look for small business opportunities in which to invest—at a significant rate of return on their investment. You can find them through your banker, financial institutions, accountant, venture-capital directories, investment brokers, and ads in metropolitan newspapers.

The SBA

One of the most noteworthy services offered by the Small Business Administration is guaranteeing loans made by bankers who would not otherwise loan money to new businesses. Take time to review their loan guarantee program and then talk with an SBA office in your region.

The Small Business Investment Act allows the SBA to license small business investment companies, or *SBICs*. An SBIC supplies equity capital to companies unable to raise funds from other sources. They are privately owned and operated for profit, and chartered under state law. Your regional SBA office can help you find local SBICs that might be able to supply additional assets.

Proprietorships and partnerships can receive long-term loans from an SBIC as long as they are secured by real estate or other collateral. Corporations can receive funds from long-term loans or equity financing. Equity financing can be in the form of stock purchased in your company by the SBIC, loans with stock as equity, or other collateral.

Stock

If you incorporate your business, you can sell shares of it to investors. The type of investment they make, the risk involved, how they receive their profits or dividends, and how dividends to them are taxed depend on the type of stock purchased. Talk with your attorney or your accountant about how to sell stock in your state to develop additional capital for your business.

Promissory notes

Many small businesses fund their start-up by offering to sign personal promissory notes to investors for terms of three, five, or seven years at rates above what banks offer depositors. Promissory note forms can be purchased at local stationery or office supply stores.

Getting a loan

The ability to get a loan when you need it is as necessary to the operation of your business as is the right equipment. Before a bank or any other lending agency will lend you money, the loan officer must feel satisfied with the answers to these five questions:

- What sort of person are you, the prospective borrower? In most cases, the character of the borrower comes first. Next is your ability to manage your business.

- What are you going to do with the money? The answer to this question will determine the type of loan and the duration.
- When and how do you plan to pay it back? Your lender's judgment of your business ability and the type of loan are the deciding factors in the answer to this question.
- Is the cushion in the loan large enough? In other words, does the amount requested make suitable allowance for unexpected developments? The lender decides this question on the basis of your financial statement, which sets forth the condition of your business, and on the collateral pledged.
- What's the outlook for business in general and for your business in particular?

Adequate financial data is a must. The lender wants to make loans to businesses that are solvent, profitable, and growing. The two basic financial statements used to determine those conditions are the balance sheet and the income statement. The balance sheet is the major yardstick for solvency and the income statement for growth. A continuous series of these two statements over a period of time is the principal device for measuring financial stability and growth potential.

In interviewing loan applicants and in studying their records, the lender is especially interested in the following facts and figures from your balance sheets and income statements:

- *General information.* Are the books and records up-to-date and in good condition? What's the condition of the accounts payable and notes payable? What are the salaries of the owner-manager and other company officers? Are all taxes being paid currently? What's the order backlog? What's the number of employees? What's the insurance coverage?
- *Accounts receivable.* Are there indications that some of the accounts receivable have already been pledged to another creditor? What's the accounts receivable turnover? Is the total accounts receivable weakened because many customers are far behind in their payments? Has a large enough reserve been set up to cover questionable accounts? How much do the largest accounts owe, and what percentage of the total accounts does this amount represent?
- *Fixed assets.* What's the type, age, and condition of the equipment? What are the depreciation policies? What are the details of mortgages or conditional sales contracts? What are the future acquisition plans?

For many people, additional capital needed to start a business comes from getting a loan from a banker, venture capitalist, supplier, friend, or relative. Once you have gathered the necessary information about your catering service, it's time to determine what types of loans are available and how to get one at the lowest rates.

Types of loans

When you set out to borrow money for your business, it is important to know the kind of money you need from a bank or other lending institution. There are three kinds of money: short term, term money, and equity capital.

Keep in mind that the purpose for which the funds are to be used is an important factor in deciding the kind of money needed. But even so, deciding what kind of money to use is not always easy. It is sometimes complicated by the fact that you might be using some of the various kinds of money at the same time and for identical purposes.

The important distinction between the types of money is the source of repayment. Generally, short-term loans are repaid from the liquidation of current assets which they have financed. Long-term loans are usually repaid from earnings.

Short-term bank loans

You can use short-term bank loans for purposes such as the financing of accounts receivable for, say, 30 to 60 days. You might also use them for purposes that take longer to pay off, such as the purchase of needed equipment. Usually, lenders expect short-term loans to be repaid after their purposes have been served. For example, accounts receivable loans should be paid off when your outstanding accounts have been paid.

Banks grant such short-term money either on an *unsecured loan*, which relies on your general credit reputation, or on a *secured loan*. The unsecured loan is the most frequently used form of bank credit for short-term purposes. You don't have to put up collateral because the bank relies on your credit reputation. The secured loan involves a pledge of some or all of your business assets. The bank requires security as a protection for its depositors against the risks involved even in business situations where the chances of success are good.

Term borrowing

Term borrowing provides money you plan to pay back over a fairly long time. Some people break it down into two forms: intermediate (covering one to five years) and long term (over 5 years). However, for your purpose of matching the kind of money to the needs of your company, think of term borrowing as money that you probably will pay back in periodic installments from earnings.

Equity capital

Some people confuse term borrowing with *equity* or *investment capital*, but there is a big difference. You don't have to repay equity money. It is money you get by selling interest in your business. You take people into your company who are willing to risk their money in it. They are interested in potential income rather than an immediate return on their investment.

Within these types of money, many types of loans are available, all with their own unique name depending on the lender. Most fall into one of the following categories:

- A *signature loan* holds nothing in collateral except your promise to pay the lender back on terms that you both agree upon. If the amount of money you need is small, you only need the money for a short time, your credit rating is excellent, and you're willing to pay a premium interest rate because you're not using physical collateral, a signature or character loan is an easy way to borrow money in a hurry.
- A *term loan* requires good credit and typically some type of collateral, either equipment or real estate. The term can be as short as a few months or as long as several years. Payments can be set up monthly, quarterly, annually, or seasonally, depending on the security involved and your business's cash flow.
- A *collateral loan* requires some type of asset put up as collateral; if you don't make payments, you lose the asset. The lender wants to make sure

that the asset is worth more than the value of the loan, which is usually 50 to 75 percent of asset value. A new catering service often does not have sufficient collateral—real estate, equipment, inventory—to secure a collateral loan unless an owner uses personal assets, such as a home.

- *Personal credit cards* have been used in many small businesses for at least some funding. Tools, equipment, materials, fees, office supplies, office expenses, and other costs can be covered with your personal credit card. However, interest rates on credit cards are extremely high—sometimes double what you might pay on a collateral loan. On the other hand, they can get you quick cash when you need it. If using your personal credit card is an option for you, talk to your credit card representative about raising your credit limit. It will be much easier to do so while you're employed by someone else instead of self-employed.

- A *line of credit* is similar to a loan, except that you don't borrow it all at once. You get a credit limit, say $50,000, that you can tap anytime you need money for business purposes. The most common is the "revolving" line of credit that you can draw from when business is off and pay back when business is good, providing that you don't exceed your limit. A line of credit is an excellent way for a catering service to work through the ups and downs of seasonal business. With some restrictions, a line of credit can be established using a portion of your home equity as collateral. Using a secured equity earns you a lower interest rate.

- A *cosigner loan* should be one of the most popular loans for small businesses, but many businesspeople never consider it. You simply find a cosigner with good credit or assets who will guarantee the loan with you. If you have a potential investor who believes in your business but doesn't want to put up the cash you need, ask him or her to cosign for a loan with you. Your chances of receiving the loan are much better. Some cosigners require that you pay them a fee of one to four percent of the balance, or a flat fee; others will do it because of your friendship, or in the hope of future business from you. In any case, consider a cosigner loan as an excellent source of capital for your new catering business.

- *Equipment loans* are made by the supplier when you're purchasing a catering vehicle, special equipment, or other assets. This type of loan often requires about 25 percent down, so be ready to come up with some cash of your own.

- Once you've completed some jobs and billed your clients, you don't have to wait for them to send you the money. You can sell your accounts receivable—at a discount, of course—called *factoring.* Or you can use your best accounts receivable as collateral for a loan. There are certainly some pluses and minuses to this method of raising capital, but it is a commonly used option. Talk to your accountant, banker, financial adviser, or another catering business owner about finding a reputable factoring broker.

- Depending on your suppliers, you can build working capital for your business by developing *trade credit.* That is, once approved, your supplier will give you additional time in which to pay your bill to them. You might start off with 60 days' credit, then earn 90 days, and even 120 days before you must pay their bill. There will typically be a finance charge on the

balance over 30 days old, but some suppliers will give you low- or no-interest "loans" of materials for this period. Compare prices versus credit terms as you shop for primary and secondary suppliers.
- The Small Business Administration offers a short-term loan guaranty program for businesses that need a *seasonal line of credit.* For more information, contact your regional SBA office.

A recent survey of small businesses indicates that 23 percent have lines of credit, 7 percent have financial leases, 14 percent have mortgage loans, 12 percent have equipment loans, and 25 percent have vehicle loans. For larger firms, the percentages about double in each category.

Collateral

As mentioned earlier, sometimes your signature is the only security lenders need when making a loan. At other times, the lender requires additional assurance that the money will be repaid. The kind and amount of security depends on the lender and on your situation. Of course, a lender will attempt to get as much security as possible, sometimes even more than is required.

If the loan required can't be justified by the borrower's financial statements alone, a pledge of security might bridge the gap. The types of security are as follows:
- *Endorsers, cosigners, and guarantors.* Borrowers often get other people to sign a note in order to bolster their own credit. These endorsers are contingently liable for the note they sign. If the borrower fails to pay up, the lender expects the endorser to make the note good. Sometimes the endorser might be asked to pledge assets or securities, too. A cosigner is one who creates an obligation jointly with the borrower. In such cases, the lender can collect directly from either the maker or the cosigner. A guarantor is one who guarantees the payment of a note by signing a guaranty commitment. Both private and government lenders often require guarantees from officers of corporation in order to assure continuity of effective management. Sometimes a manufacturer or supplier will act as a guarantor for customers.
- *Assignment of leases.* The assigned lease as security is similar to the guarantee. It is used, for example, in some franchise situations. The bank lends the money on a building and takes a mortgage. Then the lease, which the dealer and the parent franchise company work out, is assigned so that the bank automatically receives the rent payments. In this manner, the bank is guaranteed repayment of the loan.
- *Chattel mortgages.* If you buy equipment such as a refrigerator, you might want to get a chattel mortgage loan. You give the bank a lien on the equipment you're buying. The lender also evaluates the present and future market value of the equipment being used to secure the loan. How rapidly will it depreciate? Does the borrower have the necessary fire, theft, property damage, and public liability insurance on the equipment? The lender has to be sure that you protect the equipment used as chattel.
- *Real estate.* Real estate is another form of collateral for long-term loans. When taking a real estate mortgage, the lender finds out the location of the real estate, its physical condition, its foreclosure value, and the amount of

insurance carried on the property. Many catering service owners use their home as collateral for a real estate loan to begin their business.

- *Accounts receivable.* Some lenders lend money on accounts receivable. In effect, you're counting on your customers to pay your note. The lender might take accounts receivable on a *notification* or a *nonnotification plan.* Under the notification plan, your customer is informed by the bank that his or her account has been assigned to it and account payments must be made directly to the bank. Under the nonnotification plan, your customers continue to pay you the sums due on their accounts, and you pay the bank. Unfortunately, under a notification plan, your customers might assume that your business is financially unsound and reduce future business with you.
- *Savings account.* Sometimes you can get a loan by assigning a savings account to the bank. In such cases, the bank gets an assignment from you and keeps your passbook. If you assign an account in another bank as collateral, the lending bank asks the other bank to mark its records to show that the account is held as collateral.
- *Life insurance.* Banks will lend up to the cash value of a life insurance policy if you assign the policy to the bank. If the policy is on the life of an executive of a small corporation, corporate resolutions must be made authorizing the assignment. Most insurance companies allow you to sign the policy back to the original beneficiary when the assignment to the bank ends. Some people like to use life insurance as collateral rather than borrow directly from insurance companies. One reason is that a bank loan is often more convenient to obtain and can often be obtained at a lower interest rate.
- *Stocks and bonds.* If you use stocks and bonds as collateral, they must be marketable. As a protection against market declines and possible expenses of liquidation, banks usually lend no more than 75 percent of the market value of high-grade stock. On federal government or municipal bonds, they might be willing to lend 90 percent or more of their market value. The bank might ask you for additional security or payment whenever the market value of the stocks or bonds drops below the bank's required margin.

For more information on business credit, write to

The Federal Trade Commission
Washington, DC 20580
Attn: Public Reference

Ask for their booklet called "Getting Business Credit." It's free.

HOW MUCH INTEREST WILL I HAVE TO PAY?

Money is a commodity, bought and sold by lenders. Just like other products, you can often save by shopping around. Consider several points as you shop for money.

First, are there any loan fees or other charges required to set up or service the loan? Some lenders require that a loan fee of one or two percent, or more, be paid in advance. Others even roll the loan fee into the loan—so you actually pay interest upon interest. Still others deduct a monthly service fee from each payment as it is made. This arrangement is not necessarily bad; after all, the lender must get a profit from you in some manner. Just make sure that you understand what the actual cost of the loan is before you agree to it. You also need to know actual interest rates as you compare rates between lenders.

Second, consider whether your best option is *fixed rate* or *variable rate* interest. Fixed rate interest means that the interest rate charged by the lender is the same throughout the life of the loan. Variable rate interest can vary during the term of the loan based on some outside factor. This factor is usually the cost of the money to the lender. The difference between the lender's cost and what you are charged is called the *spread*. From that spread comes the lender's sales costs, office overhead, salaries, and profit. The spread is also based on the amount of risk the lender is taking in loaning the money to you. Higher risk means a higher spread. Many indexes are used to establish the "cost" of money. Review all of the options with your lender, ask which one makes the most sense for your needs, and get a second opinion.

Keep in mind that variable-rate interest reduces the amount of risk the lender is taking, especially on long-term loans. The lender is virtually assured that, unless the money market goes crazy and goes over the "cap," it will get its margin of profit from every dollar you send it. Lower risk means lower rates. The point is that you shouldn't disqualify variable rate loans from consideration. In many cases, they cost less than fixed-rate loans, and many lenders are more willing to make them.

To ensure that you pay the best interest rate available, don't jump at the first loan offer that comes to you. Shop around and compare. You might eventually decide to take that first offer, but only because you've found nothing better.

On the other hand, don't worry too much about getting the absolute lowest interest rate available. You might want to accept your regular banker's loan terms, even though it's a quarter of a percentage point higher, in order to maintain a mutually profitable relationship. That quarter point might only mean a few dollars to you, but will reinforce your business relationship with your banker.

While we're on the subject, let's talk about credit. Credit is simply someone else's faith that you will keep your promise to him or her. You buy a catering truck on credit and the lender believes that you will pay what you've borrowed—or have assets that can be sold to cover what you've borrowed. So how do you build credit? Easy. You borrow a small amount, pay it back, borrow a larger amount, pay it back, and so on. It also helps to have some assets, like stocks or land, that are already paid off, or in which you have some equity.

A good way to start building your business credit is to use personal assets—such as signature or real estate equity—as collateral for your business. One enterprising catering owner simply applied for a credit card in her business name from the same company that sponsored her long-standing personal credit card. She asked for a small credit limit, used it and paid it off, then asked for an increased credit limit. Meantime, she used the credit card as a reference for a new account with a supplier. Other new businesspeople use equity in their homes or investment land as collateral for credit with banks and suppliers, as discussed earlier.

SHOULD I LEASE EQUIPMENT?

Small businesses have difficulty raising capital, that's no secret. This difficulty has caused many small businesses to look at leasing as an alternative financing arrangement for acquiring assets. All types of equipment used by catering services—from vehicles to computers to equipment to office furniture—have become easier to lease. Smart business owners are learning more about leases and how they help them manage their business more efficiently.

A lease is a long-term agreement to rent equipment, land, buildings, or any other asset. In return for most—but not all—of the benefits of ownership, the user (*lessee*) makes periodic payments to the owner of the asset (*lessor*). The lease payment covers the original cost of the equipment or other asset and provides the lessor a profit.

Types of leases

There are three major types of leases: the financial lease, the operating lease, and the sale-and-leaseback.

Financial leases are the most common by far. A financial lease is usually written for a term not to exceed the economic life of the property or equipment. A financial lease usually requires that periodic payments be made, that ownership of the asset reverts to the lessor at the end of the lease term, that the lease cannot be canceled with the lessee having a legal obligation to continue payments to the end of the term, and that the lessee agrees to maintain the asset.

The *operating* or *maintenance lease* can usually be canceled under conditions spelled out in the lease agreement. Maintenance of the asset is usually the responsibility of the owner or lessor. Computer equipment is often leased under this kind of arrangement, with the lessor taking care of maintenance or repairs to the computer as required.

The *sale and leaseback* is similar to the financial lease. The owner of an asset sells it to another party and simultaneously leases it back to use it for a specified term. This arrangement lets you free up money otherwise tied up in an asset for use elsewhere. Buildings are often leased in this way. Your corporation might buy a building, then lease it back to you.

You might also hear leases described as *net leases* or *gross leases*. Under a net lease, the lessee is responsible for expenses such as for maintenance, taxes, and insurance. The lessor pays these expenses under a gross lease. Financial leases are usually net leases.

Finally, you might run across the term *full-payout lease*. Under a full-payout lease, the lessor recovers the original cost of the asset during the term of the lease.

Types of lessors

As the use of leasing as a method for businesses to acquire equipment and other assets has increased, the number of companies in the leasing business has increased dramatically. Leasing is now a billion dollar industry.

Commercial banks, insurance companies, and finance companies do most of the leasing. Many of these organizations have formed subsidiaries primarily concerned with equipment leasing. These subsidiaries are usually capable of making lease arrangements for almost anything. Ask your primary bank or lender whether they offer leases for equipment you require.

In addition to financial organizations, some companies specialize in leasing. Some are engaged in general leasing, while others specialize in particular equipment such as commercial vehicles, computers, or catering equipment.

Some equipment manufacturers are also in the leasing business. They often lease their equipment through their sales representatives. As you consider leasing equipment, ask your catering equipment sales rep about leases available through the manufacturer.

Advantages and disadvantages of leasing

The obvious advantage to leasing is acquiring the use of an asset without making a large initial cash outlay. Compared to a loan arrangement to purchase the same equipment, a lease usually requires little or no down payment, requires no restriction on a company's financial operations, spreads payments over a longer period than most loans, and provides protection against the risk of equipment obsolescence.

There might also be tax benefits in leasing. Lease payments are deductible as operating expenses if the arrangement is a true lease (as defined by the Internal Revenue Service). Ownership, however, usually has greater tax advantages through depreciation. Naturally, you need to have enough income and resulting tax liability to take advantage of these two benefits.

With leasing firms that specialize in equipment used by catering services, leasing has the further advantage that the leasing firm has acquired considerable knowledge about the kinds of equipment it leases. Thus, it can provide expert technical advice based on experience with the leased equipment.

Finally, one advantage of leasing you hope won't ever be necessary. In the event of your firm's bankruptcy, the lessor's claims to your assets are more restricted than those of general creditors.

So what's the downside of leasing? First, leasing usually costs more because you lose certain tax advantages that go with ownership of an asset. Leasing might not, however, cost more if you can't take advantage of these benefits because you don't have enough tax liability for them to come into play.

Obviously, you also lose the economic value of the asset at the end of the lease, since you don't own the asset. Lessees have been known to grossly underestimate the salvage value of an asset. If they had known this value from the outset, they might have decided to buy instead of lease.

Finally, never forget that a lease is a long-term legal obligation. Usually, you cannot cancel a lease agreement. If you were to cancel an equipment lease, you might find the cancellation fees were as much as if you had used the equipment for the full term of the lease.

Leases and taxes

Full lease payments are deductible as operating costs. You can make these deductions only if the Internal Revenue Service finds that you have a true lease. You cannot take a full deduction for a lease that's really an installment purchase.

Although each lease arrangement can be different, here are some general guidelines:

- In no way should any portion of the payment be construed as interest.
- Lease payments must not be large compared to the cost of purchasing the same asset.

- Any renewal option at lease end must be on terms equivalent to what a third party would offer.
- Purchase options must be at amounts comparable with fair market value.

Accounting for leases

Historically, financial leases were off-the-balance-sheet financing. That is, lease obligations often were not recorded directly on the balance sheet, but listed in footnotes instead. Not explicitly accounting for leases sometimes resulted in a failure to state operational assets and liabilities fairly.

In 1977, the Financial Accounting Standards Board (FASB), the rule-making body of the accounting profession, required that capital leases be recorded on the balance sheet as both an asset and a liability. This requirement was in recognition of the long-term nature of a lease obligation.

Cost analysis

You can analyze the cost of leasing versus purchasing through discounted cash-flow analysis. This analysis compares the cost of each alternative by considering the timing of the payments, tax benefits, the interest rate on a loan, the lease rate, and other financial arrangements. Even if you plan to have your accountant work up these numbers for you, follow through the following exercise so that you will better understand what this cost analysis tells you about buying versus leasing equipment. After all, it's you not your accountant who will make the decision.

To make the analysis, you must first make certain assumptions about the economic life of the equipment, salvage value, and depreciation. A sample problem will illustrate the process. The assumptions for the sample problem are included in Table 4-1. Table 4-2 is the analysis of the lease alternative, and Table 4-3 is an analysis of the borrow and buy option.

To evaluate a lease, you must first find the net cash outlay (not cash flow) in each year of the lease term. You find this amount by subtracting the tax savings (at

Table 4-1 Example assumptions for lease versus loan

Equipment cost: $60,000

Estimated economic life: 10 years

Lease terms: 8 annual* payments of $10,363.94 (Apr 10.5%). First payment due upon delivery. Investment tax credit to lessor. Lessee maintains equipment.

Loan terms: 5 years, 75% financing at 10% (Apr). 5 annual* payments of $11,870.89. First payment due at end of first year.

Taxes: Lessee tax rate 50%. Method of depreciation for tax purposes is straight line.

Other: Equipment needed for term of lease, 8 years. If firm purchases equipment, it can be sold at end of 8 years for book value. Average after-tax cost of capital for lessee is 9%.

* Payments have been annualized to simplify calculations. Payments are usually made monthly.

Table 4-2 Evaluation of lease cost

(1) End of year	(2) Lease payment	(3) (0.50×2) Tax saving	(4) (2–3) Net cash outlay	(5) Discount factor	(6) (4×5) Net present value
4	10,363.94	5,181.97	5,181.97	0.823	4,264.76
5	10,363.94	5,181.97	5,181.97	0.784	4,062.66
6	10,363.94	5,181.97	5,181.97	0.746	3,865.75
7	10,363.94	5,181.97	5,181.97	0.710	3,684.38
8	—	—	—	—	—
Net present value of costs of leasing					**$35,170.63**

50 percent, in this example) from the lease payment. This calculation gives you the net cash outlay for each year of the lease.

Each year's net cash outlay must next be discounted to take into account the time value of money. This discounting gives you the present value of each of the amounts.

The *present value* of an amount of money is the sum you would have to invest today at a stated rate of interest to have that amount of money at a specified future date. Suppose someone offered to give you $100 five years from now, how much could you take today and be as well off? Common sense tells you that you could take less than $100 because you'd have the use of the money for the five-year period. Naturally, how much less you could take depends on the interest rate you thought you could get if you invested the lesser amount. To have $100 five years from now at 6 percent compounded annually, you'd have to invest $74.70 today. At 10 percent, you could take $62.10 now to have the $100 at the end of five years.

Thus, the present value of the net outlay under the lease ($5181.97 after tax savings, in this example) at the end of year 6 of the lease term is something less than $5181.97. Here, the appropriate interest rate for discounting the lease payment is 5 percent (after-tax cost of 50 percent times the loan interest of 10 percent). This low rate of interest is used because of the certain nature of the payments under a lease contract. So, at an annually compounded 5 percent interest rate, you would have to invest $3865.75 today to have $5181.97 at the end of six years.

Fortunately, tables provide the discount factors for present value calculations, such as the one in Table 4-4. The factor for the present value of $1 six years from now at 5 percent is 0.746. This factor times the after-tax lease payment outlay ($5181.97) equals $3865.75, or exactly the amount you would have to invest today at 5 percent interest compounded annually to have $5181.97 six years from now. Also, relatively inexpensive business calculators and computer spreadsheets are programmed to make these calculations for you.

Signing a lease

A lease agreement is a legal document. It carries a long-term obligation. You must be thoroughly informed about just what you're committing yourself to. Find out the

Table 4-3 Evaluation of loan cost

(1) End of year	(2) Payment	(3) Interest	(4) (2–3) Principal repayment	(5) (5–4) Outstanding balance	(6) Depreciation	(7) .05×(6 + 3) Tax savings	(8) (2–7) Net cash flow	(9) Discount factor	(10) (8×9) Net present value
0	$15,000.00			$45,000.00		$6,000.00*	$9,000.00	1.000	$9,000.00
1	11,870.89	$4,500.00	$ 7,370.89	37,629.11	$6,000.00	5,250.00	6,620.89	0.952	5,303.09
2	11,870.89	3,726.91	8,107.98	29,521.13	6,000.00	4,881.46	6,989.43	0.907	6,339.41
3	11,870.89	2,952.11	8,918.78	20,602.35	6,000.00	4,476.06	7,394.83	0.864	6,389.13
4	11,870.89	2,060.24	9,810.66	10,791.69	6,000.00	4,030.12	7,840.77	0.823	6,452.95
5	11,870.86	1,079.69	10,791.69		6,000.00	3,539.59	8,331.27	0.784	6,531.72
6					6,000.00	3,000.00	(3,000.00)	0.746	(2,238.00)
7					6,000.00	3,000.00	(3,000.00)	0.711	(2,133.00)
8	(12,000.00)**				6,000.00	3,000.00	(3,000.00)	0.677	(2,031.00)
							(12,000.00)	0.502***	(6,024.00)
						Net present value of cost of purchasing			$28,590.30

* Investment tax credit = 0.10 × $60,000 – $6,000.

** Salvage value = book value = $60,000 – 8 × $6,000 = $12,000.

*** Discount factor using average after-tax cost of capital.

Table 4-4 Present value of future dollars

Year*	1%	2%	3%	4%	5%	6%	7%	8%	9%	10%
1	.990	.980	.971	.962	.952	.943	.935	.926	.917	.909
2	.980	.961	.943	.925	.907	.890	.873	.857	.842	.826
3	.971	.942	.915	.889	.864	.840	.816	.794	.772	.751
4	.961	.924	.889	.855	.823	.792	.763	.735	.708	.683
5	.951	.906	.863	.822	.784	.747	.713	.681	.650	.621
6	.942	.888	.838	.790	.746	.705	.666	.630	.596	.564
7	.933	.871	.813	.760	.711	.665	.623	.583	.547	.513
8	.923	.853	.789	.731	.677	.627	.582	.540	.502	.467
9	.914	.837	.766	.703	.645	.592	.544	.500	.460	.424
10	.905	.820	.744	.676	.614	.558	.508	.453	.422	.386

* Periods can be any time period; they do not have to be years.

lessor's financial condition and reputation. Be reasonably sure that the lease arrangements are the best you can get, that the equipment is what you need, and that the term is what you want. Remember, once the agreement is signed, it is just about impossible to change it.

The lease document spells out the provisions of the agreement. These provisions will probably include the specific nature of the financial agreement, the payment amount, terms of the agreement, disposition of the asset at the end of the term, schedule of asset value (for insurance and settlement purposes in case of damage or destruction), who is responsible for maintenance and taxes, renewal options, and cancellation penalties. In addition, the lease might include special provisions required by either you or the lessor.

As with any legally binding document, make sure that your attorney—and even your accountant—review it before you sign it to ensure that they don't have to defend it later.

SUCCESS ACTION PLAN

Money is simply a convenient way of keeping score. This chapter helps you determine how much money you will need to start and operate your catering service. It also gave you numerous valuable resources for getting needed finances. To put this chapter into action, take the following steps:

❏ Complete the capital requirements worksheet in this chapter as thoroughly and accurately as possible. You might need to set it aside for a few days as you research answers to some of the questions.

❏ Begin listing financial resources available to you, then prioritize them by opportunity. That is, if your current employer has the greatest potential for offering funding, indicate it as 1.

❏ Determine what type of loans best fit your financial requirements and your credit. List the top three options you have.

❏ Determine exactly how much money you need to borrow, how you will pay it back, and under what interest rate.

❏ Consider leasing opportunities for equipment you need.

❏ Take action on your catering business' financial requirements: sell personal assets, borrow, or lease.

5
How do I price my catering services?

You might think that the question of how much to charge is one of the most important questions of the book. It really isn't. Many other questions are just as important to the success of your business. However, this question is often the first one that new catering services ask, so let's get it answered.

First, let's consider the three *C*'s of pricing:

- Cost
- Competition
- Customer

How much does my service cost me to furnish?

Once you've established your start-up costs and your monthly operating costs, you'll have a pretty good idea of how much your catering service will cost you to furnish to your customers. But there's one more important factor that you need: your amount of available time.

A month with 20 workdays offers you approximately 160 hours of time that you can sell to customers. You might wind up working many more hours, but 160 is probably the most you'll be able to bill to clients. In fact, depending on the size and structure of your business, you might not be able to bill that many hours. One-person businesses require about a quarter of their time to market their services and to manage the business. So they're down to 120 billable hours per month, unless they do all marketing and management after normal working hours. If the operating or overhead costs calculated in the last chapter total $3000 a month, that amount is divided by 120 billable hours to come up with an hourly fee of $25. Add to this fee the cost of foods you prepare and cater.

As a rule-of-thumb, many caterers estimate that food costs, labor, and overhead/profits each make up about a third of the retail catering price. That is, if a banquet requires $5.50 per person in food costs, expect to allocate another $5.50 for labor costs and a third $5.50 for overhead and profit. That makes the catering price to the client $16.50 per person. Some caterers then add or subtract a small amount for extra marketing costs or to gain a client's business.

How much are my competitors charging?

A few telephone calls should get you the rates charged by your competitors. Of course, you must make sure that you're comparing apples with apples. Your competitors might not have your level of skill in this area, or they might have more. Your competitors might be including costs for some specialized skills or equipment that you don't have yet.

Why should you care what your competitors charge? Because your clients will probably get bids from them as well as you. You don't necessarily have to match or beat their bids, but you do need to know what their rates are so that you can help the client make a fair comparison.

How much does the customer expect to pay?

Guessing how much customers expect to pay is tough. The question isn't how much customers *will* pay, it's how much they *expect* to pay. The difference is expectations. You might get some customers to pay an excessive fee for a while, but they'll soon move to other sources. You need to find out what they think your service is actually worth to them. Most understand that, if they pay you too little, you will soon be out of business and won't be able to help them in the future. They might not admit to it, but they know it.

How can you know how much the consumer expects to pay for your skills? Ask a few of them. They might tell you what they're used to paying, what they think is a fair price, or maybe what they wish they were paying. Take them all into consideration. Ask the question of them and let them take a few minutes to explain their answer. You'll get some valuable insight into what customers expect from you, as well as what you should expect from them.

As when evaluating your competition's prices, make sure that you're comparing similar skills and similar fees. A customer might expect more skills than you can offer—or fewer.

Figure 5-1 illustrates a typical price list for a catering service, based on the answers to the three *C* questions.

PRICE VERSUS VALUE

Now you know what your time costs you, what your competitors charge for their time and skills, as well as what customers expect to pay for your time and skills. So which figure represents the right price? All and none. What you want is a price that will drive away about 20 percent of your prospects as too high, and another 20 percent as too low.

Here's a technique that makes your business more profitable, puts your business above your competitors, and keeps your customers happy: sell value, not price. How can a fancy restaurant charge five times as much as the diner next door for the exact same ingredients? They sell value. Call it "ambiance," or "image," or "snobbery," but the fancy restaurant makes the client's purchase an event rather than just a transaction. The fancy restaurant treats the client like a person rather than a number, gives extra service, uses finer dinnerware, and decorates the food to look appetizing.

You'll see the same technique—selling value rather than price—in any competitive business where one firm wants to stand out above the others. Consider the automobile industry. Chevys are sold on price; Cadillacs are sold on value—and both are built by General Motors. Value implies that, whether the price is large or small, you will get your money's worth.

PRICE LIST

123 Main Steet, Yourtown USA 12345

Date: June 30, 19xx

Code	Description	Unit Cost
SCC	Cold Cut Sandwich on White or Wheat Bread	$2.95
SPR	Pastrami Sandwich on Rye Bread	$3.50
SBL	Bacon, Lettuce and Tomato Sandwich on White Bread	$3.75
BPS	Small Pepsi Product -- 12 oz.	$0.79
BPL	Large Pepsi Product -- 24 oz.	$1.09
DBC	Brownie Cake	$1.29
DCB	Candy Bars	$0.50

5-1 A standard price list helps you ensure profitability.

So how does a catering service sell value? By offering services that other catering services do not, or by maintaining a clean and appetizing image with well-maintained vehicles and signage, or by simply turning questions of price into discussions of value.

Extra service

A valuable catering service can perform many extra services for clients. These extras don't cost much to implement, but add value to service. For example, depending on the type of work done, some catering services hire a part-time clean-up assistant—usually a high-school or college student at minimum wage—who will make sure that the serving area is cleaned well after the event. The cost to the catering business is minimal, and is usually factored into the hourly rate, but this "extra-mile" service is a courtesy that few catering services offer. Other catering services add value by offering to print invitations, serve as receptionist, or secure entertainment for the client.

Value-priced catering services can step ahead of their competition by taking on any jobs that the client might otherwise have to handle. One successful caterer selects, purchases, and arranges fresh flowers for all of her events at no additional

Price versus value   **75**

charge. This gives the caterer another chance to sell her value to the client or prospect.

What can you offer in your specialty that will set you apart from your competitors and help you sell value rather than price? First, present your service attractively. A catering portfolio is a useful tool for presenting your services to potential clients. Your catering portfolio should include color photographs of typical services and special dishes, parties that you've catered, popular menus, advertisements, awards, association affiliations, testimonials, and anything else that will help you sell your service.

Professional image

Imagine seeing a can of tomato sauce on the grocer's shelf that is discolored and dented, with a torn label. You'd probably pass it by for one that looked neat, fresh, and undamaged. Yet the contents of each might be exactly the same quality. Appearance does make a difference—especially in the catering business. For just a few dollars more, your catering business can develop a clean, professional appearance that tells prospects and customers that you offer quality.

Make sure that your vehicles are all well-painted and reasonably clean, especially if they have your business name written on them. One catering service owner paid her children a few dollars every Sunday afternoon for the weekly vehicle wash.

Signage is important. Go to your local library and check the yellow pages in out-of-state telephone books for catering service ads. Is there a design or insignia that appeals to you? Modify it to fit your own business and make it your design. Check how much local sign shops charge for designing signs for you. You'll want signs on your vehicles, your stationery, your menus, and your office. The only exception is a home office in a neighborhood that doesn't allow business signs in residential areas.

At a job site, a clean, well-painted catering vehicle with an attractive business sign tells your client and passerby that you own and manage a quality catering service that cares about its image.

Talk value

The question of price always comes up with a client or prospect. Many catering service owners dread it and would rather avoid the discussion. A successful catering firm encourages the question of price because it provides the opportunity to talk about value. The caterer wants clients to know why they should pay as much or more for his services as for a competitor's.

Price is the *cost* of something. Value is the *worth* of something. Why is your service worth something? Because you can offer the following:

- You're knowledgeable; you know about catering and how to effectively manage social events.
- You're efficient; you know how to work smart to get the job done in less time.
- You're honest; you will not knowingly mislead your client or charge for services not performed.

- You're helpful; you want to solve the client's problem, not just perform a job.
- You're fair; you charge a reasonable fee for an important service.
- You're accessible; you respond to questions, answer telephone calls, and follow up with clients.

Successful catering services don't shun the question of pricing or apologize for high rates. They look forward to the question so that they can explain why their service is worth more than that of others. They sell—and give—value.

HOW DO I ESTIMATE A CATERING JOB?

An *estimate* is a calculation of your value—the customer's cost—stated in dollars. Clients of your catering service will require written estimates, so you must learn how to write job estimates that are accurate, fair, and profitable for both you and the client. Some forms and procedures can help you estimate costs and value. Estimating forms are available through trade associations. In addition, the appendix of this book offers ready-to-use estimating forms that can be photocopied and easily customized for your catering business.

Some computer programs (discussed in chapter 3) can automate the estimating process and print out bids. These commercial programs are written especially for the catering and food-service industry to help you estimate and bill jobs.

Here are some hints from successful caterers on how to accurately estimate jobs:

- Allow more food per person for buffets than for sit-down meals.
- To reduce food costs per person at a buffet, place more expensive foods at the end of the table.
- Keep complete records for all catering jobs, including food used, food wasted, and the number of people served. Reviewing these records can help you more accurately estimate future jobs.
- Get an equipment list and fee schedule from a local party-rental service to help determine what is available as well as what you should charge for party equipment and supplies.

HOW DO I BID A CATERING JOB?

A *bid* is simply a written offer to perform a job at a specified price. A bid might also be called a *quote*, a *price quotation*, or a *proposal*. In each case, once it is accepted and signed, it is a legally binding document.

If you specialize in a segment of catering that doesn't have reprinted proposal forms, you can modify forms in this book or develop one that will serve your specific requirements. You might want to incorporate the wording of your bids into a word processing program on your computer so that you can easily develop and submit a bid in the shortest time.

A *bid record* is simply a written report of bids prepared and submitted. It gives you the opportunity to track your success as a bidder, and to determine whether specific competitors are taking too much business from you.

Types of bids

Catering services use a variety of bidding types, depending on the requirements of the customer and the marketplace. Here are the most common:

- *Labor only.* In this arrangement, the catering service furnishes labor and culinary tools, and the customer furnishes cooking equipment and raw foods. The labor charge includes the cost of labor, taxes, benefits, overhead, and a profit. The proposal in Fig. 5-2 is an example of this sort of arrangement.
- *Time and material.* Labor is billed at hourly service rates established for each worker, and material is billed at its retail price (sometimes less a discount), as shown in Fig. 5-3. Overhead costs are built into the labor rates. Profit comes from the hourly service rates as well as from the sale of foods at retail prices.
- *Fixed price.* The total price includes the cost of materials, labor, food expenses, prorated overhead costs, and profit. This method is the most common for pricing catering, either by the piece ($3.00 for a packaged sandwich) or by the person ($18.00 per banquet guest).
- *Unit price.* Total price is broken down into components: labor, food expenses, and overhead.
- *Cost plus fee.* The costs of materials, labor, and job expenses are reimbursed at actual cost, plus a fee to cover overhead and profit.
- *Cost plus percentage.* The costs of food, labor, and related expenses are reimbursed at actual cost, plus a percentage to cover overhead and profit.

After a bid is made and accepted, the customer signs a work order (Fig. 5-4) or a letter of agreement (Fig. 5-5) that you have written.

Terms

How you get paid for your job depends on the terms that you offer in the bid and upon the requirements of the bidder. Three common payment schedules are

- 100 percent due on completion of the work.
- 50 percent on signing an agreement, and 50 percent on completion.
- Bill the first of every month for work completed during the previous month.

How many bids will it take to get a job? It depends on many factors: your local market, economic conditions, your pricing, the perceived value of your bid, the presentation of your bid, and your relationship with prospects and customers. Typically, one out of five bids will probably come to a job. Based on this 20 percent factor, if you want a catering income of $200,000 in the coming year, you'd better write good bids for about $1 million. Your factor might be higher or lower, but it's a good rule of thumb.

HOW DO I PROFITABLY MANAGE MY OPERATING BUDGET?

Managing your catering business requires that you manage your business budget so you can continue to provide service, support, and employment to others as well as a profit to yourself. When you first start your business, you establish a preliminary budget. Once your business is operating, you must establish and manage an operating budget.

	PROPOSAL

ABC Catering Service

123 Main Street, Yourtown

NUMBER
1234

DATE
June 30, 19xx

Proposal Submitted to:

NAME
Smith & Jones Manufacturing

ADDRESS
876 Main St.

CITY
Yourtown

STATE
USA

ZIP CODE
12345

Job Site Information:

JOB NAME
Friday Staff Lunches

JOB LOCATION
876 Main St.

JOB PHONE
234-6666

We hereby submit specifications and estimates for:

ABC Catering Service agrees to furnish cold-service lunches to Smith & Jones Manufacturing employees attending their Friday staff meetings between 12:00 and 1:00 p.m. Smith & Jones Manufacturing agrees to place their order for thenumber of lunches and items required by 9 a.m. on Friday. Items available are from the ABC Catering Service menu and are offered at a 20% discount from retail prices. Smith & Jones Manufacturing agrees to pay ABC Catering Service in full by check when the food is delivered.

We hereby propose to furnish material and labor - complete in accoreadnce with the above specifications for

_____ dollars $ _____

Payment to be made as follows:

As noted above. _____

_____

_____

All matter is guaranteed to be as specified. All work to be completed in a workmanlike manner according to standard practices. Any alternation or deviation from above specifications involving extra costs will be executed only upon written orders, and will become an extra charge over and above the estimate. All agreements contingent upon strikes, accidents, or delays beyond Our Company. Owner is to carry necessary insurance. Our Company workers are fully covered by Workman's Compensation Insurance.

are

Authorized Signature

X _____

Note: This proposal may be withdrawn by us if not accepted within _____ days

Acceptance of Proposal. The above prices and specifications are satisfactory and hereby accepted. You are authorized to do the work as specified. Payment will be made as outlines above.

_____
Date of Acceptance

X _____
Signature

X _____
Signature

5-2 A written proposal can reduce misunderstandings between you, your clients, and your staff.

ABC Catering Service

Quotation Form

123 Main stret, Yourtown USA

Date: June 30, 19xx

Quote # 4321

Client: Don and Mary Smith
345 Valley Road
Yourtown USA 12345
234-7323

Materials

Quantity	Description	Cost Per Unit	Total
35	Three-course dinner	$28.00	$980.00
1	Four-tier Wedding Cake	$156.00	$156.00
35	Hors d'oeuvres	$5.75	$201.25
35	Complete Bar Service	$12.00	$420.00
	For Jones/Smith Wedding July 15, 19XX		
	at Murphy Hills Country Club		
		Total Cost:	$1757.25

Labor

	Hours	Description	Cost Per Hour	Total
REGULAR	12	2 Servers, 1 Bartender @ 4 hours each	$25.00	$300.00
OVERTIME				
			Total Cost:	$300.00

GRAND TOTAL $2057.25

Authorized Signature   Date

5-3 Make sure that all of your quotes are written to ensure that clients understand what they will get and how much it will cost.

80 How do I price my catering services?

A *budget* is a forecast of all cash sources and cash expenditures. It is organized in the same format as a financial statement, and most commonly covers a 12-month period. At the end of the year, the anticipated income and expenses developed in the budget are compared to the actual performance of the business, as recorded in the financial statement.

A budget can greatly enhance your chances of success by helping you estimate future needs and plan profits, spending, and overall cash flow. A budget also enables you to detect potential problems before they occur and to alter your plans to prevent those problems.

In business, budgets help you determine how much money you have and how you will use it, as well as help you decide whether you have enough money to achieve your financial goals. As part of your business plan, a budget can help convince a loan officer that you know your business and have anticipated its needs.

A budget indicates the cash required for necessary labor and materials, day-to-day operating costs, revenue needed to support business operations, and expected profit. If your budget indicates that you need more revenue than you can earn, you can adjust your plans by doing one or more of the following:

- Reducing expenditures (hiring fewer employees, purchasing less expensive furniture, eliminating a telephone line)
- Expanding sales (offering additional services, conducting an aggressive marketing campaign, hiring a salesperson)
- Lowering profit expectations

Elements of a budget

A budget has three main elements: sales revenue, total costs, and profit.

Sales are the cornerstone of a budget. It is crucial to estimate anticipated sales as accurately as possible. Base estimates on actual past sales figures. Once you target sales, you can calculate the related expenses necessary to achieve your goals.

Total costs include fixed and variable costs. Estimating costs is complicated because you must identify which costs will change—and by how much—and which costs will remain unchanged as sales increase. You must also consider inflation and rising prices as appropriate.

Variable costs are those costs that vary directly with your level of sales. Food expenses, for example, are variable costs for your catering business. *Fixed costs* are those costs that don't change, regardless of sales volume. Rent is considered a fixed cost. *Semi-variable costs*, such as office salaries, labor wages, and telephone expenses, have both variable and fixed cost components. Part of such an expense is listed as fixed (such as telephone line charges) and part is variable (the long-distance charges).

Your profit should be large enough to make a return on your cash investment and your work. Your investment is the money you put into the firm when you started it and the profit of prior years that you have left in the firm (*retained earnings*). If you can receive 10 percent interest on $25,000 by investing outside of your business, then you should expect a similar return when investing $25,000 in equipment and other assets within the business. In targeting profits, you also want to be sure you're receiving a fair return on your labor. Your paycheck should reflect what you could be earning elsewhere as an employee.

Establishing an operating budget

As you develop your budget, you'll be working with the *budget equation.* The basic budget equation is

$$Sales = Total\ Costs + Profit$$

This equation shows that every sales dollar you receive is made up partly of a recovery of your costs and partly of profit. Another way to express the basic budgeting equation is

$$Sales - Total\ Costs = Profit$$

This equation shows that, after reimbursing yourself for the cost of producing your service, the remaining part of the sales dollar is profit. For example, if you expect $1000 for a specific job and you know that it will cost $900 to market and perform this service, your profit will be $100.

In calculating an operating budget, you will often make estimates based on past sales and cost figures. Adjust these figures to reflect price increases, inflation, and other factors. For example, for the past three years, a catering service spent an average of $3500 on advertising costs. For the coming year, the owner expects a price increase of 3 percent (0.03). To calculate next year's advertising costs, the owner multiplies the average annual advertising costs by the percentage price increase ($3500 × 0.03 = $105) and adds that amount to the original annual cost ($3500 + $105 = $3605).

If your catering business is a new venture and has no past financial records, rely on your own experience and knowledge of the industry to estimate demand for and costs of your service. Your accountant or catering association might also be able to help you develop realistic estimates.

The budgeting process

Before you create an operating budget, you must answer three questions:
- How much net profit do you realistically expect your business to generate during the calendar year?
- How much will it cost to produce that profit?
- How much sales revenue is necessary to support both profit and cost requirements?

To answer these questions, consider expected sales and all direct and indirect costs associated with your catering service. To make the safest estimates when budgeting, most companies prefer to overestimate expenses and underestimate sales revenue.

Start constructing your budget with either a forecast of sales or a forecast of profits. For practical purposes, most small businesses start with a forecast of profits. In other words, decide what profit you realistically want to make, and then list the expenses you will incur to make that profit.

The steps to creating an operating budget are
1. Target desired profit.
2. Determine operating expenses.
3. Calculate gross profit margin.
4. Estimate sales revenues.
5. Adjust figures.

The sample income statement for ABC Catering Service shown in Table 5-1 illustrates the main steps in budget preparation. As you follow the steps, calculate all the figures yourself. Once you have calculated projected sales, expenses, and profits, organize the figures into a readable format.

Target desired profit

During the three-year period, ABC Catering Service averaged an annual net profit of $63,100. During Year 2, the company had its highest net profit of $65,000. In Year 3,

Table 5-1 Income statements for years 1, 2, and 3

	Year 1	Year 2	Year 3	Total	Average	Average percent of sales
Sales	$490,000	$508,333	$513,233	$1,511,566	$503,855	100%
Cost of goods sold	$343,000	$355,833	$359,263	$1,058,096	$352,698	70%
Gross profit margin	$147,000	$152,500	$153,970	$ 453,470	$151,157	30%
Operating expenses:						
Advertising	$ 3,200	$ 3,700	$ 3,600	$ 10,500	$ 3,500	0.7%
Depreciation	$ 4,000	$ 4,000	$ 4,000	$ 12,000	$ 4,000	0.8%
Insurance	$ 1,700	$ 1,700	$ 1,700	$ 5,100	$ 1,700	0.3%
Legal and accounting expenses	$ 3,400	$ 3,605	$ 3,800	$ 10,805	$ 3,602	0.7%
Office expenses	$ 2,200	$ 2,400	$ 2,650	$ 7,250	$ 2,417	0.5%
Rent	$ 24,000	$ 24,000	$ 24,000	$ 72,000	$ 24,000	4.8%
Repair and maintenance	$ 300	$ 550	$ 420	$ 1,270	$ 424	0.1%
Salaries	$ 33,000	$ 33,000	$ 33,000	$ 99,000	$ 33,000	6.6%
Telephone and utilities	$ 6,000	$ 6,350	$ 6,200	$ 18,550	$ 6,183	1.2%
Miscellaneous	$ 9,200	$ 8,195	$ 10,300	$ 27,695	$ 9,231	1.8%
Total operating expenses	$ 87,000	$ 87,500	$ 89,670	$264,170	$ 88,057	17.5%
Net profit	$ 60,000	$ 65,000	$ 64,300	$199,330	$ 63,100	12.5%

sales were up, but net profit declined. For the coming year, Year 4, the company is targeting a net profit of $65,000.

Determine operating expenses

ABC Catering Service estimates that it will have many additional expenditures in Year 4. It will award a 5 percent wage increase to its two employees and purchase a more comprehensive medical insurance package for them at an additional annual cost of $2400. The company also plans to install additional telephone services at a cost of $1500.

In addition, ABC Catering Service's accountant has advised it to plan on a 3 percent overall inflation rate next year. Taking these factors into consideration, ABC Catering Service figures its expenses as shown in the preliminary budget in Table 5-2.

Table 5-2
Preliminary budget for year 4

	Amount ($)	Percent of sales
Sales	533,730	100%
Cost of goods sold	373,611	70%
Gross profit margin	160,119	30%
Operating expenses		
Advertising	3,605	0.7%
Depreciation	4,000	0.8%
Insurance	4,100	0.8%
Legal and accounting		
expenses	4,142	0.8%
Office expenses	2,995	0.6%
Rent	24,000	4.5%
Repair and maintenance	437	0.1%
Salaries	34,650	6.5%
Telephone and utilities	7,683	1.4%
Miscellaneous	9,507	1.8%
Total operating expenses	95,119	17.8%
Net profit	65,000	12.2%

Under fixed costs, the company makes the following estimates:
- Rent will remain unchanged at $24,000 per year.
- Depreciation will remain unchanged at $4000 per year.
- Salaries will be raised by 5 percent (0.05).
- The annual insurance expense of $1700 will be increased by $2400 to provide for additional medical coverage, so will now be budgeted at $4100.

The company calculates variable costs as follows:
- Telephone and utilities expenses will be budgeted for $7683 (average annual cost plus the $1500 expected increase).
- Advertising, repair, maintenance, and miscellaneous expenses will increase by the 3 percent inflation factor.
- Due to the company's growth, office expenses will continue to increase 10 percent in the coming year, plus the 3 percent inflation factor.
- Legal and accounting expenses will continue to increase by 6 percent in the coming year, to which the 3 percent inflation factor should be added.

Calculate gross profit margin

Gross profit margin is the sum of net profit and total operating expenses, computed by working the preliminary budget backwards. ABC Catering Service's gross profit margin is obtained by adding net profit of $65,000 to operating expenses of $95,119, resulting in a gross profit of $160,119.

Estimate sales revenue

To estimate sales, analyze the gross profit margin. The income statement in Table 5-1 shows that ABC Catering Service has experienced a gross profit margin equal to 30 percent of sales for three consecutive years. Since a gross profit margin of $160,119 is expected to equal 30 percent of net sales, then targeted sales should equal $533,730.

Adjust figures

If the preliminary figure for targeted net sales seems realistic, the budget is complete. If generating the amount of targeted net sales will be a problem, the preliminary budget must be reviewed and adjusted. In the ABC Catering Service example, the management is uncomfortable with the preliminary results. They don't believe that the firm can realistically generate sales of more than $525,000. To derive a more realistic operating budget, the owner decides to do the following:
- Delay installing additional telephone services to reduce telephone expenses by $1000.
- Carefully monitor expenses to reduce miscellaneous expenses by $1000.
- Choose a similar but less expensive employee benefit package with a higher employee deductible for medical insurance to reduce benefit expenses by $1200.

After making these adjustments to its budget, ABC Catering Service's new gross profit margin is $156,919 ($65,000 + $91,919). To compute the targeted sales, the company divides the gross margin by 30 percent for a targeted sales of $523,063, as shown in Table 5-3. This figure is within the company's limit of $525,000.

The annual operating budget might have to be altered again during the year to reflect a sharp rise or drop in one or more variable expenses or in revenues. Often, annual operating budgets are divided into smaller monthly or quarterly operating budgets. Monthly budgets are used to measure actual results against budgeted goals.

For large catering firms with several departments or work functions, the annual operating budget should be expanded into a master budget. A master operating budget consists of a group of separate but interconnected operating budgets. These budgets will depend on and contribute to the company's overall plans.

Table 5-3
Final budget for year 4

	Amount ($)	Percent of sales
Sales	533,730	100%
Cost of goods sold	373,611	70%
Gross profit margin	160,119	30%
Operating expenses		
Advertising	3,605	0.7%
Depreciation	4,000	0.8%
Insurance	4,100	0.8%
Legal and accounting expenses	4,142	0.8%
Office expenses	2,995	0.6%
Rent	24,000	4.5%
Repair and maintenance	437	0.1%
Salaries	34,650	6.5%
Telephone and utilities	7,683	1.4%
Miscellaneous	9,507	1.8%
Total operating expenses	95,119	17.8%
Net profit	65,000	12.2%

An operating budget is an indispensable tool for converting plans into a successful reality. The budget helps focus your efforts on the direction in which you're headed. It indicates how much cash you have to spend, your expenses, and how much you need to earn. By planning on paper first, you minimize some of the risks of owning and operating a catering firm. A good operating budget can also build morale by helping you organize, communicate, and motivate employees to do their part in achieving the company's financial goals.

SUCCESS ACTION PLAN

Pricing is an important aspect of starting and running a money-making catering service. If your pricing is too high, business will go elsewhere; if your pricing is too low, profits will go elsewhere. Here's how you can put this chapter into action and ensure reasonable profits for your catering service:

❏ Determine how much your catering service will cost you to furnish.

❏ Find out how much your closest competitors are charging for the same services.

❏ Survey prospects to learn how much they expect to pay for catering services that you will provide.

❏ List five reasons why price should not be as important as value to your customers.

❏ Develop an accurate method of estimating catering costs and pricing for your services.

❏ Develop a bidding method that will help you sell value over price.

❏ Decide what terms you will offer customers and under what conditions.

❏ Develop your catering service's operating budget using the five steps in this chapter.

6

How do I get and keep customers?

The National Restaurant Association's off-premises catering study conducted in 1992 revealed that 42 percent of consumers reported having eaten a meal at a catered event within the previous year. In addition, 28 percent said they had eaten a meal at an event catered in a home within the previous year.

This chapter helps you find these people and keep them as good customers for your catering service. You'll learn to think like a customer, find prospects, advertise and market, and—most important—keep customers coming back.

WHO ARE MY CUSTOMERS?

Understanding your customers is so important that large corporations spend millions of dollars annually on market research. Although some formal research is important, a small catering service firm can usually avoid this expense. Typically, the owner or manager of a small business knows many of the customers personally. From this foundation, understanding your customers can be enhanced by a systematic effort.

Who are your customers? They are those recommended to you by other satisfied customers, those who have been influenced by your advertising or been solicited by your signage or sales force, former customers, newcomers to the area, customers who need immediate help, and your competitors' dissatisfied customers. They are businesses who have never before required catering services, as well as those who have decided to change caterers because of price, quality, or service.

A seller characterizes what customers are buying as goods and services—food, drills, video games, or cars. But understanding your customers starts with the realization that they purchase benefits as well as products. Consumers don't select food. Instead, some will pay to displace the feeling of hunger. Some seek pleasant taste. Others want entertainment. Or perhaps any food at a bargain price will do.

You must find out, from their point of view, what customers are buying—and why. Understanding your customers enables you to profit by providing what buyers seek: satisfaction.

If you were a rich and influential person in your community, why would you use a food catering service? What if you were a local business owner? How about an average 9-to-5 office worker? In nearly every case, you would purchase the services of a food catering firm for approximately the same reasons:

- Convenience
- Value
- Price

Everyone must eat food. After many years of doing so, it can be a drudgery or it can be enjoyable. Your job as a caterer is to make food appetizing, wholesome, enjoyable, and convenient. Convenience is very important. The primary difference between a restaurant and a caterer is that the caterer goes to where the customer is to serve the food. It might be at a home, church meeting room, an office building, or even at a sporting or entertainment event. In each case, the caterer takes the food to the customer rather than requiring the customer to come to the food.

It is this convenience that not only separates restaurateurs from caterers, it also distinguishes between caterers. One caterer selects to furnish sandwiches, drinks, and snacks to construction workers at the job site. Another caterer specializes in preparing food for wedding banquets. A third serves gourmet food at society functions.

According to The National Restaurant Association's 1992 study, men and consumers with relatively high household incomes are more likely to have eaten a catered meal within the previous year. In fact, more than half of the men between the ages of 25 and 49 and about a third of the men between 18 and 24 reported eating a meal catered at an office or other public place. More than half of the people with incomes over $40,000 had eaten a catered meal.

Your market is simply the group of people who would most benefit from your services. The first step to defining your market, as discussed earlier in this book, is defining who you are to them. You start out defining your market in broad terms, such as "I am a catering service who specializes in one-person events that can be performed with minimal equipment." Now, it's time to be more specific.

There are dozens of types of catering services—and hundreds of potential markets—so this chapter necessarily uses broad examples. You'll quickly get the idea, though, and be able to apply it to your specialty.

In the case of a one-person catering service with minimal equipment, your customers will be those whose needs don't require a large labor force or specialized equipment. The most common application of this market definition is the small catering service that works out of a catering vehicle offering sandwiches and snacks to office or construction workers at their work site.

Let's say that, based on your study of the local market, you determine that the best opportunity for you and your skills is to specialize in catering food to office workers. You look around and decide that there is enough work in your community to keep you busy for quite awhile, yet not so much as to attract lots of competition. Your customers, in this simplified example, are those who work in offices in your area, who can conveniently leave their office for lunch, and who are not currently served by other mobile catering services.

Now you need to find customers who fit this description. With a map, you drive your prospective market area during traditional lunchtime (11 a.m. to 1 p.m.), watching for food-buying patterns. Is there a lot of foot traffic during the lunch hour? Where are they going? Are there "favorite" lunch spots? Do many people brown-bag and take their lunch to a nearby park? Is the area currently served by mobile caterers or by food carts? Once you've selected a few prime spots, make actual counts of prospects, when they arrive, how long they seem to have for lunch, and what types of foods they purchase. Conduct on-the-street surveys to determine who the primary employers are in the area, the length of the typical lunch hour, where people go to get their lunches, and what they typically pay for lunch. Most important, ask them what lunch foods or services they would like from a new caterer.

Once you have this information, it's time to build your prospect database of business and factory owners in your selected market. Then, approach your prospects. Focus your attention on one goal: getting them to recognize their need for your services and your qualifications to serve them.

Your approach to prospects of a gourmet catering service would be somewhat different, but the principles will be the same. First, determine whether there is sufficient opportunity for you to build your business and whether potential competitors are already adequately serving this market. Then, focus your attention and marketing on those prospects who can best use your services. You might analyze the services of gourmet restaurants in the area, their success and weaknesses. You could then conduct a survey of people who enjoy gourmet food to determine if a catering service specializing in this area would be profitable.

Depending on your specialty, you can subscribe to local or regional newspapers, society magazines, and business publications that will keep you informed of opportunities in your market.

Some start-up catering services begin their business by serving customers who cannot be served by their current or ex-employer. By working with them, you reduce the amount of marketing you must do to develop your business. Most start-up catering services then pay a marketing fee or a finder's fee to these sources. It's another reason to maintain a good relationship with all of your past and current employers.

HOW SHOULD I MARKET MY CATERING SERVICE?

Marketing is a science. It's not a perfect science where the answer to a question is always the same; it's a science based on data, information, knowledge, and wisdom. Data is easy to get and build into information. From this information comes knowledge and, eventually, wisdom. Wisdom is what makes your business profitable. Marketing wisdom builds your business.

The purpose of marketing is to get more customers. That's it. If you're new to business, the purpose is to get your first customers. If you've established a substantial business, the purpose is to keep the customers that you have.

You can market your services to prospects and customers in dozens of ways. They include the many forms of advertising, as well as literature, direct mail, and telephone marketing.

The purpose of advertising is to tell your potential customers why they will benefit from using your services. The best way to do this is to let your other customers tell your prospects how much they gain from your service. This word-of-mouth advertising is the most valuable type of advertising there is. Unfortunately, it is also the slowest to develop. Your first satisfied client might, in conversations, mention your good food and service to prospects once or twice a month. After hearing that a number of times and when they are looking for your service, a few of these prospects might call you. By that time, though, you might be out of business due to lack of work.

Impressions

Every time prospects see or hear your name, you make an impression. It might be something small like seeing your vehicle's sign on the highway or seeing your sponsorship sign on a baseball field. Or it might be a listing in the yellow pages or a positive (or negative) comment about your last catering job made by a mutual acquaintance.

Each impression is important because they are cumulative. After several impressions, large and small, prospects might bring your name into the "possible source" parts of their brains. Then, when a legitimate need for your service arises, the prospect considers you as a supplier. Think about it. How many times did you see or hear about "Ford," "Mr. Coffee," or "Hawaii" before you even considered trying them? Probably dozens or even hundreds of impressions were made. And consider that any negative feelings are also impressions. You will need to positively impress your prospects many times and in many ways before they can be upgraded to a customer.

You can speed the process along by developing *testimonials*. That is, when you have a client who expresses satisfaction with your service, you ask the client to write you a testimonial letter. The letter describes how professional your service is and how well you respond to the needs of customers.

Unfortunately, only a small percentage of those who say they will write a testimonial letter actually do so. The problem isn't sincerity, it's time. Most customers just don't have the time to write such a letter. So some catering services hire a writer (check the local telephone book for "Writers" or "Resume Services") to interview the client and actually write the letter for the customer. You foot the bill. A well-written testimonial from a well-respected person is worth literally thousands of dollars in new business to you. Copy it and include it with your brochure, quote from it in advertisements, and pass it out to prospects. It is your best form of advertising. Of course, make sure that you have a customer's written permission to use any testimonials you quote in advertising.

To encourage satisfied customers and their testimonials, some catering services establish and promote a policy of "satisfaction guaranteed." The profits lost are usually replaced by the profits gained through this policy. It is a helpful persuasion tool when trying to close a sale.

Free advertising

You can advertise your new catering service in many ways at little or no cost. Exactly which methods you use depend somewhat on your specialization.

Once you have your business card printed, carry a stack of them with you wherever you go. Pass them out to anyone who might be or know a prospect. When you stop at the supermarket, put your business card on the market's bulletin board. Do the same if you stop at a local retailer for anything: Put your card on their bulletin board. All it costs is the price of a business card.

Many catering services overlook one of the best sources of free advertising: publicity. When you start your business, write a short article (called a *press release*) and give copies to your local newspaper, radio stations, shoppers, and other "media." Include information about your business such as owners, experience, affiliations, background, expertise, purpose, location, to whom the business sells its services, and how to contact the business. If you're not comfortable with writing, hire a local freelance writer or publicist to do the job for you.

A single sheet of paper, printed on both sides and folded, can become your first brochure describing your services and your qualifications. The cost is very small, especially if you have the skills to write and produce it yourself. You can pass your brochure out at chambers of commerce meetings, local service club meetings, or anywhere where you would pass out your business card. Your brochure doesn't have to be slick and expensive, but a few dollars spent on a neat and accurate brochure can bring you many hundreds of dollars in new business. That's a good return on your investment. If you need help, contact a local "Desktop Publishing Service" through the yellow pages or a copy shop.

While business signs aren't free, they offer a second "free" benefit beyond their main purpose of informing. They repeat their message whenever they are seen. So you want signs that are frequently seen. One excellent reason for selecting a delivery van as your catering vehicle is that a van offers space on its side for a large sign. Using a picture, a graphic image, or a logo in your sign helps viewers better identify and remember what you do. Some enterprising catering services park their work vehicles over the weekend at locations that offer high visibility: shopping centers, prominent job sites, and park-and-ride lots near major highway intersections. Make sure, though, that your vehicle is securely locked, especially if you keep your equipment in it.

Other catering services buy or make their own standing sign that they place at the job site (with permission), announcing, for example, "another quality event catered by Jones Catering Service." Regular passers-by see the sign daily. Each time they see it is another impression for your business. Even if they are not potential clients, the impression might be passed on verbally to someone who is—" I sure see a lot of signs for Jones Catering Service. They must be good."

Traditional advertising

When most people think of advertising, they think of billboards, large newspaper ads, catchy radio ads, and the like. Should catering services use this type of advertising to develop their business? In most cases, no. The cost is typically too high for the results derived.

Let's say that you purchase a quarter-page ad in your local daily newspaper and it's seen by 100,000 people for a price of just $500. That's just a half-cent per impression, which might seem pretty cheap. However, of those 100,000 people, suppose only 50 are true prospects for your service. Then the price goes to $10 per impression. You'd be better off spending your money for an article that appears in the paper's business section, or mailing your brochures and a personalized letter to each of those 50 prospects.

Newspaper advertising
Almost every home in the U.S. and Canada receives a newspaper. From the advertiser's point of view, newspaper advertising can be convenient because production changes can be made quickly, if necessary, and you can often insert a new adver-

tisement on short notice, depending on the frequency of the publication. Another advantage is the large variety of ad sizes newspaper advertising offers.

The disadvantages to newspaper advertising include the cost of a large ad that's required to stand out among other large ads, the short throw-away life of a newspaper, and the poor printing quality. If you do select to advertise in newspapers, establish a consistent schedule rather than a hit-and-miss advertising program. Most importantly, ensure that the program is realistically within your budget.

Radio and tv advertising

Radio is a relatively inexpensive way of reaching people. Radio has a more selective audience than newspapers because stations aim at specific age groups and genders as their primary target, where newspapers typically do not. However, a radio ad cannot be reviewed later. Once it is played, it is gone. So, during the 30 or 60 seconds it airs, you must make sure that listeners hear something they can easily remember.

Advertising on TV is just not financially practical for most catering services—at least until they grow.

Yellow pages advertising

Depending on your specialty, an ad in the yellow pages might be one of your best sources of new business. In most locations, if you purchase a required business telephone line, you get a listing in one category of your local telephone book. In some areas, this is optional. The listing can be as simple as

> ABC Catering Service, 123 Main St.------------------------------------555-1234

Or the firm name can be in capital letters such as:

> ABC CATERING SERVICE
> 123 Main St.--555-1234

You can also include information on your specialty, and even an alternate telephone number, like this:

> ABC Catering Service
> Fine European Foods In Your Home
> 123 Main St.--555-1234
> If no answer--555-2345

Many businesses upgrade their listings with *space ads*. A space ad is simply an advertisement that takes up more space than a line or two and is usually surrounded by a box.

To determine the size and cost of an appropriate space ad, check your local and nearby telephone book's yellow pages under headings for "Caterers," and related topics. Look for your competitors. When potential clients look in their yellow pages, which ads stand out the best? Which have the greatest eye-appeal? Which are easiest to read? Remember that you don't need the largest ad in the telephone book, you need the one that's most cost-effective for you.

The last few pages in your yellow pages section frequently has information on how to select a space ad. You'll learn terms like "double half," "double quarter,"and "triple quarter," as well as "columns." It's actually quite easy to follow. Most larger telephone books have four vertical columns per page; community telephone books in rural areas are half-size with only two columns per page. So a "triple quarter" is three columns wide and a quarter-page long; a "double half" is two columns wide and a half-page long.

At the end of the yellow pages section, there will often be a toll-free telephone number for ordering a space ad or listing. You might also find the number in the front of the book under "Business Telephone Service" or a similar title. The firm that produces your telephone book will help you design and write your ad—with input from you. Ask them about the cost and availability of color in your ad, and any other special requirements you have. Then they will supply a *layout* of the ad and a contract for you to sign. Most yellow pages listing or space ad contracts are for one year and can be paid in monthly installments.

One more thing about yellow pages ads: Make sure you include any state or local licensing information. Some ads include the phrase "Licensed—Bonded—Insured" while others include a state license board number such as "Professional License #12345." Some catering services also include information about affiliations, including the logo of catering associations.

The American Marketing Association is an excellent resource for additional information and data on marketing your catering service. Contact them at

250 South Wacker Dr.
Chicago, IL 60606

What features and benefits do I offer?

So what is it that you are promoting? An alternative to starvation? Not exactly. You are actually promoting the benefits of the features of your catering business. That is, customers don't want food, they want prestige. They're not buying tiny-pigs-in-a-blanket, they're buying service.

The difference between a *feature* and a *benefit* is relative. A feature is what you provide to a customer; a benefit is what the customer gets from it. A benefit is expressed from the viewpoint of the customer rather than you. If you want to be successful, talk about benefits rather than features. It's the difference between selling a 12-ounce USDA Choice cut of meat (feature) and a sizzling, juicy, satisfying steak (benefit).

For example, a catering service offers such benefits as convenience, value, taste, simplicity, time saving, variety, ease of selection, prestige, appetite satisfaction, aroma, color, service, and entertainment.

HOW CAN I FIND AND DEVELOP PROSPECTS?

A prospect, as mentioned earlier, is someone who could potentially use your service but hasn't done so yet. They might not have heard of your service, or they might not know enough about it to determine its value, or they simply haven't been asked.

Who is a prospect for your catering service? Of course, that depends on what service you perform for customers. If you're a catering service specializing in company picnics, your prospects are companies in the area that sponsor or would like to sponsor such events. To turn these prospects into customers, you must first think like they think, only faster. For example, they begin planning a summer picnic in the spring by calling caterers to ask for costs. If you contact them in the early spring with a description of the benefits your firm offers, you might have a sale. At least you have a prospect.

The U.S. Census Bureau is an excellent source of statistical data for market surveys. Based on the national census conducted every ten years, the Bureau divides large cities into census tracts of about 5000 residents within *Standard Metropolitan Statistical Areas* (SMSAs). Data on these tracts cover income, housing, and related information that can be valuable to you. Results of the 1990 census are now available. For this and other market information, contact

The Office of Business Liaison
U.S. Department of Commerce
Washington, DC 20230

The Bureau of the Census offers business statistics, data, and special demographic studies among its services.

Qualifying prospects

In the case of a caterer who provides staff picnics, any business with a staff of 10 or more in the area would be a prospective customer. None should be overlooked. By digging through local records and calling area businesses, the catering business owner is *qualifying* the prospect to determine the chances for turning the prospect into a customer. The catering service owner can call businesses to determine if they sponsor social events among staff where food would be required, and, if not, whether they would be interested in doing so if a catering service managed the details for them.

Qualifying, or determining the need of prospects, depends on your specialty. If you work primarily as a wedding-reception caterer, you will have a different set of qualifications to look for, such as event date, number of guests, budget per guest, opportunities for related services, catering services currently used, and the name of the person who decides which bids are accepted.

Keeping track

There are many ways to keep track of prospects, depending on how many you have and how you plan to market to them. Some catering business owners use 3×5-inch file cards available at any stationery store. A sample card will include basic information—name, address, telephone number, event, etc.—as well as qualifying information and notes from prospecting contacts, such as

- *August 22: found out that Ms. Helen Hostess is hosting a party for 20–30 guests at her home on September 30.*
- *August 26: submitted an agreement letter to Ms. Hostess for her 9/30 party: 25 guests @ $18 ea. = $450.*

Other new catering services use their business notebook, described in chapter 1, to list prospecting information and contacts.

If you're using a computer to automate your business records, "contact management" software programs can help you keep track of prospects. They range from about $50 for a simple system to $500 or more for a specialized prospecting system that can even help you write personalized sales letters and fill out orders. A good contact management program gives you standard "fields" or areas where you can type the firm name, contact name(s), address, telephone number, names of mutual friends or associations, information about contacts. If you're making regular telephone calls to prospects, the program might help you schedule call-backs, maintain records of conversations, and help you write personalized proposals that can be quickly printed for mailing or even faxed to your prospects while they're still thinking about you.

HOW CAN I KEEP PROFITABLE CUSTOMERS?

One of the most satisfying aspects of becoming a successful catering service is helping your customers solve problems, such as the need for a cost-effective meal for a stockholder's meeting at the end of the month. In each case, they have a problem that requires a solution you offer.

The more customers you can help, the more they will help you succeed. As you've learned, the best advertising is word-of-mouth, where your satisfied customers tell your prospects about the value you give. The real key to keeping customers is keeping them happy.

Of course, keeping your customers happy doesn't mean that you always have to agree with them or that they are always right—but they are always your customer and deserve your respect and best efforts.

Remember that, to many businesses, you're the customer. Your bank, utility companies, grocery and hardware stores, suppliers, and other businesses want to keep you as their customer. How do they do it? Are they successful? What would it take for you to switch to the services of a competing business? What's the most important services these businesses give you? How do they make you feel as a customer?

The golden rule of business success is: Treat your customers as you wish your suppliers to treat you.

Customer satisfaction

Your customers must be satisfied with the value of your service or they will no longer be your customers. You might have some customers who are temporarily dissatisfied, but will soon get satisfaction either from you or from one of your competitors. If you don't have any significant competitors, customer dissatisfaction might breed them. Your catering business cannot afford dissatisfied customers.

So how do you continue to make sure that your customers are satisfied with your service? Listen to them. Watch how they pay their bills, call them up for a friendly chat to learn what business problems they're facing, ask other customers if they've heard of anyone who is dissatisfied with your services. Here are some of the questions that smart catering business owners periodically ask their customers:

- Is everything going well with our project?
- Have you seen anything that we can do better?
- Are any of my employees doing an exceptional or inadequate job for you?
- How can I get more great customers like you?

Why should you, a busy business owner, take time out of your day to ask these questions of customers? Because, if you don't, someone else will, and you might soon lose valuable customers. Remember that it is much less expensive to keep an existing customer satisfied than to find a new one.

Repeat customers

A repeat customer is simply one who hires you for more than one job. If the customer is satisfied and needs your services again, you have a good chance of getting a repeat customer. You didn't have to go out and spend additional money on advertising or work extra hours to promote your business. Your quality of business promotes itself.

The best way to get repeat business is to ask for it. As you call up your clients to determine their satisfaction, also ask them the following questions:

- Do you have any other events coming up that might need catering services?
- Would you like us to bid on them?
- What services do you expect to need from us in the coming year?
- Are there any related services that we could implement for you in the future?

You can also build repeat business by continually trying to sell your services to them. It is more productive to get more business from current customers than to find new ones. Here's how some successful catering services build repeat business:

- Write a monthly newsletter to all customers with new information on the events you're catering and new services you offer.
- Perform extra services that other local catering businesses don't do for their customers, like giving the hostess or host a free bottle of fine wine with your compliments.
- Serve as a consultant at no charge to clients, providing such services as arranging entertainment for the party with no obligation.

Referral customers

Earning referrals is one of the most powerful types of business promotion. A referral is simply having one of your satisfied customers sell your services to prospective buyers. The word of a trusted businessperson is much more believable to prospects than is the word of an unknown businessperson or salesperson.

Get your customers to refer prospects to you by asking them to do so. In fact, it should be an automatic question that you ask: "Do you know anyone who might also need our catering services?" Ask it right after you schedule an event, as you start an event, as you complete a catered event, and—especially—whenever anyone compliments an aspect of your business, like this:

Client: "I really appreciate the way you served the 12 last-minute wedding guests so easily."

You: "I'm glad to hear that. Is there anyone you know who might also need our catering services?"

In addition, once your customer has referred others to you, many feel a stronger obligation to continue to use your services. It not only helps your business grow, but also helps you keep the customers that you have.

WHAT DO CUSTOMERS EXPECT FROM MY CATERING SERVICE?

One of the most important, and overlooked, aspects of keeping customers satisfied is making sure you understand what they expect from you. Until you know, you won't be able to satisfy their needs. Here are some questions to ask about your customers:

- What are their expectations?
- Do customers expect immediate response to calls, or do most customers need your services "sometime in the next 30 days"?
- Do customers expect "instant credit" from you, or do they usually pay all or some of the costs in advance?
- Do customers expect you to be on-call 24 hours a day or only during normal business hours?
- Do customers expect to talk to "the boss" when they call, or can an office person handle most calls?
- Do your customers expect discounts for off-season jobs or for paying cash in advance?
- Do your customers expect to pay you in payments or within 30, 60, or 90 days of completion?
- Do your customers expect bids that are priced by the head, by the hour, by the event, or by another pricing structure?

How can you know what your customers expect? Simply ask them. Spend some time in person or on the telephone with your customers—large and small—talking about what they expect from you. In fact, you can develop prospects into customers by telling them you're conducting a survey for your new catering business and would like to learn what the expectations of potential customers are. Finally, you can also ask, "Is your current catering service meeting your expectations?"

Think about what you want as a customer. You have distinct expectations when you buy from someone. If you buy stationery from office supply stores, you expect hard-to-find products from one vendor and lowest prices on stock items from another. From a food supplier, you want vegetables that are fresh as well as cost-effective. You might also want fast service or a broad inventory from which to choose. In fact, you might use one supplier for fast delivery of common food items and another for specialty or ethnic foods.

Of course, the next question to ask yourself—and your customers and prospects—is, "Are these expectations realistic?" That is, you might want to pay less than wholesale price for hard-to-get items, but that isn't a realistic expectation. Or a customer might say that he or she "expects" you to be available 24 hours a day for questions about an upcoming event when you know that responding to questions within an hour during business hours is a realistic expectation.

Of course, if you find sufficient customers expressing the same unmet expectation—such as 24-hour event-planning—you might consider this as an expectation that you can meet.

SUCCESS ACTION PLAN

Without customers, you don't have a catering business. So the key to your business's success and growth is treating customers as you wish to be treated. To learn more about your prospective customers, take these actions:

❏ Describe your catering service in terms that interest prospective customers: convenience, value, and price.
❏ Define your typical customer in terms of economics, social status, work or living site, interests, occupation, goals, needs, and opportunities.

❏ Describe how best to market your catering services to this typical customer. What type of advertising or promotion would reach them? If you can, talk over your ideas with another catering service owner or with a marketing or advertising expert.

❏ List the features and benefits that your catering service offers to the typical customer.

❏ Describe how you can keep your best customers coming back to you as well as referring good prospects to you.

❏ Learn as much as you can about your customers and prospects. They are the key to your success as a catering service.

7

How do I find good employees?

A good employee can make the difference between profit and loss for your catering service. If you are your business's only employee, you know you will work hard. As you hire others to prepare and serve food, however, you will be compromising your quality and service—unless you select and keep employees who are skilled and motivated. That's the challenge.

This chapter shows you how to select, hire, train, motivate, and keep employees who will help your catering business succeed. You'll also discover the numerous legal and taxation requirements for managing employees, and how to comply with these regulations. Finally, you'll learn how to develop an employee handbook that saves you time and frustration.

WHAT TYPE OF EMPLOYEE SHOULD I LOOK FOR?

The trick to getting the right person for the job is deciding what kind of skills are needed to perform the job. Once you know what it takes to do the job, you can match the applicant's skills and experience to the job's requirements. This step will probably come easy for you if you're hiring a catering worker, but how about office help or other support personnel?

The first step in analyzing a job is to describe it. Suppose, as the owner of a growing catering business, you decide to hire someone to relieve you of some of your administrative or sales duties. Look at the many functions you perform and decide what your stronger and weaker areas are.

Further, suppose that you have decided that you will need help in the office. The telephone is always ringing. Letters that need answering are piling up. Bids must be typed and mailed.

Once you have a job description on paper, decide what skills the person must have to fill the job. What's the lowest level of skill you will accept? Suppose that you decide initially to hire a secretary, but discover that secretaries are hard to find and expensive. Likewise, in your area, stenographers are almost as scarce and expensive as secretaries. Perhaps you could get by with a typist, which you determine would be both easier and cheaper than hiring a secretary or stenographer. Many high school students are well-qualified as typists, and many are seeking part-time work.

When you start looking for someone to fill your job, make sure you describe exactly what you want. Suppose you advertise for an "office manager." What, exactly, do you want this person to do? They might do any or all of the following:

- Answer the telephone and take messages
- Contact you at the job site
- Type correspondence
- Write correspondence
- Sort mail
- Pay bills
- Prepare bills for payment
- Keep accounting records
- Produce invoices
- Mail monthly statements
- Manage collection of past-due accounts
- Read catering magazines and mark important articles for you
- Order supplies and foods
- Manage payroll
- Prepare the books for your accountant
- Make quarterly tax payments

Finding job applicants

When you know the kinds of skills you need in your new employee, you're ready to contact sources who can help you recruit job applicants.

If you are a union shop, you can work with the union to find skilled apprentices and journeymen. An advantage to apprentices is that their pay ranges from 35 to 85 percent of the wage of a journeyman, depending on the local union contract, the apprenticeship program, and the time served in the apprenticeship.

Each state has an employment service (Department of Employment, Unemployment Bureau, or Employment Security Agency). All are affiliated with the United States Employment Service, and local offices are ready to help businesses with their hiring problems. The state employment service screens applicants for you by giving aptitude tests (if any tests are available for the skills you need). Passing scores indicate the applicant's ability to learn the work. So, be as specific as you can about the skills you want.

Private employment agencies can also help in recruitment. However, the employee or the employer must pay a fee to the private agency for its services. This fee can be from a month's to as much as a year's salary.

Another source of applicants is a "Help Wanted" sign in your office window (if you have one). Of course, a lot of unqualified applicants might inquire about the job, and you cannot simultaneously interview an applicant and talk on the phone to a customer. Newspaper advertisements are another source of applicants. You reach a large group of job seekers, and if you used a blind box address, you can screen them at your convenience. If you list an office telephone number, you might end up spending your day on the telephone with applicants instead of with customers.

Job applicants are also readily available from local schools. Your local high school might have a distributive or cooperative education department where the students work in your office part-time while taking home economics, culinary, or business courses at school. Many part-time students continue with their employer after they finish school. Consider local and regional business schools as well. The students are often more mature and more motivated than high school students.

You might also find job applicants by contacting friends, neighbors, customers, suppliers, current employees, local associations, service clubs, or even a nearby armed forces base where people are leaving the service. However, don't overlook the problems of such recruiting. What happens to the goodwill of these sources if they recommend a friend who you do not hire, or if you have to fire the person they recommend?

Your choice of recruitment method depends on what you're looking for, your location, and your method of managing your business. You have many sources available to you. A combination might best serve your needs. The important thing is to find the right applicant with the correct skills for the job you want to fill, whatever the source.

Labor laws

As you begin the search for qualified employees, certain federal and state laws come into play:

- The *Social Security Act of 1935, as amended,* is concerned with employment insurance laws, as well as retirement insurance.
- The *Fair Labor Standards Act of 1938, as amended*, establishes minimum wages, overtime pay, recordkeeping, and child labor standards for most businesses.
- The *Occupational Safety and Health Act (OSHA) of 1970* is concerned with safety and health in the workplace and covers almost all employers. Specific standards, regulations, and reporting requirements must be met.

Your local state employment office can assist you in learning the requirements of these laws and other laws that might concern your business. Contact your local state employment office to determine the requirements for hiring disadvantaged workers, federal service contracts, employee pension and welfare benefit plans, and the garnishment of employee's wages. State and local health laws also dictate training and managing food handlers.

In addition, the Immigration Reform and Control Act of 1986 prohibits employing illegal aliens. Employers must require every employee to fill out the Employment Eligibility Verification Form (Form 19) within three days of the date of hire (if hired after November 7, 1987). Fines are levied for noncompliance. For more information, contact the nearest office of the Immigration and Naturalization Service.

The application form

The hardest part of the hiring process, once you've listed the required skills, is finding and hiring the one right employee. You need some method of screening the applicants and selecting the best one for the position.

Use the application form in Fig. 7-1 to make your tasks of interviewing and selection easier. The form can be photocopied and adapted as needed. The form should have blank spaces for all the facts you need as a basis for judging the applicants. You will want a fairly complete application so you can get sufficient information. However, keep the form as simple as you can. Have the applicants fill out the application before you talk to them; it makes an excellent starting point for the interview. It is also a written record of experience and former employers' names and addresses.

The Civil Rights Act of 1964 prohibits discrimination in employment practices because of race, religion, sex, or national origin. Public Law 90-202 prohibits discrimination on the basis of age with respect to individuals who are between 40 and 70 years of age. Federal laws also prohibit discrimination against the physically handicapped. Your state employment office can help you in understanding the laws regarding applicants and employment. In addition, firms like the following offer catalogs of human relations supplies: job applications, personnel folders, labor law posters, attendance controllers, employee awards, and related materials.

G. Neil
720 International Pkwy.
Sunrise, FL 33345

HR Direct
122 14th St.
Mendota, IL 61342-0951

When an applicant has had work experience, other references are typically not as important. However, if the level of work experience is limited, additional references can be obtained from other individuals such as school counselors, who might be able to offer objective information. Personal references are almost useless; applicants only list people who have a kind word for them. Some employers use them, though, to open a discussion with such questions as these:

- What would this reference say were your greatest skills and traits?
- What would this reference say were skills and traits that you needed to work on?

The interview

The objective of the job interview is to find out as much information as you can about the job applicant's work background, especially work habits and skills. Your major task is to get the applicants to talk about themselves and about their work habits. The best way is to ask each applicant specific and identical questions:

- What did you do on your last job?
- How did you do it?
- Why was it done?
- What were the results?

As you go along, evaluate the applicants' replies. Do they know what they are talking about? Are they evasive or unskilled in the job tasks? Can they account for discrepancies in their employment record?

When the interview is over, ask the applicant to check back with you later, if you think you might be interested in him or her. Never commit yourself until you have interviewed all likely applicants. You want to be sure that you select the best available applicant for the job.

EMPLOYMENT APPLICATION

ABC Catering Service

123 Main Street, Yourtown USA 12345

Position Applied For	Type of Employment		Date
Chef	Full Time ☑ Summer ☐	Part Time ☐ Temporary ☐	30 Jun 19xx

Name of Applicant (please indicate how you wish to be addressed)

Surname	First Name	Initial (s)
Johnson	Robert	L.

Address (No., Street, City, State, Zip Code)
987 River Road, Yourtown, USA 12345

Social Security Number	Telephone Number (Home)	Business
123-45-6789	234-8282	234-9870

Previous Address In the United States
666 Main Street, Apt. 3-A, Yourtown, USA 12345

Some positions in the company require that staff be bonded.
Are you bondable?   YES ☑   NO ☐
Have you ever been bonded?   YES ☑   NO ☐

Are you legally entitled to work in th e United States? ☑ YES ☐ NO	Are you willing to relocate? ☑ YES ☐ NO

Do you have a valid driver's license?   ☑ YES   ☐ NO   Class

Education

Secondary School attended and location. Yourtown High School Yourtown USA	Highest grade successfully completed. 12th	Year Graduated 1979

University attended and location.	No. of years completed	Year graduated	Degrees

Major subjects of specialization.
College Preparation

Community College attended and location. Yourtown Community College Yourtown USA	No. of years completed	Year graduated	Degrees
	2	1981	Associate of Arts

Major subjects of spelcialization.

Culinary Arts

Other Educational Training/Courses.

Banquet Chef, Ethnic Food Preparation, Food Management

Office/Secretarial Applications

Skill/Aptitude	Years of Experience	Words per minute	List secretarial training courses completed and any other training which may be helpful in considering your application.
Typing			
Shorthand			

EMPLOYMENT APPLICATION   Page 1.

7-1 Standard employment application.

EMPLOYMENT HISTORY (List present or most recent positions first)

1. Name of Employer	Address	No.	Street	City
Bonzo's Restaurant	789 Main St., Yourtown, USA			

Type of Business	Department	Your Position
Restaurant and Catering Service	Food Preparation	Head Chef

Duties   Responsible for menu development, food purchasing, hiring and firing cooks, and bidding all catering jobs.

Name and Position of Immediate Supervisor

Bill Bonzalini, Owner

Date Employed (Day, Mo, Yr)	Date Left (Day, Mo, Yr)	Starting Salary	Final Salary
19 Nov 1988		$1,800.00	$2,400.00

Reason for leaving.

Prefer to work for full-service caterer. Want to eventually become part of management or part-owner in leading catering firm.

2. Name of Employer	Address	No.	Street	City
Denny's Restaurant	987 Main St., Yourtown, USA			

Type of Business	Department	Your Position
Restaurant	Food Preparation	Cook

Duties   Prepare meals per standards established by Denny's International franchise. Rose to head cook and food-orderer.

Name and Position of Immediate Supervisor

Jim Loggan

Date Employed (Day, Mo, Yr)	Date Left (Day, Mo, Yr)	Starting Salary	Final Salary
1 Apr 1981	10 Nov 1988	$1,200.00	$1,800.00

Reason for leaving

Reached highest salary level offered by Denny's Restaurants.

3. Name of Employer	Address	No.	Street	City

Type of Business	Department	Your Position

Duties

Name and Position of Immediate Supervisor

Date Employed (Day, Mo, Yr)	Date Left (Day, Mo, Yr)	Starting Salary	Final Salary

Reason for leaving

MAY WE ASK YOUR PRESENT EMPLOYER FOR A REFERENCE   ☑ YES   ☐ NO

REFERENCES (Please do not list relatives or former employers)

Name	Occupation	Address
Martin Franklin	College Instructor	654 River St., Yourtown
John Jones	Baker/Kiwanis President	333 Main St., Yourtown
Ben Hopper	Pastor	567 Main St., Yourtown

Whom do you know in this company?
Judy Richards, owner

7-1 Continued.

Scholarships

Activities/Interests (Student, Professional, Community, etc.)
Yourtown Kiwanis, vice president

Publication, patents and thesis subjects

Languages (spoken, written, read) Note fluency

Other interests or hobbies
Fishing

Special talents

| Medical | Do you agree to take a medical exam at company expense related to the essential requirements of the position. | ✓ YES | ☐ NO |

We appreciate your interest in seekin employment with us - please feel free to make any additional remarks in the space provided remarks in the space provided below or attach any additional information that would be helpful in evaluating your qualifications.

Additional Remarks

Member of National Association of Catering Executives (NACE). Recently Completed requirements for Certified Catering Executive (CCE) designation.

Please Read Carefully

I hereby certify that to the best of my knowledge and belief the answers given by me to the foregoing questions and all statements made by me in the application are correct.

If employed, I agree that all material created and produced whether in written, graphic or broadcasting form, all inventions new or changes in processes developed during my employment are the exclusive property of the company to use and/or sell and that subsequent to my employment with this company I will not disclose, use or reveal any confidential information related to the company without first obtaining written consent from an officer of the company.

I hereby apply for employment upon the basis and understanding that such employment may be termnated at any time upon notice given to me personally or sent to my last known address.

I consent to   ABC CateringService   obtaining such personal and job-related information as required in connection with this application.
for employment

_____   _____
Date   Signature of applicant

This application form complies with all Human Rights Legislation.

EMPLOYMENT APPLICATION Page 3.

7-1 Continued.

Next, verify the information you've obtained. A previous employer is usually the best source. Sometimes a previous employer will give out information over the telephone, but, if you have the time, it is usually best to request your information in writing and get a written reply.

To help ensure a prompt reply, you should ask previous employers a few specific questions about the applicant that can be answered yes or no, or with a very short answer. Consider these examples:

- How long did the employee work for you?
- Was his or her work: poor, average, or excellent?
- Why did the employee leave your employment?

Also, make sure that you include a self-addressed stamped envelope for their reply.

After you have verified the information about all of your applicants, you're ready to make your selection. The right employee can help you make money; the wrong one will cost you much in wasted time and provisions, and might even drive away your customers. Be sure that, once you've decided on the most appropriate applicant, you document in writing why you selected a specific applicant (Fig. 7-2) and why you did not select other applicants. Make sure that all decisions and comments are relative to job requirements and not other factors. Then, if you're challenged about your fair employment practices, you have the documentation that will keep you from being sued or paying large fines.

SHOULD I HIRE TEMPORARY HELP?

How does your catering business cope with unexpected personnel shortages? Many businesses are facing this question because of seasonal peak business, the illness or unavailability of several employees at once, or an unexpected increase in business. For some skills, many catering services hire and use independent contractors. A growing number, though, hire help through temporary personnel services. In fact, many new catering services start their business by "renting" part-time temporary help instead of hiring full-time employees.

A temporary personnel service, listed in your telephone book's yellow pages under "Employment Contractors-Temporary Help," is not an employment agency. Like many service firms, it hires people as its own employees and assigns them to companies requesting assistance. When you use such a service, you're not hiring an employee; you're buying the use of their time. The temporary personnel firm is responsible for payroll, bookkeeping, tax deductions, workers' compensation insurance, fringe benefits, and all other similar costs connected with the employee. You're relieved of the burden of recruiting, interviewing, screening, and basic skill training.

Most national temporary personnel companies also offer performance guarantees and fidelity bonding at no added cost to their clients. Just as importantly, you're relieved of the need for government forms and for reporting withholding tax, social security insurance, and unemployment compensation insurance. If you need people for six months or more, however, it's usually more cost-effective to hire a full-time employee than to use temporaries. Also, if the task requires skills or training beyond basic office skills, it might cost you less to pay overtime to an employee with those skills.

The key to successful use of temporary employees is in planning what type of help you will need, how much, and when. The accurate information you give to the

ABC Catering Service

123 Main street, Yourtown USA

Date June 30, 19XX

Social Security Number 123-45-6789	Employee Number 17	Sex	Worker's Comp.	Job Cat.

Birth Date (YY MM DD) January 9, 1961	Code Reason Desc. Rehire ☐ New Hire ☒	Employment Date (YY MM DD) July 1, 19xx	Fair Non exempt ☐ Exempt ☐

Name (Last Name, First Name, Middle Initial)
Robert L. Johnson

Legal Address (Street, Apt. No., City, State and Zip Code)
987 River Road, Yourtown USA 12345

Mailing Address (Street, Apt. No., City, State and Zip Code)
Same

Bulk Mailing Address (No., P.O Box Address) (Street, City, State and Zip Code)
Same

Check Mailing Address (Street, Apt. No., City, State and Zip Code)
Same

Department Name (City, State and Zip Code are also needed)

Emergency Contact Name Linda Johnson	Relationship Wife	Telephone 234-8282

Marital Status Single ☐ Married ☒	Home Phone No. 234-8282	Review/Raise date	Annual Salary $ 36,000.00

Salary Date July 1, 19xx	Code Reason Desc. Rehire ☐ New Hire ☒	Hourly Rate 18.00	Pay Period Hours 40 Hrs

Job Date July 1, 19xx	Reason Rehire ☐ New Hire ☐	Job Code	Job Title HeadChef

Salary Grade	Location Code	Location Code Description

Requisition Number	Addition ☐ Replacement ☒	Person Replaced Bob Smithers

REHIRES ONLY

Previous Hire Date YY/MM/DD	Previous Termination Date YY/MM/DD	Term Code

COMMENTS

Very creative and talented chef with experience with the preparation of thnic foods. Will handle all food ordering.

APPROVALS

Operations Administrator/Immediate Supervisor	Date	PAYROLL USE ONLY
Department Head/V P	Date	
Human resources	Date	
Human resources	Date	

7-2 Make sure that information about a new hire or rehire gets to the people on your staff who need to know.

temporary service firm improves their efficiency in supplying the correct person for your needs.

Before your temporary employee arrives on the job, there are a few things you should do. First, appoint one of your permanent employees to supervise the temporary employee and check on the progress of the work. Be sure this supervisor understands the job to be done and just what the responsibilities are. Next, let your permanent staff know that you're taking on extra help and that it will be temporary. Explain why the extra help is needed and ask them to cooperate with the new employee in any way possible.

Have everything ready before the temporary employee arrives. The work to be done should be organized so that the employee can begin producing with a minimum of time spent in adjusting to the job and the surrounding. Also, don't set up schedules that are impossible to complete within the time you allot. Try to stay within the time limits you gave the temporary help service, but plan to extend the time if necessary, rather than hurry the employee.

Finally, furnish detailed instructions. Describe your type of business and the services you offer. Help the temporary worker feel comfortable and as part of your team. Many temporary employees have broad food-service experience and can easily adapt to your requirements—if they know what those requirements are.

SHOULD I HIRE INDEPENDENT CONTRACTORS?

Depending on your business structure, your workload, and your specialty, you might decide to hire independent contractors for specific jobs. You can do this effectively much like you hire an employee. Here are some of the questions you should ask the subcontractor and yourself:

- How long have you been in business?
- Are you reliable and prompt?
- How would you manage the job?
- Have you done this type of work before?
- What size crew will be working on the job?
- Do you have references? Can I contact them?
- What warranties do you provide?
- Do you have the necessary skills and equipment?
- Do you have quick access to provisions?
- What's the rate for your services?
- Why do you want to be hired to subcontract this job?
- Are you efficient? How?
- How do you expect to be paid?

If selected carefully, an independent contractor or subcontractor cannot only help you during a busy time, but can also furnish you with an alliance that can help you in your growing catering business.

HOW SHOULD I ESTABLISH FAIR PERSONNEL POLICIES?

More and more, the government is requiring written personnel policies, even for the smallest firms. A written personnel-policy manual makes your life, as an owner/manager of a catering service, easier as well. Fortunately, there are specific books and computer programs that help you write policies that are clear, consistent, conform with current laws.

Writing the policy manual

The first rule of writing personnel policies is to know yourself and your business. Know your own personal abilities and weaknesses, and try to anticipate how you will deal with the situations that you expect to arise in the daily operation of your catering business.

Then, formulate your policies in writing. Include all matters that would affect employees. Matters such as the following should be included, not left to whim:

- *Hours of work.* Unless dictated by a labor contract, indicate the number of hours to be worked per week, the number of days per week, evening and holiday work, and the time and method of payment for both regular and overtime work. Will you allow employees time off for personal reasons, emergencies in the family, holidays, Saturday or Sunday holidays?
- *Time recordkeeping.* Use weekly or monthly time reports (Fig. 7-3 and Fig. 7-4) to track hours worked by employees.
- *Paid holidays and vacations.* How long will vacations be? Will you specify the time of the year they may be taken? With or without pay? How does an employee schedule vacation time? What's your policy if vacation time goes unused or if additional time is requested?
- *Separation and probation procedures.* Define the period (usually 30, 60, or 90 days) during which a new employee can be dismissed without a hearing on the cause, if allowed by state laws. Even though severance is a distasteful matter to most business owners, it is important to have a written policy regarding layoffs, seniority rights, severance pay, and the conditions that warrant summary discharge.
- *Training.* You must make sure that each employee is given adequate training for the job. In a small catering office, the training responsibility normally falls to the owner/manager. If you have to employ supervisors, each one should recognize the importance of being a good teacher and should schedule time to teach or review the requirements of the job with new employees.
- *Dress regulations.* Are any employees required to wear uniforms? Who pays for them? How must they be maintained?
- *Compensation system.* Most of your employees will be paid a salary or hourly wage competitive with the pay offered by similar food-service businesses in your area. Try to relate any pay incentives to both your goals and the goals of your employees. Whatever plan and level of compensation you use, be sure each employee understands it completely.
- *Overtime.* Are Saturday and Sunday normal workdays? Unnecessary payment of overtime at premium rates is a source of needless expense. By planning ahead, you might be able to organize your employees' work to keep overtime to a minimum. When peak periods do occur, you can often handle them by using part-time help paid at regular rates or temporary help.
- *Personnel review and promotion.* Will you periodically review your employee's performance? If so, what factors will you consider? Will you

ABC Catering Service

WEEKLY TIME REPORT

123 Main Street, Yourtown USA 12345

LOCATION /ORG. UNIT

DATE   June 30, 19xx

NAME	HOURS	CLASSIFICATION	DESCRIPTION OF WORK
Bill Franklin	42	Chef	Manages food purchasing and preparation
Jim Jackson	32	Head Server	Manages food service and fills in as required
Fran Mitchell	40	Office Manager	Telephone, bookkeeping, payroll, records
Roger Reed	28	Bartender	Sets up bar, serves drinks, cleans up bar
Donna Smith	36	Server	Serves food and beverages
Jack Gilbert	20	Server-part-time	Serves food and beverages on part-time (evenings) basis

REMARKS

The undersigned employee certifies that the above and foregoing is the actual, correct number of hours worked by him/her on the day stated, and that he/she has not been told or instructed by anyone having authority over him/her to incorrectly state the number of hours actually worked.

Employee's Signature _____

Supervisor's Signature _____

7-3 A weekly time report summarizes the hours and tasks of your employees for reference and payment.

TIME SHEET

123 Main Street, Yourtown USA 12345

PERIOD END	MONTH	DAY	YEAR	PERSONNEL #	NAME	DIV
	06	30	xx	12	Bill Franklin	Shop

Description of Work	TIME DISTRIBUTION FOR PERIOD																Total Hours
	1 16	2 17	3 18	4 19	5 20	6 21	7 22	8 23	9 24	10 25	11 26	12 27	13 28	14 29	15 30	31	
Ryerson wedding		6	2														8
Murphy banquet			7	4		3											14
Jake's Catering Truck				2	7	4				6		3					22
		1	3						4								8
Morgan Accounting: catered lunch						2							5				7
					3						3						6
Simpson: banquet									8	2	1	1					12
	4																4
Rowley: wedding reception dinner																	
	2	6	3	8													19
Batterson: Italian meal																	
					7		6	4	4	1							22
Franklin: bar mitzvah											8	9	6	6	1		30
Holiday																	
Personal Illness - Approved							8										8
Overtime																	
													Total Hours				160

FOR INTERNAL USE ONLY

List of Expenses and Dollar Value (attach receipts)					Overtime Approved By	Time Report Audited
Description	$	Description	$			
		Total Expenses				

PAGE   OF

7-4 A monthly time sheet can be used to allocate employees' hours to specific catering jobs.

make salary adjustments or training recommendations? Consider such matters as normal increases of wages and salaries, changes of job titles, and the effects that your business' growth will have on your employees and their careers.

- *Pension and retirement plan.* What are your plans for retirement-age benefits, such as social security insurance, pension plans, and annuity plan insurance?
- *Benefits.* You might consider offering your employees free or reduced-cost life insurance, health insurance, pension plan, and tuition payments at schools and colleges. You might also look into joining with other catering services in a group disability plan and a group workers' compensation insurance plan. Such a plan could mean a considerable savings in your premium costs. Indicate when benefits will begin: upon employment, the first day of the month following employment, upon completion of a specific number of hours of work, or at some other time.
- *Grievance procedures.* Expect conflicts with employees, regardless of the quality of employment you offer. The best course of action is to plan for them and establish a procedure for handling grievances. Consider the employee's rights to demand review and establish provisions for third-party arbitration. If you hire through a union, these procedures are spelled out for you in your labor contract.

Employment and training procedures must be established so that you have a better chance of getting the job done the way you want it. Once you've developed your personnel policies into a manual, give each staff member a copy. For a small catering service office, this manual might consist of just one or two typed pages.

Setting fair wages

Pay administration is a management tool that enables you to control personnel cost, increase employee morale, and reduce work force turnover. A formal pay system provides a means of rewarding individuals for their contributions to the success of your firm while making sure that your firm receives a fair return on its investment in employee pay.

There are two good reasons to establish a fair employee pay plan: your business and your employees. A formal pay plan, one that lets employees know where they stand and where they can go as far as take-home pay is concerned, won't solve all your employee relations problems. It will, however, remove one of those areas of doubt and rumor that might keep your work force anxious and unhappy.

What's in it for you? Let's face it—in a catering business, good employees can make the difference between success and failure. Many people enjoy a good "mystery," but not when it's about how their pay is established. Employees under a pay plan they understand can see that it's fair and consistent rather than at the whim of the owner. They know what to expect and what they can hope to earn in the future. So a good pay plan helps you recruit, keep, and motivate employees. It can help you build a solid foundation for a successful business. If you're hiring union members, the local labor union will assist you in defining job descriptions and establishing pay levels and incentives.

Overtime

In most cases, overtime should not be required because the typical job will be bid based on a normal workday. However, as business increases, seasonally, or as modified schedules require, you might want to consider overtime.

To do so, first consider your employment policy or union requirements regarding payment for overtime hours. Depending on the standard workday and the number of hours required beyond that day, overtime can typically cost from 25 to as much as 200 percent more than standard pay.

In addition, efficiency decreases as overtime increases. One source has developed a table of overtime efficiency rates stating that, with five 10-hour days on the same job, the efficiency rate for the last two hours of the day are reduced to 87.5 percent. With five 12-hour days on the same job, the efficiency rate for the last four hours of the day are reduced to 75 percent. If the worker of five 12-hour days must move to another job after 8 hours, the efficiency rate for the 4 hours at the second job drop to 68.8 percent. The point is that employee costs go up and efficiency goes down during overtime.

If overtime is required to complete a job, make sure that you consider the costs of both overtime pay and reduced efficiency as you bid, schedule, and manage the job. Also, make sure that your employee handbook communicates your policies regarding overtime.

Writing the pay plan

As your catering business grows beyond a single employee, you will need to take time to consider a formal pay plan. Developing a written pay plan doesn't have to cost you a lot of time and money. In fact, an elaborate plan is difficult to put into practice, communicate, and manage.

The most important aspect of setting up a formal pay administration plan is to get acceptance, understanding, and support of your management and supervisory employees. (Of course, for a small catering office, that's you.) The steps in setting up a successful pay plan are:

- Define the jobs.
- Evaluate the jobs.
- Price the jobs.
- Install the plan.
- Communicate the plan to employees.
- Appraise employee performance under the plan.

Defining the jobs

Unless you know each job's specifications and requirements, you can't compare them for pay purposes. It's no surprise, therefore, that the initial step in installing a formal pay plan is preparing a job description for each position.

You might be able to write these job descriptions yourself, since at one time or another you might have worked at just about every job. However, the best and easiest way to put together such job information is simply to ask employees to describe their jobs. Supervisors, if you have them, should be asked to review these descriptions. Prepare a simple form to be filled out by the employee or by someone, such as a supervisor, interviewing the employee. The form should include the following:

- Job title
- Reporting relationship
- Specifications
- Primary function
- Main duties (by importance and percent of time spent)
- Other duties
- Job requirements (training, experience, responsibilities, unusual working conditions)

It will probably take some time to prepare job descriptions from the information you get from your employees, but what you learn might have other uses besides comparing jobs for pay purposes. For example, you might discover that some employees are not doing what you thought they were, or what they were hired to do. You might find you want to make some changes in their work routines. The information might also be useful for hiring, training, and developing employees; realigning duties in your firm; comparing job data for salary surveys; assuring compliance with various employment practice and pay rate laws; and evaluating job performance based on assigned duties.

Evaluating the jobs

Nobody has yet come up with a precise way of deciding exactly how much a particular job is worth to a company. Human judgment is the only way to put a dollar value on work. A good job evaluation method for smaller firms is called *simple ranking*.

Under the simple-ranking system, job descriptions are compared against each other. They are ranked according to difficulty and responsibility. Using your judgment, you end up with an array of jobs that shows the relative value of each position to the company.

After you have ranked the job descriptions by value to the firm, the next step is to group jobs that are similar in scope and responsibility into the same pay grade. Then you arrange these groups in a series of pay levels from highest to lowest. The number of pay levels depends on the total number of jobs and types of work in your organization, but for a small firm, 6 to 12 pay levels is the typical range to cover everyone from the janitor to the president.

Pricing the jobs

So far in establishing a pay system, you've looked only inside your company. To put an accurate dollar value on each of your pay levels, you should also look outside at the going rates for similar work in your area. Since you have ranked and grouped your jobs in pay levels, you won't have to survey each job. Survey those on each level that are easiest to describe and are most common in the industry.

A survey of who's paying how much for what in your locality is the best way of finding out how much you ought to pay for each of your jobs. You probably have neither the time nor the money to conduct such a survey yourself. That shouldn't be a problem; you should be able to get the data you need from sources such as a local catering service or restaurant association, a union local, the local chamber of commerce, major firms in your area, or from national sources such as the National

Caterers Roundtable Association, the Mobile Industrial Caterers' Association, the National Association of Catering Executives, or the National Restaurant Association. You can also contact the U.S. Bureau of Labor Statistics at this address:

Department of Labor
441 G St., NW, Room 2421
Washington, DC 20212

Or contact:

The American Management Association
135 W. 50th St.
New York, NY 10020

After you're satisfied that you are comparing apples and apples, you can compute an average rate for each job and enter it on a worksheet. You might need to adjust the average rates somewhat to keep a sufficient difference between pay levels. The going rates you find for each pay level can then become the midpoints of your pay ranges. You can, of course, set your midpoints above or below the survey averages based on your firm's ability to pay, the length of your work week, the type and value of your firm's benefits program, and the local job market.

You then build a pay range for each pay level, with a minimum, a midpoint, and a maximum. Typically, the minimum rate in a level is 85 percent of the midpoint rate, and the maximum rate is 115 percent of the midpoint. With this arrangement, a new employee can increase his or her earnings by 30 percent without a job change, thus having performance incentives even if the employee is not promoted.

Such a pay range enables you to tell where your employees' pay and pay potential stand in relation to the market rates for their kinds of work. It should show you at a glance where you need to make changes to achieve rates that are fair within your organization and pay that's competitive with similar businesses in your community. With a planned pay structure, you can tie the individual rates of pay to job performance and contribution to company goals, while providing enough flexibility to handle special situations.

Installing the plan

At this point you have a general plan, but you don't, of course, pay in general. You pay each employee individually. You must now consider how the plan will be administered to provide for individual pay increases.

In administering the pay increase feature of your plan, you can use several approaches:

- Merit increases, granted to recognize performance and contribution
- Promotion increases for employees assigned to different jobs in higher pay levels
- Progression to minimum for employees who are below the minimum rate for the pay level
- Probationary increases for newer employees who have attained the necessary skills and experience to function effectively
- Tenure increases for time with the company
- General increases, granted employees to maintain real earnings as economic factors require and to keep pay competitive

These are the most common approaches, but there are many variations. Most annual increases are made for cost of living, tenure, or employment market reasons. You might use several, all, or combinations of the various increase methods.

Communicating the plan

After you've set your pay administration plan into place, you have to consider how to tell employees about it. Setting up a good pay administration program is almost useless if you don't communicate it to your employees.

Two of the more successful methods of communicating your decision include personal letters to each employees and staff meetings to explain the plan and answer general questions. However you tell your employees, you must clearly, honestly, and openly explain the way the plan works. It is a prime opportunity for you to enhance good relations with your employees. Be sure that your supervisors, if any, understand and can explain the plan to their people. Explaining the plan to new hires is also essential, as well as reviewing the plan periodically with all employees to handle questions and concerns.

Appraising the employee

The majority of employees in the labor force are under a merit increase pay system, though most of their pay increases result from other factors. This approach involves periodic review and appraisal of how well employees perform their assigned duties.

An effective employee appraisal plan improves two-way communications between the manager and the employee. It also relates pay to performance and results, while showing the employee how to improve by helping him or her understand job responsibilities and expectations. An employee appraisal plan also provides a standardized approach to evaluating job performance.

Such a performance review helps not only the employee whose work is being appraised, it also helps the manager doing the appraising to gain insight into the organization. An open exchange between employee and manager can show the manager where improvements in equipment, procedures, or other factors might improve employee performance. Try to foster a climate in which employees can discuss progress and problems informally at any time throughout the year.

To get the best results, use a standardized written form for appraisals. An appraisal form should cover the results achieved, quality of performance, volume of work, effectiveness in working with others in the firm and with customers and suppliers, initiative, job knowledge, and dependability.

To keep your pay administration plan up-to-date, you should review it at least annually. Make adjustments where necessary, and don't forget to retrain supervisory personnel. This plan can't be set up and then forgotten. During your annual review, ask yourself if the plan is working for you. That's the most important question. Are you getting the kind of employees you want or are you just making do? What's the employee turnover rate? Do employees seem to care about the business? Most importantly, does your pay administration plan help you achieve the objectives of your business?

WHAT EMPLOYEE BENEFITS SHOULD I OFFER?

Employee benefits play an important role in the lives of employees and their families, and they have a significant financial impact on your business. Catering services cannot be competitive employers if they don't develop a comprehensive benefit program. However, if not managed, an employee benefit program can quickly eat up a small firm's profits.

A comprehensive employee-benefits program can be broken down into four components: legally required benefits, health and welfare benefits, retirement benefits, and prerequisites. Legally required benefit plans are mandated by law. The systems necessary to administer such plans are well-established. These plans include social security insurance (FICA), workers' compensation insurance, and unemployment compensation insurance (FUTA).

Health, welfare, and retirement benefits can be viewed as benefits provided to work in conjunction with statutory benefits to protect employees from financial hazards such as illness, disability, death, and retirement. Health and welfare plans are perhaps the most visible of all the benefit program components. They include medical care, dental care, vision care, short-term disability, long-term disability, life insurance, accidental death and dismemberment insurance, dependent care, and legal assistance.

Retirement plans are established to help ensure that employees are able to maintain their accustomed standard of living upon retirement. Retirement-benefit plans basically fall into two categories: defined-contribution plans that provide employees with an account balance at retirement, and defined-benefit plans that provide employees with a projected amount of income at retirement.

Prerequisite benefits are any other benefits an employer promises, such as a company vehicle, professional association or club membership, paid tuition, sabbatical, extra vacation, personal expense account, credit cards, financial counseling services, or other benefits of employment.

Selecting an employee-benefit program

Designing and implementing an employee-benefit program can be a complicated process. Many small businesses contract with employee-benefit consulting firms, insurance companies, specialized attorneys, or accounting firms to assist in this task. As you establish your program yourself or with a professional, consider the following questions:

- What should the program accomplish in the long run?
- What's the maximum amount you can afford to spend on a program?
- Are you capable and knowledgeable in administering the program?
- What kind of program will best fit the needs of your employees?
- Should you involve your employees in the design and selection of the benefit program? If so, how much and at what stage?

Health and welfare plans

When purchasing a health and welfare plan, select a professional whose clientele is made up primarily of small businesses. In fact, if you can find one in your area, select one that's used and recommended by other catering services or restaurateurs. Your insurer needs to be aware of the special problems that small businesses face, especially in food service.

Generous plans might look attractive and logical today, but can become a financial burden for your growing company. Remember that it is much easier to add benefits than to take them away.

Medical plans are usually the greatest concern of employers and employees. There are essentially two kinds of traditional medical plans. *Major medical* plans cover 100 percent of hospital and inpatient surgical expense, as well as a percentage (typically 80 percent) of all other covered expenses. *Comprehensive medical* plans cover a percentage (again, generally 80 percent) of all medical expenses. In both types of plans, the employee is usually required to pay part of the premium, particularly for dependents, as well as a deductible. Deductibles often range from $100 to $500 for single coverage and from $200 to $1000 per person for family coverage. A comprehensive medical plan is typically less expensive because more of the cost is shifted to the employee. Any plan you design should include features for containing costs.

As an alternative to a traditional medical plan, you might contract with a *health maintenance organization* (HMO) to provide employees with medical services. The main difference between a traditional medical plan and an HMO is that the traditional plan allows employees to choose their medical providers, while HMOs often provide medical services at specified clinics or through "preferred" doctors and hospitals. HMOs reduce flexibility for lower costs that are often passed on to the employee through reduced or eliminated deductibles or through lower rates. If your catering firm has 25 or more employees, you might be legally required to offer your employees the option of coverage under an HMO. Discuss current requirements with your insurer.

Disability insurance is an important but often overlooked benefit in small businesses. Disability insurance prevents a drain of financial resources to support an employee if he or she cannot continue working.

Group life insurance is a benefit employees have come to expect in many regions and trades. Such insurance is usually a multiple of an employee's salary. Be aware that an amount of insurance over a legally specified amount is subject to taxation as income to the employee. Call the IRS to determine the latest limitation and rules.

Recent legislation provides that employers who maintain medical and dental plans must provide certain employees the opportunity to continue coverage if they otherwise become ineligible through employment termination or other causes. In addition, new rules state that if a firm's health and welfare plan discriminates in favor of key employees, the benefits to those employees are taxable as income. Talk to your plan administrator about current laws and requirements.

Retirement benefit plans

Retirement benefit plans are either *qualified* or *unqualified* plans. A plan is qualified if it has met certain standards mandated by law. Qualified retirement plans are popular benefits because contributions are currently deductible, earnings on plan assets are tax-deferred, benefits earned are not considered taxable income until received, and certain distributions are eligible for special tax treatment. Of the various qualified plans, profit-sharing plans, 401(k) plans, and defined-benefit plans are the most popular.

A *profit-sharing plan* is a defined-contribution plan in which you, the sponsoring employer, agree to contribute a discretionary or set amount to the plan. Any contributions made to the plan are generally allocated pro rata to each participant's plan account based on compensation. You make no promise as to the dollar amount a participant will receive at retirement. The focus in a profit-sharing plan, and in defined-contribution plans, is on the contribution. What a participant receives at retirement depends on the contributions made to the plan and the earnings on such contributions during the participant's employment. At retirement, profit-sharing plan participants receive the balance in their account. Profit-sharing plans are favored by employers because they allow employers the ability to retain discretion in determining the amount of the contribution made to the plan.

In a *401(k) plan*, participants agree to defer a portion of their pretax salary as a contribution to the plan. In addition, you, as the employer, might decide to match all or a portion of the participant deferrals. You might even decide to make a profit-sharing contribution to the plan. As with profit-sharing, the focus is on the contribution to the plan. At retirement, participants receive their account balance.

Special nondiscrimination tests apply to 401(k) plans that might reduce the amount of deferrals highly compensated employees are allowed to make and that somewhat complicate plan administration. Still, 401(k) plans are popular because they enable employees the ability to save for retirement with pretax dollars, and they can be designed to be relatively inexpensive.

In direct contrast to a defined-contribution plan, a *defined-benefit plan* promises participants a benefit specified by a formula in the plan. The focus of a defined-benefit plan is the retirement benefit provided instead of the contribution made. Plan sponsors must contribute to the actuarially determined amounts necessary to meet the dollar amounts promised to participants. Generally, benefits are paid at retirement over the remainder of the employee's life, so a defined-benefit plan guarantees a certain flow of income at retirement.

Selecting the right plan

As you can see, certain plans are more suitable for catering services than others based on your financial situation and the demographics of your employees. As a new business unsure of future income, you probably will not want to start a defined-benefit plan requiring a specific level of contributions. However, if your employees are fairly young, a profit-sharing plan or 401(k) plan can result in a more significant and more appreciated benefit than a defined-benefit plan.

You can also set up your own retirement plan as a self-employed business owner, called a Keogh or HR 10 plan. For more information on Keoghs and SEPs (simplified employee pension plans), request Publication 560, "Retirement Plans for the Self-Employed," from your regional IRS office. It's free.

SUCCESS ACTION PLAN

Having been an employee yourself, you understand how an employee thinks as well as how to motivate her or him. You have practical experience. Now that you are an employer, you will be sensitive to the value of each employee and to the necessity to help each one develop potential. Even if you don't plan on adding employees soon, you should begin developing an employee plan and gathering further information. Here's how to put this chapter into action:

- ❏ List the different jobs that your catering service will need in the coming year, such as chef, food preparer, food server, delivery person, and assistant manager.
- ❏ For each of these jobs, list the qualifications that will be required, such as health card, certification, special training, attitude, and special skills.
- ❏ List resources you can use to develop applicants.
- ❏ Talk with your state employment office to determine requirements and to ensure compliance.
- ❏ Find or develop an application form that will help you analyze the abilities and best use for applicants.
- ❏ List questions that you should and can ask during the employment interview.
- ❏ Consider whether you will use a temporary employment service and, if so, which ones.
- ❏ Consider whether you will hire independent contractors and, if so, where you will find them. Make certain that they are truly independent according to state employment department definitions.
- ❏ Establish your firm's wage and benefits package.
- ❏ Develop your personnel policy manual.
- ❏ As needed, establish health, welfare, and retirement plans to your employees.

8
How do I keep accurate records?

There are many reasons to keep good records. When you are just starting a catering business, an adequate recordkeeping system helps increase the chances of survival and reduces the probability of early failure. When you have an established catering service, you can enhance your chances of staying in business and of earning increased profits with a good recordkeeping system.

How do good accounting records decrease the chances of failure and increase the likelihood of remaining in business and making a profit? Here are some of the things that good business records can tell you:

- How much cash do I have on hand and in the bank?
- Do these amounts agree with what records tell me I should have, or is there a shortage?
- How much business am I doing?
- How much credit am I extending?
- How much is tied up in receivables?
- How much of my receivables are more than 60, 90, or 120 days overdue?
- How are my collections?
- What are my losses from credit sales?
- Who owes me money?
- Who is delinquent?
- Should I continue extending credit to delinquent accounts?
- How soon can I anticipate a return on my accounts receivable?
- How much is my investment in provisions?
- How often do I turn over my inventory?
- How much do I owe my suppliers and other creditors?
- Have I received all of my outstanding credits for returned provisions?
- How much gross profit or margin did I earn?
- What are my expenses, including those not requiring cash outlays?
- What's my weekly payroll?
- Do I have adequate payroll records to meet the requirements of workers' compensation insurance, wage-and-hour laws, social security insurance, unemployment compensation insurance, and withholding taxes?
- How much net profit have I earned?
- How much income taxes do I owe?
- What's my capital?

- Are my sales, expenses, profits, and capital showing improvements, or did I do better last year than this?
- How do I stand as compared with two periods ago?
- Is my business' position about the same, improving, or deteriorating?
- On what services am I making a profit, breaking even, or losing money?
- Am I taking full advantage of cash discounts for prompt payments?
- How do my discounts taken compare with my discounts given?
- How do the financial facts of my catering business compare with those of similar businesses?

Get the point? Your business requires a good recordkeeping system to help you work smarter rather than harder.

Keeping accurate and up-to-date business records is, for many people, the most difficult and dull aspect of operating a business. If this area of business management is one that you believe will be hard for you, plan now how you will handle this task. Don't wait until tax time or until you're totally confused. Take a course at a local community college, ask a volunteer SCORE representative, or hire an accountant to advise you on setting up and maintaining your recordkeeping system.

You will need your records to prepare tax returns, make business decisions, and apply for loans. Set aside a special time each day or week to update your records. It will pay off in the long run with more deductions and fewer headaches.

What business expenses are deductible? There's a long list. The best answer is found in a free publication offered by the Internal Revenue Service, "Business Expenses." Ask for Publication 535.

WHAT RECORDS DO I NEED?

So what do you need for a good recordkeeping or accounting system? A good recordkeeping system should be
- Simple to use
- Easy to understand
- Reliable
- Accurate
- Consistent
- Timely

Several published systems and software systems provide simplified records, usually in a single record book. These systems cover the primary records required for all businesses; some are even modified specifically for the catering business.

A good recordkeeping system identifies the sources of your receipts, keeps track of deductible expenses, figures depreciation allowances, records details of assets, determines earnings for self-employment tax purposes, and supports items reported on tax returns. Simply, your records should tell you these three facts:
- How much cash you owe
- How much cash is owed to you
- How much cash you have on hand

To keep track of everything, you should have these basic journals:
- A check or *cash disbursements register* (Fig. 8-1) shows each check disbursed, the date of the disbursement, number of the check, to whom it was made out (the payee), the amount of money disbursed, and for what purpose.

Date	Check Number	Account Number	Amount	Name
June 4	3456	6666	$221.34	Myerson Wholesale Grocery–May groceries
June 7	3457	9942	$1,721.43	Mack McLean–Payroll
June 13	3458	2123	$891.21	Internal Revenue Service–Estimated Taxes
June 19	3459	9827	$76.14	Petty Cash–Replenish Petty Cash Fund
June 25	3460	3260	$389.19	Bigtown Insurance Agency–Business Insurance
June 29	3461	1975	$192.20	Tools R Us–Equipment Lease
June 30	3462	1111	$2,156.60	Capital Draw–Owner's Salary

8-1 A cash disbursements register tracks the money you pay out.

- *Cash receipts* show the amount of money received, from whom, and for what (Figs. 8-2 and 8-3).
- A *sales journal* shows each sale you make, the date, the customer, the amount of the invoice, how much you spent for labor and materials, and any applicable sales tax.
- A *general journal* is used for noncash transactions and those involving the owner's equity in the business.
- A *voucher register* records bills, money owed, the date of the bill, to whom it is owed, the amount, and the service.

In addition, you need the following other records in your business:

- *Accounts receivable* is the record of accounts on which you will receive money because you have sold them something, but they haven't paid for it all.
- *Accounts payable* is the record of accounts for which you will have to pay money because you have purchased a product or service, but you haven't paid for it all.
- *Inventory* is a record of your firm's investment in foods or provisions that you intend to resell (Fig. 8-4).

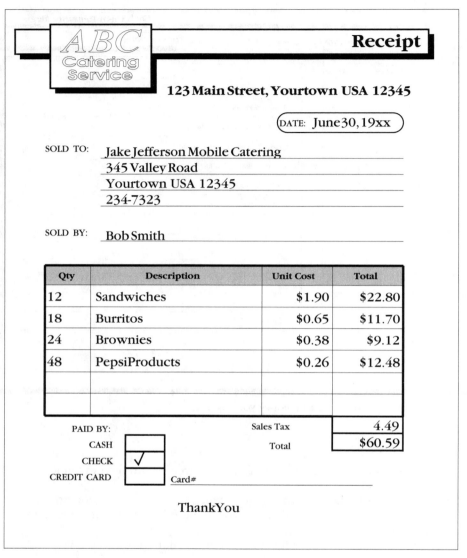

Receipt

ABC Catering Service

123 Main Street, Yourtown USA 12345

DATE: June 30, 19xx

SOLD TO: Jake Jefferson Mobile Catering
345 Valley Road
Yourtown USA 12345
234-7323

SOLD BY: Bob Smith

Qty	Description	Unit Cost	Total
12	Sandwiches	$1.90	$22.80
18	Burritos	$0.65	$11.70
24	Brownies	$0.38	$9.12
48	PepsiProducts	$0.26	$12.48

PAID BY:

CASH [ ]

CHECK [✓]

CREDIT CARD [ ] Card#

Sales Tax	4.49
Total	$60.59

ThankYou

8-2 You should have some type of receipt, with a copy, for every transaction.

- *Equipment* is a record of your firm's investment in equipment that you will use in providing your service and will not normally resell.
- *Payroll* is a record of the wages of employees and their deductions for income, FICA, and other taxes as well as other payroll deductions (Fig. 8-5).

Some businesses combine all of these journals into one. In fact, many good "one-write" systems are available that allow you to make a single entry for each transaction.

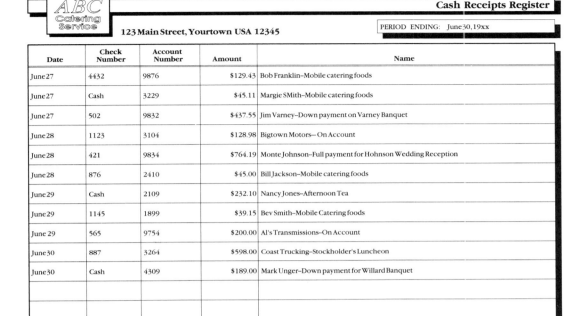

Date	Check Number	Account Number	Amount	Name
June 27	4432	9876	$129.43	Bob Franklin–Mobile catering foods
June 27	Cash	3229	$45.11	Margie SMith–Mobile catering foods
June 27	502	9832	$437.55	Jim Varney–Down payment on Varney Banquet
June 28	1123	3104	$128.98	Bigtown Motors– On Account
June 28	421	9834	$764.19	Monte Johnson–Full payment for Hohnson Wedding Reception
June 28	876	2410	$45.00	Bill Jackson–Mobile catering foods
June 29	Cash	2109	$232.10	Nancy Jones–Afternoon Tea
June 29	1145	1899	$39.15	Bev Smith–Mobile Catering foods
June 29	565	9754	$200.00	Al's Transmissions–On Account
June 30	887	3264	$598.00	Coast Trucking–Stockholder's Luncheon
June 30	Cash	4309	$189.00	Mark Unger–Down payment for Willard Banquet

8-3 A cash receipts register tracks the money you receive.

Single-entry vs. double-entry systems

There are two ways to record transactions in your business: with a single entry or with a double entry. The primary advantage to single-entry recordkeeping is that it is easy. As the name implies, you make a single entry that records the source of each income or the destination of each expense. Each entry is either a plus or a minus to the amount of cash that you have. For example, receiving a check on an outstanding account is a plus. Paying for a supplies order is a minus. As long as you have a limited number of transactions, single-entry accounting is adequate.

As your business grows in complexity, however, you will want a check-and-balance system that ensures accurate records. Double-entry accounting requires that you make two offsetting entries that balance each other, as shown in Fig. 8-6. In double-entry accounting, a check received on an outstanding account is a debit to "cash" and a credit to "accounts receivable." Paying for a supplies order is a debit to "supplies" and a credit to "cash."

Every account in a double-entry system has two sides: a left, or *debit*, side and a right, or *credit*, side. The posted debits must always equal the posted credits. Some types of accounts are called *debit accounts* because their balance is typically a debit. Asset accounts (typically cash and accounts receivable) are debit accounts. Liability

ABC Catering Service

123 Main Street, Yourtown USA 12345

Date	June 30, 19xx	
Page	4	of 4

Department : Food Inventory

Location : Refrigerator #2

Item#	Qty	Description	Price	Total
89345	120	Quarter-Pound Hamburger Patties	$0.43	$51.60
89333	92	Sesame Seed Hamburger Buns--Large	$0.12	$11.04
88444	7	Potato Salad--Pounds	$2.45	$17.15
88555	3	Mustard--Pounds	$2.60	$7.80
87666	3	Mayonnaise--Pounds	$3.10	$9.30
			TOTAL	96.89

Priced By:	Bob Smith	Called By:	Ed Jones
Checked By:		Entered By:	

8-4 An accurate inventory record helps you reduce waste as well as ensure that you are getting the most from your purchases.

[3]——EMPLOYEE COMPENSATION RECORD

NAME __John E. Marks__
ADDRESS __1 Elm St., Newark, NJ__
PHONE __555-6075__

FULL TIME _____
PART TIME ____X____

SOC. SEC. NO. ___567-00-8901___
DATE OF BIRTH ___12-21-65___
NO. OF EXEMPTIONS __Single - 1__

Pay Period Ending	Hours Worked S M T W T F S S M T W T F S	Total Reg. Hours	Over-time	Earnings Regular Rate	Earnings Overtime Rate	Earnings Total	Deductions Social Security	Deductions Medicare	Deductions Fed. Income Tax	Deductions State Income Tax	Deductions Other	Net Pay
1-4-92	5 5 5 5 5 5 4 6	40		6.50		$260.00	$16.12	$3.77	$20.00	$6.00		$214.11
1-18-92	4 4 4 4 2 4 3 4 4 3	40		6.50		260.00	16.12	3.77	20.00	6.00		214.11
		80				$520.00	$32.24	$7.54	$40.00	$12.00		$428.22
QUARTERLY TOTALS												

8-5 Employment compensation record.

General Journal

Date	Description of Entry	Post Ref.	Debit	Credit
Oct. 5	Rent Expense		780 00	
	Cash			780 00

8-6 Typical general ledger double-entry.

accounts (such as accounts payable and notes payable) usually carry a credit balance. Income carries a credit balance, while expenses carry a debit balance. Everything else in double-entry bookkeeping is based on these rules. Here are some examples of common double entries:

- Cash income = Debit cash and credit income
- Accrued income = Debit accounts receivable and credit income
- Cash expense = Debit the expense account and credit cash
- Accrued expense = Debit the expense account and credit accounts payable
- Prepaid expense = Debit prepaid expenses and credit cash

If, at the end of the month, the debits don't equal the credits, look for debits erroneously posted as credits, credits erroneously posted as debits, transposition of numbers (such as *123* to *132*), and incorrect math.

Assets, liabilities, and net worth

Assets include not only cash, inventory, land, building, equipment, machinery, furniture, and the like, but also money due from individuals or other businesses (known as *accounts receivable* or *notes receivable*).

Liabilities are funds acquired for a business through loans or the sale of property or services to the business on credit. Creditors do not acquire ownership in your business, but promissory notes to be paid at a designated future date (known as *accounts payable* or *notes payable*).

Net worth (or shareholders' equity or capital) is money put into a business by its owners or left in it as retained earnings for use by the business in acquiring assets.

The following formula shows the relationship of assets, liabilities, and net worth:

$$\text{Assets} = \text{Liabilities} + \text{Net worth}$$

That is, the total funds invested in assets of the business equals the funds supplied to the business by its creditors plus the funds supplied to the business by its owners. If a business owes more money to creditors than it possesses in value of assets owned and retained earnings, the net worth or owner's equity of the business will be a negative number.

This accounting formula can also be expressed as follows:

$$\text{Assets} - \text{Liabilities} = \text{Net worth}$$

Cash or accrual?

Many small businesses are operated primarily on a cash basis. The customer buys products with cash or check, the merchant buys inventory with cash or short-term credit. As businesses become larger and more complicated, many keep records on the accrual basis. The dividing line between a cash basis and accrual basis business might depend on whether or not credit is given to customers, as well as the amount of inventory required.

An accrual-basis accounting system is, according to the government, "a method of recording income and expenses in which each item is reported as earned or incurred, without regard as to when actual payments are received or made." For example, charge sales are credited at once to sales and charged to accounts receivable. When the bills are collected, the credit is to accounts receivable.

Accruals should also be made for larger expense items payable in the future, such as annual or semiannual interest on loans.

If you're comfortable with accounting, accrual can be the most accurate basis for records, but the cash basis is easier to understand. As long as you don't prepay many of your expenses and are not incorporated, a cash basis is fine for your new catering business.

Accounts receivable

As mentioned, income not paid to you is called accounts receivable. Follow these few rules to help keep your accounts receivable current. First, be sure bills are prepared immediately after the service is performed. Make sure that the statement is mailed to the correct person and address. Make sure your invoice has sufficient information to fully identify the source and purpose of the charge because some businesses simply set aside any bills that they question.

At the end of each month, "age" your accounts receivable. That is, list accounts and enter the amounts that are current, unpaid for 30 days, and those 60 days and over. (Most accounts receivable computer programs automatically produce reports on aged receivables.) Then, call each account in the 60+ days column and find out why the bill is unpaid. Keep an especially close watch on larger accounts.

To ensure that you get paid promptly, pay close attention to customers' complaints about bills. If a complaint is justified, offer an adjustment and reach an agreement with the customer. Then get a date from the customer when you can expect to receive the payment.

When you get a new customer who asks for credit, use a simple form listing name, address, telephone number, employment, and bank and credit references. Credit application forms such as the one in Fig. 8-7 are available at many office supply and stationery stores. (A blank sample is included in the appendix for your use.) Make sure that the customer is worthy of credit before you grant it.

Managing payroll records

Quarterly and yearly reports of individual payroll payments must be made to federal and, in many cases, state governments. Each employee must receive a W-2 form after the end of the calendar year showing total withholding payments made for the employee during the previous year.

A payroll summary should be made each payday showing the employee's name, employee number, rate of pay, hours worked, overtime hours, total pay, and amount of deductions for FICA (social security insurance), Medicare insurance, state and federal withholding taxes, deductions for insurance, pension, savings, and child support, as required. Also maintain a running total of earnings, pay and deductions for each individual employee. In addition, if your business employs union members, you might have additional deductions for union dues, pensions, and other fees.

To ensure that you maintain adequate records for this task, keep an employee card or computer file for each employee of your firm showing the full legal name, social security insurance number, address, telephone number, name of next of kin and their address, marital status, number of exemptions claimed, and current rate of pay. A federal W-4 form completed and signed by the employee should also be attached to the employee card or record.

To begin your payroll system, contact the Internal Revenue Service to request the "Employer's Tax Guide" (Circular E) and get a nine-digit Employer Identification Number. The IRS will then send you deposit slips (Form 8109) with your new ID number printed on them. Use these deposit slips each time you pay your payroll taxes. Payroll taxes are paid within a month of the ending of a quarter; that is, January 31, April 30, July 31, and October 31. As your business grows, you might be required to pay payroll taxes more frequently. By then, your accountant will help you determine need and the process.

Petty cash fund

Most business expenses are paid by business check, credit card, or placed on account with the seller. However, sometimes small expenses will be paid by an em-

CREDIT APPLICATION

123 Main Street, Yourtown USA 12345

DATE: June 30, 19xx

BUSINESS INFORMATION	
NAME OF BUSINESS	Franklin Mobile Catering
LEGAL (IF DIFFERENT)	
ADDRESS	345 Main Street
CITY	Yourtown
STATE USA	ZIP 12345 PHONE 234-5678

DESCRIPTION OF BUSINESS

NO. OF EMPLOYEES	CREDIT REQUESTED	TYPE OF BUSINESS
2	2000.00	Mobile Catering

IN BUSINESS SINCE 1987

BUSINESS STRUCTURE

☐ CORPORATION ☐ PARTNERSHIP ☑ PROPRIETORSHIP
☐ DIVISION/SUBSIDIARY
NAME OF PARENT
COMPANY _____
HOW LONG IN BUSINESS

COMPANY PRINCIPALS RESPONSIBLE FOR BUSINESS TRANSACTIONS

NAME :	TITLE:	ADDRESS:	PHONE:
Tom Franklin	Owner	999 9th St., Yourtown	234-8765
NAME:	TITLE:	ADDRESS:	PHONE:
NAME:	TITLE:	ADDRESS:	PHONE:

BANK REFERENCES

NAME OF BANK	Bank of Yourtown	NAME TO CONTACT	Betty Johnson
BRANCH	Uptown	ADDRESS	456 Main Street, Yourtown
CHECKING ACCOUNT NO.	3456-7890	TELEPHONE NUMBER	234-4321

TRADE REFERENCES

FIRM NAME	CONTACT NAME	TELEPHONE NUMBER	ACCOUNT OPEN SINCE
Smith Grocers	Mack Smith	234-9876	1989
State Wholesale Foods	Mary Rivers	992-7654	1990
Yourtown Stationery	Joe Johnson	234-7654	1992

CONFIRMATION OF INFORMATION ACCURACY AND RELEASE OF AUTHORITY TO VERIFY

I hereby certify that the information in this credit application is correct. The information included in this credit application is for use by the above firm in determining the amount and conditions of credit to be extended. I understand that this firm may also utilize the other sources of credit which it considers necessary in making this determination. Further I hereby authorize the bank and trade references listed in this credit application to release the information necessary to assist this firm in establishing a line of credit.

X _____   _____   June 30, 19xx
SIGNATURE   TITLE   DATE

POLICY STATEMENT: INITIAL ORDER FROM NEW ACCOUNTS WILL NOT BE PROCESSED
UNLESS ACCOMPANIED BY THE ABOVE REQUESTED INFORMATION.
TERMS: NET 30 DAYS FROM DATE OF INVOICE UNLESS OTHERWISE STATED.

8-7 Typical credit application.

ployee or with cash that requires reimbursement. Because the amount is typically small, the fund from which the reimbursement comes is usually known as *petty cash.*

A petty cash fund should be set up to be used for payments of small amounts not covered by invoices. A check should be drawn for, say, $50 or $100. The check is cashed and the fund placed in a box or drawer. When small cash payments are made for such items as postage, freight, or bus fares, the items are listed on a printed form or even a slip of paper. When the fund is nearly exhausted, the items are summarized and a check drawn to cover the exact amount spent. The check is cashed and the fund replenished. The cash in the drawer plus the listed expenditures should always equal the established amount of the petty cash fund. (A sample petty cash form is included in the appendix.)

Equipment records

Keep an accurate and up-to-date list of permanent equipment used in your catering business. Especially, keep track of equipment useful for a year or longer, and of appreciable value. Equipment records should show the date purchased, name of supplier, description of the item, check number of the payment(s), and amount of purchase including tax. If you own a number of items, keep a separate list for vehicles, tools and related work equipment, and office furniture and fixtures. Use these records to develop a depreciation worksheet (Fig. 8-8) and provide supporting information for fixed asset accounts.

For depreciation and other accounting purposes, a *calendar year* is 12 consecutive months beginning January 1 and ending December 31. A *fiscal year* is 12 consecutive months ending on the last day of any month other than December. A *short tax year* is less than 12 months because your firm was not in business a full year or you have changed your tax year.

Insurance records

Insurance helps to safeguard your business against losses from fire, illness, injury, and other hazards. You cannot operate without it. Your catering business will have several types of insurance. Each policy should be listed showing the type of insurance coverage (such as automotive, fire, theft, or bonding), name of the insurance company and agent, expiration date, and premiums (monthly and annual). In fact, keep a file with all of your insurance policies in them, or separate files for the types of policies. In addition to fire, theft, and hazard insurance, some of the most common types of business insurance are the following:

- Liability coverage protects you in case a service you perform leads to an injury of the user.
- Auto liability insurance is needed for any vehicle that you use in your business in any way.
- Medical insurance pays if someone is injured while at your place of business
- Workers' compensation insurance covers people who work for you in case of on-the-job injury.
- Business-interruption insurance covers you in case your business is damaged by fire, flood, or some other hazard that requires you to totally or partially suspend operation.

Depreciation Worksheet

Description of Property	Date Placed in Service	Cost or Other Basis	Business/ Investment Use %	Section 179 Deduction	Depreciation Prior Years	Basis for Depreciation	Method/ Convention	Recovery Period	Rate or Table %	Depreciation Deduction
Equipment–Transmission Jack	1/2/92	1,366	100%	—	—	1,366	200 DB/HY	7	14.29%	195
Pickup Truck (Used)	1/2/92	3,500	100%	2,000	—	1,500	200 DB/HY	5	20%	300
Heavy Duty Tow Truck	1/2/92	18,000	100%	8,000	—	10,000	200 DB/HY	5	20%	2,000
Equipment – Engine Hoist	1/2/92	1,600	100%	—	—	1,600	200 DB/HY	7	14.29%	229
										2,724

8-8 Depreciation worksheet.

- Disability income protection is a form of health insurance in case you become disabled.
- Business life insurance provides funds for transition if you die.

Be sure to keep all of your insurance records and policies in a safe place—either with your accountant or in a safe-deposit box at your bank. If you keep your records in your office for convenience sake, give your policy numbers and insurance company names to your accountant or attorney, or put them in your safe-deposit box.

OUTSIDE ACCOUNTING SERVICES

Many new catering services have the right skills for plying their trade, yet fail because of poor financial management. Sometimes the best decision is to hire the services of a public accounting firm. An accountant can design records, set up ways for maintaining them, draw off vital information, and help relate that information to a profitable operation.

Daily bits of information will flow into your catering business. As customers are served, pieces of information are generated about sales, cash, equipment, purchase expenses, payroll, accounts payable, and, if credit is offered to customers, accounts receivable. To capture these facts and figures, a system is necessary. If you don't feel comfortable with setting up and managing such a system, don't be shy about hiring an accounting or recordkeeping service to help you control finances and make profitable decisions.

Once a system of records has been set up, the question is: Who should keep the books? The accounting service that has set up the books might keep them. However, if you have a general understanding of recordkeeping, you can do them yourself and save some money, while using your accountant for checking and analyzing your records. Once your business has grown, you might consider hiring someone to keep your records and perform other office functions. Or maybe your spouse or other relative can assist you.

In addition to recordkeeping, an accountant can advise you on financial management. He or she can provide you with cash-flow requirements, budget forecasts, borrowing, business organization, and tax information.

On cash-flow requirements, an accountant helps you work out the amount of cash needed to operate your firm during a specific period—for example, three months, six months, or the next year. He or she considers how much cash you will need to carry customer accounts receivable, to buy equipment and supplies, to pay current bills, and to repay loans. In addition, an accountant can determine how much cash will come from collection of accounts receivable and how much will have to be borrowed or pulled from an existing line of credit. While working out the cash requirements, your accountant might point out danger spots, such as accounts that are past due.

When you borrow, your accountant can assemble financial information such as a profit-and-loss statement, an income statement, and a balance sheet. The purpose of such data is to show the lender the financial position of your business and its ability to repay the loan. Using this information, your accountant can advise you on whether you need a short-term or long-term loan. The financial data that your accountant compiles includes the following:
- Assets you will offer for collateral
- Your current debt obligations

- A summary of how you will use the money you borrow
- A schedule of how you intend to repay the money borrowed

If you have never borrowed before, your accountant can help you by introducing you to a banker who knows and respects the accountant's reputation. This, alone, might be worth the cost of hiring an accountant to advise and help you.

Taxes are another area in which an accountant can contribute advice and assistance. Normally, a recordkeeping system that provides the information you need for making profitable decisions will suffice for tax purposes. However, if you purchase a lot of equipment that requires special depreciation, have employees who handle cash or require payroll taxes, or have extensive bad debts, a good accountant can help you identify the problems, suggest a method of keeping good records, and help you minimize your tax obligation by "writing off" bad debts as a business expense.

FINANCIAL REPORTS

As the owner of a catering firm, you need accurate information on a regular basis to ensure that your business is running smoothly. As a single-person firm, you might have all the information you need in your head. But as your firm grows, you will need some information daily, other information weekly, and still other data on a monthly basis. Let's take a look at what you will need and when.

Daily report

To manage your catering firm, you need the following information daily:
- Cash on hand
- Bank balance
- Daily summary of sales and cash receipts
- Daily summary of monies paid out by cash or check
- Correction of any errors from previous reports

This information is summarized in the daily report shown in Fig. 8-9. You can prepare this information yourself, have your office employee prepare it for you, or rely on your accountant. While daily records do not show you trends, they help you get a feel for the level of business that you're doing. And you'll be able to spot problems before they become serious.

Weekly report

Once a week, you or someone in your employ should prepare a weekly report on your firm. While still not sufficient for long-term planning, weekly figures help you make small corrections in the course of your business. Weekly, you'll want the following information:
- Accounts receivable report listing accounts that require a call because they are over 60 days overdue
- Accounts payable report listing what your business owes, to whom, and if a discount is offered for early payment
- Payroll report including information on each employee, the number of hours worked during the week, rate of pay, total wages, deductions, net pay, and related information
- Taxes and reports required to be sent to city, state, and federal governments

Daily Summary of Cash Receipts

January 2, 19

Cash Sales		263 60
Sales Tax		4 20
Total Receipts		267 80
Cash on Hand		
Cash in Register (Including unspent petty cash)		
Coins	23 75	
Bills	143 00	
Checks	134 05	
Total Cash in Register		300 80
Petty Cash Slips		17 00
Total Cash		317 80
Less: Change and Petty Cash		
Petty Cash Slips	17 00	
Coins and Bills (unspent petty cash)	33 00	
Total Change and Petty Cash Fund		50 00
Total Cash Receipts		267 80

8-9 Daily summary of cash receipts.

Your weekly reports should be prepared by the end of business on Friday so you can review them over the weekend or early Monday morning.

Monthly reports

Once a month, you should review a number of pieces of information that have accumulated through your daily and weekly reports, but were too small to analyze clearly. Now that they are part of a full month, information about cash flow, accounts receivable, and other parts of your business make more sense—and can be more easily acted upon. Here are some of the reports and information you will want to see every month:

- Monthly summary of daily cash receipts and deposits (Fig. 8-10)
- General ledger including all journal entries
- Income statement showing income for the prior month, expenses incurred in obtaining the income, overhead, and the profit or loss received
- Balance sheet showing the assets, liabilities, and capital or current worth of the business
- Check reconciliation (Fig. 8-11) that shows what checks were deposited or applied by payees against your business checking account, and that verifies that the cash balance is accurate
- Petty cash fund report ensuring that paid-out slips plus cash equals the beginning petty cash balance
- Tax payment report showing that all federal tax deposits, withheld income, FICA taxes, state and other taxes have been paid
- Aged receivables report showing the age and balance of each account (30, 60, 90 days, past due, etc.)
- Summary of Schedule C tax-form entries (Fig. 8-12)

Your balance sheet

Your balance sheet is a summary of the status of your business—its assets, liabilities, and net worth—at an instant in time. By reviewing your balance sheet along with your income statement and your cash-flow statement, you will be able to make informed financial and business-planning decisions.

The balance sheet is drawn up using the totals from individual accounts kept in your general ledger. It shows what you have left when you pay all your creditors. The assets and liabilities sections must balance—hence the name "balance sheet." Remember: Assets less liabilities equal capital or net worth.

Your balance sheet can be produced quarterly, semiannually, or at the end of each calendar or fiscal year. If your recordkeeping is manual, you will be less likely to frequently update your balance sheet. Many accounting software programs, on the other hand, can give you a current balance sheet in just a few minutes.

While your accountant will be most helpful in drawing up your balance sheet, it is your responsibility to understand it.

Your income statement

Your income statement is a detailed, month-by-month tally of the income from sales and the expenses incurred to generate the sales. It is a good assessment tool because it shows the effect of your decisions on profits. It is a good planning tool because you can estimate the impact of decisions on profit before you make them.

Your income statement includes four kinds of information:

- Sales information lists the total revenues generated by the sale of your service to clients.
- Direct expenses include the cost of labor and materials to perform your service.

Monthly Summary of Cash Receipts

Date 19		Net Sales	Sales Tax	Daily Receipts	Deposit
Jan	2	263 60	4 20	267 80	
	3	212 00	3 39	215 39	
	4	194 40	3 10	197 50	680 69
	6	222 40	3 54	225 94	
	7	231 15	3 68	234 83	
	8	137 50	2 13	139 63	600 40
	9	187 90	2 99	190 89	
	10	207 56	3 31	210 87	401 76
	11	128 95	2 05	131 00	
	13	231 40	3 77	235 17	
	14	201 28	3 21	204 49	
	15	88 01	1 40	89 41	660 07
	16	210 95	3 36	214 31	
	17	221 80	3 53	225 33	439 64
	18	225 15	3 59	228 74	
	21	221 93	3 52	225 45	
	22	133 53	2 13	135 66	589 85
	23	130 84	2 08	132 92	
	24	216 37	3 45	219 82	352 74
	25	220 05	3 50	223 55	
	27	197 80	3 15	200 95	
	28	272 49	4 34	276 83	701 33
	29	150 64	2 40	153 04	
	30	224 05	3 56	227 61	
	31	133 30	2 13	135 43	516 08
		4865 05	77 51	4942 56	4942 56

8-10 Monthly summary of cash receipts.

- Indirect expenses are the costs you have even if your service is not sold, including salaries, rent, utilities, insurance, depreciation, office supplies, taxes, and professional fees.
- Profit is shown as pretax income and aftertax, or net, income.

Check Reconciliation as of
January 31, 19

Balance shown on bank statement				1458	12
Add deposits not credited:					
1/28		701	33		
1/31		516	08		
				1217	41
				2675	53
Subtract outstanding checks:					
No. 89		66	70		
90		9	80		
93		150	00		
94		300	00		
				526	50
Adjusted balance per bank statement				2149	03
Balance shown in checkbook				2153	03
Add: Deposit of $600.40 for 1/8					
entered as $594.40 (difference)				6	00
				2159	03
Subtract:					
Bank service charge				10	00
Adjusted checkbook balance				2149	03

8-11 Reconciliation of bank statement.

Annual Summary for Schedule C Entries

	Cash Receipts	Materials/ Supplies	Gross Payroll	FICA Taxes	Bank Charges	Electric	Interest	Insurance	Rent	Telephone	Truck/Auto	Advertising	Office Expenses	Taxes/ Licenses	Miscellaneous
January	4866.05	1063.50	526.00	39.79	10.00	175.30	118.09	21.00	300.00	27.00	45.00	85.00	36.00	100.08	39.00
February	3476.32	874.03	235.40	17.66	17.50	153.10	118.09	21.00	300.00	21.50	20.50				
March	3742.00	724.00	507.00	38.08	11.25	145.91	118.09		300.00	52.10	51.20				
April	4077.02														
May	4066.32														
June	4151.62														
July	3912.12														
August	3741.12														
September	4126.52														
October	5017.72														
November	3645.42														
December	3656.52														
Totals	47446.95	11021.00	5434.00	406.09	92.50	1642.37	1217.08	452.00	3600.00	324.09	571.46	85.00	140.00	1218.00	344.00
Enter on Schedule C	Line 1	Line 22	Line 26	Line 23	Line 27a	Line 25	Line 16b	Line 15	Line 20b	Line 25	Line 10	Line 8	Line 18	Line 23	Line 27a

8-12 Keeping track of your Schedule C entries throughout the year helps you ensure that you don't pay too much, nor too little, income taxes.

Your cash-flow statement

Your business must have a healthy cash flow to survive. Cash flow is the amount of money available in your business at any given time. To keep tabs on cash flow, forecast the funds you expect to disburse and receive over a specific time. Then you can predict any deficiency or surplus in cash and decide how best to respond.

A cash-flow statement like the one in Fig. 8-13 serves one other very useful purpose in addition to planning. As the actual information becomes available to you, compare it to the monthly cash-flow estimates you previously made to see how accurately you are estimating. As you do this, you will be giving yourself on-the-spot business training in making more accurate estimates and plans for the coming months. As your ability to estimate improves, your financial control of the business will increase.

HOW CAN I PROFITABLY MANAGE CASH?

If your catering business has only one employee—you—you'll have no problem with one of the greatest enemies of business: employee theft. However, as your business grows and you hire others to handle some of your tasks, you will need to manage them to ensure that employee theft doesn't become a major problem.

			Date:		Date:		Date:	
			ESTIMATE	ACTUAL	ESTIMATE	ACTUAL	ESTIMATE	ACTUAL
FOR INTERNAL USE ONLY	Opening Balance							
	Collections From Trade							
	Misc. Cash Receipts							
	TOTAL CASH AVAILABLE							
	DISBURSEMENTS							
	Payroll							
	Trade Payables							
	Other							
	Capital Expenses							
	Income Tax							
	Bank Loan Payment							
	TOTAL DISBURSEMENTS							
	Ending Balance							
	Less Minimum Balance							
	CASH AVAILABLE							

ABC Catering Service — 123 Main Street, Yourtown USA 12345 — Cash Flow Forecast
DATE: / FOR TIME PERIOD: / APPROVED BY: / PREPARED BY:

8-13 Tracking cash flow is one of your most important tasks, especially during the first two years of business.

Here are some ideas for handling cash and checks within your business:

- The person who handles your cash receipts shouldn't be the person who makes bank deposits. Cash is too easily misappropriated. Don't tempt an employee by letting him or her handle both of these duties.
- For the same reason, the person who writes the checks should not also sign them or have the authority to sign them. Whenever checks are signed, the signer should view the bill being paid and then write the check number on the bill.
- Deposit your daily cash receipts in the bank each day.
- Set up and use a petty cash fund and voucher system for small cash outlays.
- Use only prenumbered checks and maintain records of all canceled or voided checks.
- The monthly bank reconciliation should be done by the owner or an outside accountant.

Remember that human error is more common than dishonesty, but that both can damage your business.

Improving cash flow

All businesses, no matter how small or large, function on cash. Many businesses become insolvent because they don't have enough cash to meet their short-term obligations. Bills must be paid in cash, not potential profits. Sufficient cash is, therefore, one of the keys to maintaining a successful business. Thus, you must understand how cash moves or flows through the business and how planning can remove some of the uncertainties about future requirements.

Catering services face a continual cycle of events that increase or decrease the cash balance. Cash is decreased in the acquisition of provisions and services. It is reduced in paying off the amounts owed to suppliers (accounts payable). Services or food is sold, generating money owed from customers (accounts receivable). When customers pay, accounts receivable is reduced and the cash account is increased. However, the cash flows are not necessarily related to the sales in that period because customers might pay in the next period.

Catering services must continually be alert to changes in working capital accounts, the cause of these changes, and their implications for the financial health of the company.

Net working capital

As discussed earlier, current assets are those resources of cash and those assets that can be converted to cash within one year or as a normal business cycle. These assets include cash, marketable securities, accounts receivable, and inventories. Current liabilities are obligations that become due within one year or a normal business cycle. These liabilities include accounts payable, notes payable, and accrued expenses payable. Consider current assets as the source of funds to reduce current liabilities.

One way to measure the flow of cash and the firm's ability to maintain its cash or liquid assets is to compute working capital, the difference between current assets and current liabilities. The change in this value from period to period is called *net working capital*, as shown in the example in Table 8-1.

Table 8-1 Example of net working capital

	Year 1	Year 2
Current Assets	$100,000	$200,000
Less Current Liabilities	-70,000	-112,000
Working Capital	40,000	88,000
Net Working Capital Increase	$48,000	

Cash-flow statement

While net working capital shows only the changes in the current position, a "flow" statement explains the changes that have occurred in any account during any time period. The cash-flow statement is an analysis of the cash inflows and outflows.

Accurately forecasting cash requirements helps you become a more efficient catering service owner. If you can determine the cash requirements for any period, you can establish a bank loan in advance, or you can reduce other current asset accounts so that the cash will be available. Also, when you have excess cash, you can put this cash into productive use to earn a return.

The change in the cash can be readily determined if you know net working capital and the changes in current liabilities and current assets other than cash. To compute the cash flow, let

$$NWC = \text{Net working capital}$$
$$CA = \text{Change in current assets other than cash}$$
$$CL = \text{Change in current liabilities}$$
$$Cash = \text{Change in cash}$$

Because net working capital is the difference between the change in current assets and current liabilities, the following formulas are true:

$$NWC = CA + Cash - CL$$
$$Cash = NWC - CA + CL$$

These relationships state that if you know the net working capital (NWC), the change in current liabilities (CL), and the change in current assets less cash (CA - Cash), you can calculate the change in cash. The change in cash is then added to the beginning balance of cash to determine the ending balance.

Suppose you forecast that catering income will increase $50,000 and the following will correspondingly change:

- Receivables increase by $25,000
- Inventory increase by $70,000
- Accounts Payable increase by $30,000
- Notes Payable increase by $10,000

Using net working capital of $48,000, you can project the change in cash as follows:

$$Cash = NWC - CA + CL$$
$$= 48,000 - 25,000 - 70,000 + 30,000 + 10,000$$
$$= -7000$$

Over this period of time, under the condition of increasing sales volume, cash decreases by $7000. Is there enough cash to cover this decrease? That depends upon the beginning cash balance.

At any given level of sales, it's easier to forecast the required accounts payable, receivables, and inventory, than net working capital. To forecast net working capital account, you must trace the sources and application of funds. Sources of funds increase working capital. Applications of funds decrease working capital. The difference between the sources and applications of funds is the net working capital.

The following calculation is based on the fact that the balance sheet is indeed in balance. That is, the total assets equal total liabilities plus owner's equity:

$$\text{Current assets} + \text{Noncurrent assets} + \text{Retained earnings}$$
$$= \text{Current liabilities} + \text{Long-term liabilities} + \text{Equity}$$

Rearranging this equation produces the following:

$$\text{Current assets} - \text{Current liabilities} =$$
$$\text{Long-term liabilities} + \text{Equity} - \text{Noncurrent assets} - \text{Retained earnings}$$

Because the left side of the equation is working capital, the right side must also equal working capital. A change in either side is the net working capital. If long-term liabilities and equity increase or noncurrent assets decrease, net working capital increases. This change would be a source of funds. If noncurrent assets increase or long-term liabilities and equity decrease, net working capital decreases. This change would be an application of funds.

Typical sources of funds or net working capital are funds provided by operations, disposal of fixed assets, issuance of stock, and borrowing from a long-term source.

To obtain the figure for "funds provided by operations," subtract all expense items requiring funds from all revenues that were sources of funds. You can also obtain this result in an easier manner: Add back expenses that don't result in inflows or outflows of funds to reported net income.

The most common nonfund expense is *depreciation*, the allocation of the cost of an asset as an expense over the life of the asset against the future revenues produced. Adjusting net income with depreciation is much simpler than computing revenues and expenses that require funding. Again, depreciation is not a source of funds.

The typical applications of funds or net working capital are the purchase of fixed assets, payment of dividends, retirement of long-term liabilities, and repurchase of equity.

Planning for cash flow

Cash flow can be used not only to determine how cash flowed through the business, but also as an aid to determine the excess or shortage of cash. Suppose your analysis of cash-flow predicts a potential cash deficiency. You might respond in several ways, such as increasing borrowings (through loans or stock issuance), reducing current asset accounts (receivables and inventory), and reducing noncurrent asset accounts (by selling fixed assets or postponing expansion).

Use a cash-flow statement to determine if sufficient funds are available to finance activities, show funds generated from all sources, and show how these funds were applied. Using and adjusting the information gained from this cash-flow analysis helps you know in advance if there will be enough cash to pay suppliers' bills, bank loans, interest, and dividends.

Increasing cash flow

As you can see, to expand your catering business you need cash. Once you've analyzed cash flow and determined that you need more of it, what can you do? Depending on the specific type of catering business you own, you can find increased cash in your accounts receivable and in your inventory.

Accounts receivable represent the extension of credit to support sales. In your catering business, the types and terms of credit you grant are set by established competitive practices. As an investment, the accounts receivable should contribute to overall return on investment (*ROI*).

Excessive investment in accounts receivable can hurt ROI by tying up funds unnecessarily. One good way to judge the extent of accounts receivable is to compare your average collection period with that of rivals or the industry average. If your average collection period is much higher than your competitors' or the industry norm, your accounts receivable might be excessive. If they are excessive, it might be that you're not keeping tight control of late payers. Develop an aging schedule as shown in Fig. 8-14 to show whether accounts receivable are on time or late.

Failure to closely monitor late payments ties up investment and weakens profits. The more overdue your accounts become, the greater the danger that they will be uncollectable and will have to be written off against profits. If the aging schedule does not reveal excessive late accounts, your credit policy is probably more liberal than most. If this policy translates into more competitive sales and greater profits, it might not be a problem. Otherwise, you should rethink your credit program.

Remember, the bottom line is: the bottom line.

WHAT TAXES DO I NEED TO PAY?

Like it or not, the government is your business partner. And, as your partner, they receive a portion of your profits—even before you do. However, government can also help you make a profit through the Small Business Administration, Department of Commerce, state corporate divisions, and other business services.

You play two roles in managing the taxes of your catering service. In one role, you're a debtor. In the other, you're an agent or tax collector.

As a debtor, you're liable for various taxes, and you pay them as part of your business obligations. For example, each year you owe federal income taxes, which you pay out of the earnings of your business. Other tax debts include state income taxes and real estate taxes.

As an agent, you collect various taxes and pass the funds on to the appropriate government agency. If you have employees, you deduct federal income taxes, social security insurance or FICA taxes, and (in most states) state income taxes from the wages of your employees. If your state requires sales tax on your catering services, you also collect it from your customers.

If you are a sole proprietor, you pay your income tax as any other individual citizen. Your income, expenses, and profit or loss are calculated on Schedule C (Fig.

123 Main Street, Yourtown USA 12345

Period Ending: June 30, 19xx

Invoice Date	Invoice #	Acct #	Customer Name	30 days	60 days	90+ days	Total
February 11	12345-67	1111	Jim Johnson	110.00	110.00	110.00	$330.00
March 19	23456-78	2222	Smith Mobile Catering		465.00		$465.00
April 2	34567-89	3333	William Jones	292.20			$292.20
April 23	45678-90	4444	Betty Doe	121.92			$121.92
			TOTALS	524.12	575.00	110.00	$1,209.12
			GRAND TOTAL DUE				$2,418.24

8-14 Make sure you know who owes you money, how much, and the age of the debt.

8-15) that's filed with your annual Form 1040. A partnership files its own tax forms (Fig. 8-16) and passes the profits on to the partners for filing on their personal income tax forms (Fig. 8-17). A corporation files an IRS Form 1120 (Fig. 8-18) or short form 1120A (Fig. 8-19). Subchapter-S corporations file an IRS Form 1120S (Fig. 8-20). Self-employment tax—social security insurance for the self-employed—is reported on your IRS 1040 using Schedule SE (Fig. 8-21).

Individual proprietors and partners are required by law to pay federal income tax and self-employment tax on a pay-as-you-go basis. That is, you file a "Declaration of Estimated Tax" (Form 1040 ES) on or before April 15, then make payments on April 15, June 15, September 15, and January 15.

Income tax returns from a corporation are due on the 15th of the third month following the end of its taxable year, which might not coincide with the calendar year. To find out more about your tax obligations, contact your regional IRS office (or call 1-800-829-3676) for the following publications:

- "Tax Guide for Small Business" (Publication 334)
- "Guide to Free Tax Services" (Publication 910)
- "Your Federal Income Tax" (Publication 17)
- "Employer's Tax Guide" (Circular E)
- "Taxpayers Starting a Business" (Publication 583)
- "Self-Employment Tax" (Publication 533)
- "Retirement Plans for the Self-Employed" (Publication 560)
- "Tax Withholding and Estimated Tax" (Publication 505)
- "Business Use of Your Home" (Publication 587)

In addition, you'll need a number of federal forms for good recordkeeping and accurate taxation:

- "Application for Employer Identification Number" (Form SS-4) if you have employees
- "Tax Calendars" (Publication 509)
- "Employer's Annual Unemployment Tax Return" (Form 940)
- "Employer's Quarterly Federal Tax Return" (Form 941)
- "Employee's Withholding Allowance Certificate" (W-4) for each employee
- "Employer's Wage and Tax Statement" (W-2) for each employee
- "Reconciliation/Transmittal of Income and Tax Statements" (W-3)
- Instructions for Forms 1120 and 1120A for corporate taxes

HOW DO I PLAN FOR THE FUTURE?

There is one simple reason why you should understand and explore financial planning in your business—to avoid failure. Many new businesses fail primarily because of the lack of good financial planning.

Financial planning affects how and on what terms you will be able to attract the funding you need to establish, maintain, and expand your business. Financial planning determines the human and physical resources you will be able to acquire to operate your business. It is a major factor in whether or not you will be able to make your hard work profitable.

The balance sheet and the income statement are essential to your business, but they are only the starting point for successful financial management. The next step is called *ratio analysis*. Ratio analysis enables you to spot trends in your business and

SCHEDULE C
(Form 1040)

Department of the Treasury
Internal Revenue Service (T)

Profit or Loss From Business
(Sole Proprietorship)
▶ Partnerships, joint ventures, etc., must file Form 1065.
▶ Attach to Form 1040 or Form 1041. ▶ See Instructions for Schedule C (Form 1040).

OMB No. 1545-0074

1993

Attachment
Sequence No. 09

Name of proprietor	Social security number (SSN)
Susan J. Brown	111 00 1111

A	Principal business or profession, including product or service (see page C-1)	B Enter principal business code
	Catering	(see page C-6) ▶ 3 9 1 3

C	Business name. If no separate business name, leave blank.	D Employer ID number (EIN), if any
	ABC Catering	1 0 1 2 3 4 5 6 7

E Business address (including suite or room no.) ▶ 725 Big Sur Drive
City, town or post office, state, and ZIP code   Franklin, NY 18725

F Accounting method: (1) ☐ Cash (2) ☑ Accrual (3) ☐ Other (specify) ▶ ....

G Method(s) used to value closing inventory: (1) ☑ Cost (2) ☐ Lower of cost or market (3) ☐ Other (attach explanation) (4) ☐ Does not apply (if checked, skip line H)

		Yes	No
H	Was there any change in determining quantities, costs, or valuations between opening and closing inventory? If "Yes," attach explanation		✓
I	Did you "materially participate" in the operation of this business during 1993? If "No," see page C-2 for limit on losses.	✓	
J	If you started or acquired this business during 1993, check here . . . . ▶ ☐		

Part I   Income

1	Gross receipts or sales. Caution: If this income was reported to you on Form W-2 and the "Statutory employee" box on that form was checked, see page C-2 and check here . . . . . . ▶ ☐	1	397,742
2	Returns and allowances	2	1,442
3	Subtract line 2 from line 1	3	396,300
4	Cost of goods sold (from line 40 on page 2)	4	239,349
5	Gross profit. Subtract line 4 from line 3	5	156,951
6	Other income, including Federal and state gasoline or fuel tax credit or refund (see page C-2)	6	
7	Gross income. Add lines 5 and 6 . . . . ▶	7	156,951

Part II   Expenses. Caution: Do not enter expenses for business use of your home on lines 8–27. Instead, see line 30.

8	Advertising	8	3,500	19	Pension and profit-sharing plans	19	
9	Bad debts from sales or services (see page C-3)	9	479	20	Rent or lease (see page C-4):		
				a	Vehicles, machinery, and equipment	20a	
10	Car and truck expenses (see page C-3)	10	3,849	b	Other business property	20b	12,000
11	Commissions and fees	11		21	Repairs and maintenance	21	964
12	Depletion	12		22	Supplies (not included in Part III)	22	1,203
				23	Taxes and licenses	23	5,727
13	Depreciation and section 179 expense deduction (not included in Part III) (see page C-3)	13	2,731	24	Travel, meals, and entertainment:		
				a	Travel	24a	
14	Employee benefit programs (other than on line 19)	14		b	Meals and entertainment		
15	Insurance (other than health)	15	238	c	Enter 20% of line 24b subject to limitations (see page C-4)		
16	Interest:			d	Subtract line 24c from line 24b	24d	
a	Mortgage (paid to banks, etc.)	16a		25	Utilities	25	3,570
b	Other	16b	2,633	26	Wages (less jobs credit)	26	59,050
17	Legal and professional services	17		27	Other expenses (from line 46 on page 2)	27	8,078
18	Office expense	18	216				

28	Total expenses before expenses for business use of home. Add lines 8 through 27 in columns. . . ▶	28	104,238
29	Tentative profit (loss). Subtract line 28 from line 7	29	52,713
30	Expenses for business use of your home. Attach Form 8829	30	
31	Net profit or (loss). Subtract line 30 from line 29.
• If a profit, enter on Form 1040, line 12, and ALSO on Schedule SE, line 2 (statutory employees, see page C-5). Fiduciaries, enter on Form 1041, line 3.
• If a loss, you MUST go on to line 32.	31	52,713
32	If you have a loss, check the box that describes your investment in this activity (see page C-5).
• If you checked 32a, enter the loss on Form 1040, line 12, and ALSO on Schedule SE, line 2 (statutory employees, see page C-5). Fiduciaries, enter on Form 1041, line 3.
• If you checked 32b, you MUST attach Form 6198.	32a ☐ All investment is at risk.
32b ☐ Some investment is not at risk.	

For Paperwork Reduction Act Notice, see Form 1040 instructions.   Cat. No. 11334P   Schedule C (Form 1040) 1993

8-15 A proprietor completes a Schedule C, Profit or Loss From Business, to be filed with the 1040.

Form **1065**

Department of the Treasury
Internal Revenue Service

U.S. Partnership Return of Income

For calendar year 1993, or tax year beginning .... , 1993, and ending .... , 19 ....

▶ **See separate instructions.**

1993

A Principal business activity	
B Principal product or service	Use the IRS label. Other-wise, please print or type.
C Business code number	

10-9876543   DEC93   D71

AbleBaker
334 West Main Street
Orange, MD 20904

one.)

D Employer identification number
10 : 9876543

E Date business started
10-1-79

F Total assets (see Specific Instructions)
$ 45,391

G Check applicable boxes: **(1)** ☐ Initial return   **(2)** ☑ Final return   **(3)** ☐ Change in address   **(4)** ☐ Amended return

H Check accounting method: **(1)** ☐ Cash   **(2)** ☑ Accrual   **(3)** ☐ Other (specify) ▶ ....

I Number of Schedules K-1. Attach one for each person who was a partner at any time during the tax year ▶ 2

Caution: Include only trade or business income and expenses on lines 1a through 22 below. See the instructions for more information.

Income

1a Gross receipts or sales	**1a**	409,465	
b Less returns and allowances	**1b**	3,365	**1c** 406,100
2 Cost of goods sold (Schedule A, line 8)			**2** 267,641
3 Gross profit. Subtract line 2 from line 1c			**3** 138,459
4 Ordinary income (loss) from other partnerships and fiduciaries *(attach schedule)*			**4**
5 Net farm profit (loss) *(attach Schedule F (Form 1040))*			**5**
6 Net gain (loss) from Form 4797, Part II, line 20			**6**
7 Other income (loss) (see instructions) *(attach schedule)*			**7** 559
8 **Total income (loss).** Combine lines 3 through 7			**8** 139,018

Deductions (see instructions for limitations)

9a Salaries and wages (other than to partners)	**9a**	29,350	
b Less employment credits	**9b**	-0-	**9c** 29,350
10 Guaranteed payments to partners			**10** 25,000
11 Repairs and maintenance			**11** 1,125
12 Bad debts			**12** 250
13 Rent			**13** 20,000
14 Taxes and licenses			**14** 3,295
15 Interest			**15** 1,451
16a Depreciation (see instructions)	**16a**	1,174	
b Less depreciation reported on Schedule A and elsewhere on return	**16b**		**16c** 1,174
17 Depletion (Do not deduct oil and gas depletion.)			**17**
18 Retirement plans, etc.			**18**
19 Employee benefit programs			**19**
20 Other deductions *(attach schedule)*			**20** 8,003
21 **Total deductions.** Add the amounts shown in the far right column for lines 9c through 20			**21** 89,648
22 **Ordinary income (loss)** from trade or business activities. Subtract line 21 from line 8			**22** 49,370

Please Sign Here

Under penalties of perjury, I declare that I have examined this return, including accompanying schedules and statements, and to the best of my knowledge and belief, it is true, correct, and complete. Declaration of preparer (other than general partner) is based on all information of which preparer has any knowledge.

▶ *Frank W. Able*   ▶ 3-12-94
Signature of general partner   Date

Paid Preparer's Use Only

Preparer's signature		Date	Check if self-employed ▶ ☐	Preparer's social security no.
Firm's name (or yours if self-employed) and address ▶			E.I. No. ▶ ZIP code ▶	

For Paperwork Reduction Act Notice, see page 1 of separate instructions.   Cat. No. 11390Z   Form **1065** (1993)

8-16 A partner files a Form 1065 on earnings from a partnership.

SCHEDULE K-1 (Form 1065) Department of the Treasury Internal Revenue Service	Partner's Share of Income, Credits, Deductions, etc. ▶ See separate instructions. For calendar year 1993 or tax year beginning ___, 1993, and ending ___, 19 ___	OMB No. 1545-0099 **1993**

Partner's identifying number ▶ *123-00-6789* | Partnership's identifying number ▶ *10 9876543*

Partner's name, address, and ZIP code	Partnership's name, address, and ZIP code
Frank W. Able *10 Green Street* *Orange, MD 20904*	*Able Baker* *334 West Main Street* *Orange, MD 20904*

A This partner is a ☑ general partner ☐ limited partner
  ☐ limited liability company member
B What type of entity is this partner? ▶ *Individual*
C Is this partner a ☑ domestic or a ☐ foreign partner?
D Enter partner's percentage of:

	(i) Before change or termination	(ii) End of year
Profit sharing	%	*50.* %
Loss sharing	%	*50.* %
Ownership of capital	%	*50.* %

E IRS Center where partnership filed return: *Philadelphia*

F Partner's share of liabilities (see instructions):
  Nonrecourse . . . . $ ....
  Qualified nonrecourse financing $ ....
  Other . . . . $ *10,900*
G Tax shelter registration number . ▶ *N/A*
H Check here if this partnership is a publicly traded partnership as defined in section 469(k)(2) . . . . ☐
I Check applicable boxes: (1) ☐ Final K-1 (2) ☐ Amended K-1

J Analysis of partner's capital account:

(a) Capital account at beginning of year	(b) Capital contributed during year	(c) Partner's share of lines 3, 4, and 7, Form 1065, Schedule M-2	(d) Withdrawals and distributions	(e) Capital account at end of year (combine columns (a) through (d))
14,050		*24,460*	(*26,440*)	*12,070*

		(a) Distributive share item		(b) Amount	(c) 1040 filers enter the amount in column (b) on:
Income (Loss)	**1**	Ordinary income (loss) from trade or business activities . . .	**1**	*24,685*	
	2	Net income (loss) from rental real estate activities	**2**		See Partner's Instructions for Schedule K-1 (Form 1065).
	3	Net income (loss) from other rental activities	**3**		
	4	Portfolio income (loss):			
	a	Interest	**4a**		Sch. B, Part I, line 1
	b	Dividends	**4b**	*75*	Sch. B, Part II, line 5
	c	Royalties	**4c**		Sch. E, Part I, line 4
	d	Net short-term capital gain (loss)	**4d**		Sch. D, line 5, col. (f) or (g)
	e	Net long-term capital gain (loss)	**4e**		Sch. D, line 13, col. (f) or (g)
	f	Other portfolio income (loss) (attach schedule)	**4f**		Enter on applicable line of your return
	5	Guaranteed payments to partner	**5**	*20,000*	See Partner's Instructions for Schedule K-1 (Form 1065).
	6	Net gain (loss) under section 1231 (other than due to casualty or theft)	**6**		
	7	Other income (loss) (attach schedule)	**7**		Enter on applicable line of your return
Deductions	**8**	Charitable contributions (see instructions) (attach schedule) . .	**8**	*325*	Sch. A, line 13 or 14
	9	Section 179 expense deduction	**9**		See Partner's Instructions for Schedule K-1 (Form 1065).
	10	Deductions related to portfolio income (attach schedule) . . .	**10**		
	11	Other deductions (attach schedule)	**11**		
Investment Interest	**12a**	Interest expense on investment debts	**12a**		Form 4952, line 1
	b	(1) Investment income included on lines 4a, 4b, 4c, and 4f above	**b(1)**	*75*	See Partner's Instructions for Schedule K-1 (Form 1065).
		(2) Investment expenses included on line 10 above	**b(2)**		
Credits	**13a**	Credit for income tax withheld	**13a**		See Partner's Instructions for Schedule K-1 (Form 1065).
	b	Low-income housing credit:			
		(1) From section 42(j)(5) partnerships for property placed in service before 1990	**b(1)**		
		(2) Other than on line 13b(1) for property placed in service before 1990	**b(2)**		
		(3) From section 42(j)(5) partnerships for property placed in service after 1989	**b(3)**		Form 8586, line 5
		(4) Other than on line 13b(3) for property placed in service after 1989	**b(4)**		
	c	Qualified rehabilitation expenditures related to rental real estate activities (see instructions)	**13c**		
	d	Credits (other than credits shown on lines 13b and 13c) related to rental real estate activities (see instructions)	**13d**		See Partner's Instructions for Schedule K-1 (Form 1065).
	e	Credits related to other rental activities (see instructions) . .	**13e**		
	14	Other credits (see instructions)	**14**		

For Paperwork Reduction Act Notice, see Instructions for Form 1065.   Cat. No. 11394R   Schedule K-1 (Form 1065) 1993

8-17 Schedule K-1 is filed by partners to show how income is distributed within the partnership.

Form **1120**			U.S. Corporation Income Tax Return			OMB No. 1545-0123	

Department of the Treasury
Internal Revenue Service

For calendar year 1993 or tax year beginning ...., 1993, ending ...., 19 ...
▶ Instructions are separate. See page 1 for Paperwork Reduction Act Notice.

1993

A Check if a:	Use IRS label. Otherwise, please print or type.		B Employer identification number
1 Consolidated return (attach Form 851) ☐		10-0395674 DEC93 071 3998	
2 Personal holding co. (attach Sch. PH) ☐		ABC CATERING	**C Date incorporated**
3 Personal service corp. (as defined in Temporary Regs. sec. 1.441-4T— see instructions) ☐		36 DIVISION STREET ANYTOWN, IL 60930	3-1-72
			D Total assets (see Specific Instructions) $879,417

E Check applicable boxes: (1) ☐ Initial return   (2) ☐ Final return   (3) ☐ Change of address

Income

1a	Gross receipts or sales **2,010,000** b Less returns and allowances **20,000** c Bal ▶	1c	1,990,000	
2	Cost of goods sold (Schedule A, line 8)	2	1,520,000	
3	Gross profit. Subtract line 2 from line 1c	3	470,000	
4	Dividends (Schedule C, line 19)	4	10,000	
5	Interest	5	5,500	
6	Gross rents	6		
7	Gross royalties	7		
8	Capital gain net income (attach Schedule D (Form 1120))	8		
9	Net gain or (loss) from Form 4797, Part II, line 20 (attach Form 4797)	9		
10	Other income (see instructions—attach schedule)	10		
11	**Total income.** Add lines 3 through 10 ▶	11	485,500	

Deductions (See instructions for limitations on deductions.)

12	Compensation of officers (Schedule E, line 4)	12	70,000	
13a	Salaries and wages **44,000** b Less employment credits **6,000** c Bal ▶	13c	38,000	
14	Repairs and maintenance	14	800	
15	Bad debts	15	1,600	
16	Rents	16	9,200	
17	Taxes and licenses	17	15,000	
18	Interest	18	27,200	
19	Charitable contributions (see instructions for 10% limitation)	19	23,150	
20	Depreciation (attach Form 4562)	20	17,600	
21	Less depreciation claimed on Schedule A and elsewhere on return	21a	12,400	21b 5,200
22	Depletion	22		
23	Advertising	23	8,700	
24	Pension, profit-sharing, etc., plans	24		
25	Employee benefit programs	25		
26	Other deductions (attach schedule)	26	78,300	
27	**Total deductions.** Add lines 12 through 26 ▶	27	277,150	
28	Taxable income before net operating loss deduction and special deductions. Subtract line 27 from line 11	28	208,350	
29	**Less:** a Net operating loss deduction (see instructions)	29a		
	b Special deductions.(Schedule C, line 20)	29b 8,000	29c	8,000

Tax and Payments

30	**Taxable income.** Subtract line 29c from line 28	30	200,350	
31	Total tax (Schedule J, line 10)	31	55,387	
32	Payments: a 1992 overpayment credited to 1993	32a		
b	1993 estimated tax payments	32b 69,117		
c	Less 1993 refund applied for on Form 4466	32c	d Bal ▶ 32d 69,117	
e	Tax deposited with Form 7004	32e		
f	Credit from regulated investment companies (attach Form 2439)	32f		
g	Credit for Federal tax on fuels (attach Form 4136). See instructions	32g	32h 69,117	
33	Estimated tax penalty (see instructions). Check if Form 2220 is attached ▶ ☐	33		
34	**Tax due.** If line 32h is smaller than the total of lines 31 and 33, enter amount owed	34		
35	**Overpayment.** If line 32h is larger than the total of lines 31 and 33, enter amount overpaid	35	13,730	
36	Enter amount of line 35 you want: **Credited to 1994 estimated tax** ▶ 13,730 Refunded ▶	36		

Please Sign Here

Under penalties of perjury, I declare that I have examined this return, including accompanying schedules and statements, and to the best of my knowledge and belief, it is true, correct, and complete. Declaration of preparer (other than taxpayer) is based on all information of which preparer has any knowledge.

▶ *James O. Barclay*   Signature of officer | 3-7-94 Date | *President* Title

Paid Preparer's Use Only

Preparer's signature ▶		Date	Check if self-employed ☐	Preparer's social security number
Firm's name (or yours if self-employed) and address ▶			E.I. No. ▶	
			ZIP code ▶	

8-18 Form 1120 is the income tax return for corporations.

Form 1120-A — U.S. Corporation Short-Form Income Tax Return

Form 1120-A
Department of the Treasury
Internal Revenue Service

U.S. Corporation Short-Form Income Tax Return
See separate instructions to make sure the corporation qualifies to file Form 1120-A.
For calendar year 1993 or tax year beginning .... , 1993, ending .... , 19.....

OMB No. 1545-0890

1993

A Check this box if the corp. is a personal service corp. (as defined in Temporary Regs. section 1.441-4T—see instructions) ▶ ☐

Use IRS label. Otherwise, please print or type.

10-2134567   DEC93   D92   5995
XYZ CATERING
38 SUPERIOR LANE
FAIR CITY, MD   20715

Employer identification number

Date incorporated
R 7-1-82

Total assets (see Specific Instructions)
$ 65,987

E Check applicable boxes: (1) ☐ Initial return (2) ☐ Change of address
F Check method of accounting: (1) ☐ Cash (2) ☑ Accrual (3) ☐ Other (specify) ▶

	Income					
1a	Gross receipts or sales	248,000	b Less returns and allowances	7,500	c Balance ▶ 1c	240,500
2	Cost of goods sold (see instructions)				2	144,000
3	Gross profit. Subtract line 2 from line 1c				3	96,500
4	Domestic corporation dividends subject to the 70% deduction				4	
5	Interest				5	942
6	Gross rents				6	
7	Gross royalties				7	
8	Capital gain net income (attach Schedule D (Form 1120))				8	
9	Net gain or (loss) from Form 4797, Part II, line 20 (attach Form 4797)				9	
10	Other income (see instructions)				10	
11	Total income. Add lines 3 through 10 ▶				11	97,442

	Deductions (See instructions for limitations on deductions)					
12	Compensation of officers (see instructions)				12	23,000
13a	Salaries and wages	24,320	b Less employment credits		c Bal ▶ 13c	24,320
14	Repairs and maintenance				14	
15	Bad debts				15	
16	Rents				16	6,000
17	Taxes and licenses				17	3,320
18	Interest				18	1,340
19	Charitable contributions (see instructions for 10% limitation)				19	1,820
20	Depreciation (attach Form 4562)		20			
21	Less depreciation claimed elsewhere on return		21a		21b	
22	Other deductions (attach schedule) (Advertising)				22	3,000
23	Total deductions. Add lines 12 through 22 ▶				23	62,800
24	Taxable income before net operating loss deduction and special deductions. Subtract line 23 from line 11				24	34,642
25	Less: a Net operating loss deduction (see instructions)		25a			
	b Special deductions (see instructions)		25b		25c	
26	Taxable income. Subtract line 25c from line 24				26	34,642
27	Total tax (from page 2, Part I, line 7)				27	5,196

	Tax and Payments					
28	Payments:					
a	1992 overpayment credited to 1993	28a				
b	1993 estimated tax payments	28b	6,000			
c	Less 1993 refund applied for on Form 4466	28c (	) Bal ▶ 28d	6,000		
e	Tax deposited with Form 7004	28e				
f	Credit from regulated investment companies (attach Form 2439)	28f				
g	Credit for Federal tax on fuels (attach Form 4136). See instructions	28g				
h	Total payments. Add lines 28d through 28g				28h	6,000
29	Estimated tax penalty (see instructions). Check if Form 2220 is attached ▶ ☐				29	
30	Tax due. If line 28h is smaller than the total of lines 27 and 29, enter amount owed				30	
31	Overpayment. If line 28h is larger than the total of lines 27 and 29, enter amount overpaid				31	804
32	Enter amount of line 31 you want: Credited to 1994 estimated tax ▶ 804 Refunded ▶				32	

Please Sign Here
Under penalties of perjury, I declare that I have examined this return, including accompanying schedules and statements, and to the best of my knowledge and belief, it is true, correct, and complete. Declaration of preparer (other than taxpayer) is based on all information of which preparer has any knowledge.

Signature of officer: George Rose   Date: 2-15-94   Title: President

Paid Preparer's Use Only

Preparer's signature ▶		Date	Check if self-employed ▶ ☐	Preparer's social security number
Firm's name (or yours if self-employed) and address ▶			E.I. No. ▶	
			ZIP code ▶	

For Paperwork Reduction Act Notice, see page 1 of the instructions.   Cat. No. 11456E   Form 1120-A 1993

8-19 Form 1120-A is the short-form income tax return for corporations.

Form 1120S

Department of the Treasury
Internal Revenue Service

U.S. Income Tax Return for an S Corporation

19 ..... **1993**

For cal

A Date of election as an S corporation
12-1-92

B Business code no. (see Specific Instructions)
5008

Use IRS label. Otherwise, please print or type.

10-4487965   DEC93   D74   3070

StratoTech, Inc.
482 Winston Street
Metro City, OH 43705

C Employer Identification number
10 448 7965

D Date incorporated
3-1-75

E Total assets (see Specific Instructions)
$ *771,334*

F Check applicable boxes: (1) ☑ Initial return   (2) ☐ Final return   (3) ☐ Change in address   (4) ☐ Amended return

G Check this box if this S corporation is subject to the consolidated audit procedures of sections 6241 through 6245 (see instructions before checking this box) ► ☐

H Enter number of shareholders in the corporation at end of the tax year . . . . ► *6*

Caution: *Include only trade or business income and expenses on lines 1a through 21. See the instructions for more information.*

Income

1a Gross receipts or sales *1,545,700*	b Less returns and allowances *21,000*	c Bal ►	1c *1,524,700*
2 Cost of goods sold (Schedule A, line 8)			2 *954,700*
3 Gross profit. Subtract line 2 from line 1c			3 *570,000*
4 Net gain (loss) from Form 4797, Part II, line 20 *(attach Form 4797)*			4 *-0-*
5 Other income (loss) (see instructions) *(attach schedule)*		►	5 *-0-*
6 Total income (loss). Combine lines 3 through 5		►	6 *570,000*

Deductions (See instructions for limitations.)

7 Compensation of officers			7 *170,000*
8a Salaries and wages *144,000*	b Less jobs credit *6,000*	c Bal ►	8c *138,000*
9 Repairs and maintenance			9 *800*
10 Bad debts			10 *1,600*
11 Rents			11 *9,200*
12 Taxes and licenses			12 *15,000*
13 Interest			13 *14,200*
14a Depreciation (see instructions)	14a *15,200*		
b Depreciation claimed on Schedule A and elsewhere on return .	14b *-0-*		
c Subtract line 14b from line 14a			14c *15,200*
15 Depletion (Do not deduct oil and gas depletion.)			15 *-0-*
16 Advertising			16 *8,700*
17 Pension, profit-sharing, etc., plans			17 *-0-*
18 Employee benefit programs			18 *-0-*
19 Other deductions (see instructions) *(attach schedule)* . .		►	19 *78,300*
20 Total deductions. Add lines 7 through 19		►	20 *451,000*
21 Ordinary income (loss) from trade or business activities. Subtract line 20 from line 6 . . .			21 *119,000*

Tax and Payments

22 Tax:			
a Excess net passive income tax *(attach schedule)*	22a		
b Tax from Schedule D (Form 1120S)	22b		
c Add lines 22a and 22b (see instructions for additional taxes)			22c *-0-*
23 Payments:			
a 1993 estimated tax payments	23a		
b Tax deposited with Form 7004	23b		
c Credit for Federal tax paid on fuels *(attach Form 4136)* . .	23c		
d Add lines 23a through 23c			23d *-0-*
24 Estimated tax penalty (see instructions). Check if Form 2220 is attached. . . . . ► ☐			24
25 Tax due. If the total of lines 22c and 24 is larger than line 23d, enter amount owed. See instructions for depositary method of payment . . . . ►			25 *-0-*
26 Overpayment. If line 23d is larger than the total of lines 22c and 24, enter amount overpaid ►			26 *-0-*
27 Enter amount of line 26 you want: Credited to 1994 estimated tax ► Refunded ►			27 *-0-*

Under penalties of perjury, I declare that I have examined this return, including accompanying schedules and statements, and to the best of my knowledge and belief, it is true, correct, and complete. Declaration of preparer (other than taxpayer) is based on all information of which preparer has any knowledge.

Please Sign Here

► *John H. Green*   Signature of officer   Date *3-10-94*   ► *President*   Title

Paid Preparer's Use Only

Preparer's signature ►		Date	Check if self-employed ► ☐	Preparer's social security number
Firm's name (or yours if self-employed) and address ►			E.I. No. ►	
			ZIP code ►	

For Paperwork Reduction Act Notice, see page 1 of separate instructions.   Cat. No. 11510H   Form **1120S** (1993)

8-20 Subchapter S corporations file income tax on Form 1120S.

SCHEDULE SE
(Form 1040)

Department of the Treasury
Internal Revenue Service (T)

Self-Employment Tax

▶ See Instructions for Schedule SE (Form 1040).

▶ Attach to Form 1040.

OMB No. 1545-0074

1993

Attachment
Sequence No. **17**

Name of person with **self-employment** income (as shown on Form 1040)	Social security number of person with **self-employment** income ▶
Susan J. Brown	*111 : 00 : 1111*

Who Must File Schedule SE

You must file Schedule SE if:

- Your wages (and tips) subject to social security AND Medicare tax (or railroad retirement tax) were less than $135,000; **AND**
- Your net earnings from self-employment from other than church employee income (line 4 of Short Schedule SE or line 4c of Long Schedule SE) were $400 or more; **OR**
- You had church employee income of $108.28 or more. Income from services you performed as a minister or a member of a religious order is **not** church employee income. See page SE-1.

Note: *Even if you have a loss or a small amount of income from self-employment, it may be to your benefit to file Schedule SE and use either "optional method" in Part II of Long Schedule SE. See page SE-3.*

Exception. If your only self-employment income was from earnings as a minister, member of a religious order, or Christian Science practitioner, **AND** you filed Form 4361 and received IRS approval not to be taxed on those earnings, **DO NOT** file Schedule SE. Instead, write "Exempt–Form 4361" on Form 1040, line 47.

May I Use Short Schedule SE or MUST I Use Long Schedule SE?

Did you receive wages or tips in 1993?

No → Are you a minister, member of a religious order, or Christian Science practitioner who received IRS approval not to be taxed on earnings from these sources, but you owe self-employment tax on other earnings? — **Yes** →

No ↓ Are you using one of the optional methods to figure your net earnings (see page SE-3)? — **Yes** →

No ↓ Did you receive church employee income reported on Form W-2 of $108.28 or more? — **Yes** →

No ↓ **YOU MAY USE SHORT SCHEDULE SE BELOW**

Yes → Was the total of your wages and tips subject to social security or railroad retirement tax plus your net earnings from self-employment more than $57,600? — **Yes** →

No ↓ Was the total of your wages and tips subject to Medicare tax plus your net earnings from self-employment more than $135,000? — **Yes** →

No ↓ Did you receive tips subject to social security or Medicare tax that you did not report to your employer? — **No** / **Yes** →

YOU MUST USE LONG SCHEDULE SE ON THE BACK

Section A—Short Schedule SE. Caution: *Read above to see if you can use Short Schedule SE.*

1	Net farm profit or (loss) from Schedule F, line 36, and farm partnerships, Schedule K-1 (Form 1065), line 15a	**1**
2	Net profit or (loss) from Schedule C, line 31; Schedule C-EZ, line 3; and Schedule K-1 (Form 1065), line 15a (other than farming). Ministers and members of religious orders see page SE-1 for amounts to report on this line. See page SE-2 for other income to report	**2** *52,713*
3	Combine lines 1 and 2	**3** *52,713*
4	**Net earnings from self-employment.** Multiply line 3 by 92.35% (.9235). If less than $400, do not file this schedule; you do not owe self-employment tax . . . . ▶	**4** *48,680*
5	**Self-employment tax.** If the amount on line 4 is:	
	• $57,600 or less, multiply line 4 by 15.3% (.153) and enter the result.	
	• More than $57,600 but less than $135,000, multiply the amount in excess of $57,600 by 2.9% (.029). Then, add $8,812.80 to the result and enter the total.	
	• $135,000 or more, enter $11,057.40.	
	Also enter on **Form 1040, line 47.** (Important: You are allowed a deduction for **one-half** of this amount. Multiply line 5 by 50% (.5) and enter the result on **Form 1040, line 25.)**	**5** *7,448*

For Paperwork Reduction Act Notice, see Form 1040 instructions.   Cat. No. 11358Z   **Schedule SE (Form 1040) 1993**

8-21 As a self-employed person, you pay self-employment tax rather than Social Security tax. Because you are both the employer and the employee, you pay all portions of the tax.

to compare its performance and condition with the average performance of other catering services as well as with your own ratios over several years. Ratio analysis can be the most important early warning indicator for solving business problems while they are still manageable.

Members of some catering associations will share their balance-sheet, income-statement, and management ratios with other members through studies and reports published by the association. It's one more good reason to join one of the local or national catering trade associations. For example, one business association issues a summary of income and expense for members every other year. According to the Internal Revenue Service, the typical food service with assets of under $100,000 will have costs like this:

- Cost of operations, 42%
- Labor and other expenses, 33%
- Owner's compensation, 5%
- Bad debts, 0.5%
- Rent, 7%
- State and local taxes, 4.5%
- Depreciation, 3%
- Advertising, 2%
- Net profit before federal taxes, 3%

These percentages can help you determine whether your catering business is being operated as efficiently as other firms in your industry.

Balance sheet ratio analysis

Important balance sheet ratios measure *liquidity* (a business' ability to pay its bills as they come due) and *leverage* (measuring the business' dependency on creditors for funding). Liquidity ratios indicate the ease of turning assets into cash. They include the current ratio, quick ratio, and working capital.

The current ratio is one of the best-known measurements of financial strength. It is figured like this:

Current ratio = Total current assets ÷ Total current liabilities

The main question this ratio answers is whether your business has enough current assets to meet the payment schedule of its current debts with a margin of safety. A generally acceptable current ratio is 2:1, that is, twice as many current assets as current liabilities.

Let's say that you—or your lender—decide that your current ratio is too low. What can you do about it? Try one or more of the following:

- Pay some debts.
- Combine some of your short-term debts into a long-term debt.
- Convert fixed assets into current assets.
- Leave in earnings or put profits back into the business.
- Increase your current assets with new equity (bring some more cash into the business).

An ideal current ratio for catering services is 1:1.

The *quick ratio* is sometimes called the "acid test" ratio. It is one of the best measurements of liquidity. It is figured like this:

Quick ratio = (Cash + Securities + Receivables) ÷ Total current liabilities

The quick ratio is a much more exacting measure than the current ratio. By excluding inventories (typically small in catering businesses), it concentrates on the really liquid assets with value that's fairly certain. It helps answer the question, "If all sales revenues should disappear, could my business meet its current obligations with the readily convertible funds in hand?"

A ratio of 1:1 is considered satisfactory unless the majority of your quick assets are in accounts receivable and the pattern of collection lags behind the schedule for paying current liabilities.

Working capital, as discussed earlier, is more a measure of cash flow than a ratio. The result of the following calculation must be a positive number:

$$\text{Working capital} = \text{Total current assets} - \text{Total current liabilities}$$

Bankers look at net working capital over time to determine a company's ability to weather financial crises. Bank loans are often tied to minimum working capital requirements.

A general rule about these three liquidity ratios is that the higher they are, the better, especially if your business is relying heavily on creditor money or financed assets. As a related indicator, the ideal ratio of gross revenue to working capital is 10:1.

The *leverage* or *debt/worth ratio* indicates your business's reliance on debt financing (loans) rather than owner's equity. Here's how to figure it:

$$\text{Leverage ratio} = \text{Total liabilities} \div \text{Net worth}$$

Generally, the higher this ratio, the more risky a creditor will consider your loan to be. The ideal ratio is 1:1.

Income statement ratio analysis

Two commonly used ratios derived from your income statement or similar report are the gross margin ratio and the net profit margin ratio.

The *gross margin ratio* is valuable if your catering service stocks and resells its inventory rather than just selling its services. The ratio is the percentage of sales dollars left after subtracting the cost of goods sold from net sales. It measures the percentage of sales dollars remaining to pay the company's overhead. Comparing your business's gross margin ratio to those of other catering services will reveal the relative strengths or weaknesses in your business. Here's how to calculate it:

$$\text{Gross margin} = \text{Gross profit} \div \text{Net sales}$$

Note that gross profit is calculated by deducting the cost of goods sold from net sales.

The *net profit margin ratio* is a percentage of sales dollars left after subtracting the cost of goods sold and all expenses, except income taxes. It provides a good opportunity to compare your company's "return on sales" with the performance of other companies in the industry. It is calculated before income tax because tax rates and tax liabilities vary from company to company for a variety of reasons. The net profit margin ratio is calculated like this:

$$\text{Net profit margin ratio} = \text{Net profit before tax} \div \text{Net sales}$$

According to one source, the net profit for a typical catering business ranges from 3.5 percent of sales for firms doing over $6 million in annual sales to about 4.5 percent for firms with sales under $1 million.

Management ratios

Other important ratios, often referred to as management ratios, are also taken from information on the balance sheet and the income statement. They can help you manage your business better.

If your catering business requires the resale of inventory, the *inventory turnover ratio* reveals how well your inventory is being managed. It is important because the more times inventory can be turned over in a given period, the greater the profit. Here's how to calculate it:

Inventory turnover ratio = Net sales ÷ Average inventory at cost

The *accounts receivable turnover ratio* shows you how well accounts receivable are being collected. If receivables are not collected reliably and on time, you should reconsider your credit policies. If receivables are too slow to convert to cash, your business might not be adequately "liquid." The ratio is figured like this:

Daily credit sales = Net credit sales per year ÷ 365 days

then,

Accounts receivable turnover (in days) = Accounts receivable ÷ Daily credit sales

The *return on investment ratio* is perhaps the most important ratio of all. It is a percentage of the return on the money invested in the business by its owners. In short, this ratio tells you whether or not all the effort you put into the business has been worthwhile. If the ROI is less than the rate of return on a risk-free investment (such as a certificate of deposit or a bank savings account), you should consider selling the business and putting the money in a savings account. Here's how to calculate ROI:

Return on investment = Net profit before taxes ÷ Net worth

A goal for many successful businesses is a 25% ROI, depending on equity, market position, and risk.

Sources of ratios

As mentioned earlier, catering trade associations can often supply you with "typical" current, quick, working capital, leverage, gross margin, net profit margin, inventory turnover, accounts receivable, and return on investment ratios. In addition, check your local or regional library for the following books on ratios:

- *Key Business Ratios*, Dun & Bradstreet, Inc.
- *Almanac of Business and Industrial Financial Ratios* by Leo Troy (Prentice-Hall)
- *Annual Statement Studies* by Robert Morris Associates.

Your accountant or tax preparer might also be able to furnish you with these ratios in your specialty.

SUCCESS ACTION PLAN

Accurate records are vital to your business' success. They can also be a time-eating chore. The key is to develop a record system that complies with legal requirements while giving you the information you need to efficiently manage your catering service. Here's how you can begin today to establish an effective recordkeeping system:

❏ Consider whether you will do your own recordkeeping or have an accountant do some or all of it.

❏ Decide whether a single- or double-entry system is most appropriate for your business, and whether you will use a paper or computer recordkeeping system.

❏ Decide whether your records will be cash or accrual.

❏ Establish a cash disbursements register, a cash receipts journal, sales or income journal, and a general journal for your business. As an option, set up a computerized recordkeeping system using software such as Quicken or Managing Your Money.

❏ Establish a payroll system for your business.

❏ Set up and manage a simple petty cash system.

❏ Make sure you keep equipment and insurance records up-to-date.

❏ Establish your financial report requirements as outlined in this chapter.

❏ Set up a workable system for handling cash in your business.

❏ Decide how you can improve cash flow by developing a cash-flow statement.

❏ Get information on all federal, state, and local taxes you must pay or collect. Make sure you understand your tax obligations and how to comply.

❏ Use your records to plan for a profitable future with financial ratios appropriate to your business.

9
How can I keep costs down?

Costs have a way of increasing faster than income; it's a natural law of business. How can you combat this law? Successful caterers have found a number of ways to keep costs down. First, they carefully analyze their expenses for reducible costs. They especially analyze overhead costs that eat away at profits. They find ways of earning valuable discounts. They use depreciation to reduce taxes. They enhance the flow of cash into their business and reduce bad debts. And they learn to better manage their time.

HOW DO I KNOW WHAT COSTS I CAN CUT?

The object of reducing costs in your catering business is to increase profits. Increasing profits through cost reduction must be based on the concept of an organized, planned program. Unless you maintain adequate records through an efficient and accurate accounting system, there can be no basis for analyzing costs.

Cost reduction is not simply attempting to slash any and all expenses. You must first understand the nature of expenses and how they interrelate with sales, inventories, overhead, gross profits, and net profits. Nor does cost reduction mean only the cutting specific expenses. You also achieve greater profits through more efficient use of your expense dollar. Some ways to achieve greater profits are increasing the average sale per customer, getting a larger return for your promotion and sales dollar, and improving your internal methods and procedures.

For example, one small catering service was quite pleased when, in a single year, sales went from $200 thousand to $1 million. However, at the end of the year, records showed that net profit the prior year, with lower sales, was actually higher than it was with increased sales. Why? Because the expenses of doing business grew at a faster rate than the income.

Analyze your expenses

Your goal should be to pay the right price for prosperity. Determining that price for your operation goes beyond knowing what your expenses are. Reducing expenses to increase profit requires that you obtain the most efficient use of your expense dollars.

Checking job records, you might determine that one of your employees is significantly less efficient than other employees performing the same tasks. You can then reduce expenses by increasing this employee's efficiency through training. By watching this employee perform his or her job, you can determine where the inefficiencies are and help the employee overcome them. If done with consideration for the person, he or she will appreciate it, and so will your profit line.

Understanding the worth of each expense item comes from experience and an analysis of records. Adequate job and expense records tell what's happening. Analyzing them provide facts that can help you set realistic cost and profit goals.

Sometimes, even when you cannot cut an expense item, you can get more from it and thus increase your profits. In analyzing your expenses, you should use percentages rather than actual dollar amounts. For example, if you increase sales and keep the dollar amount of an expense the same, you have decreased that expense as a percentage of income. When you decrease your cost percentage, you increase your percentage of profit.

On the other hand, if your sales volume remains the same, you can increase the percentage of profit by reducing a specific item of expense. Your goal, of course, is to do both: Decrease specific expenses and increase their productive worth at the same time.

Before you can determine whether cutting expenses will increase profits, you need information about your operation. This information can be obtained only through adequate recordkeeping. Your records provide the figures to prepare an income statement, a budget, break-even calculations, and evaluations of your operating ratios compared with those of similar types of business.

If you do much business-related traveling, an expense report (Fig. 9-1) or automobile travel log (Fig. 9-2) helps to keep track of costs. Blank forms that you can use are included in the appendix of this book.

Break-even analysis is useful for making expense comparisons. The break-even is the point at which gross profit equals expenses. In a business year, it is the time at which your sales volume has become sufficient to enable your overall operation to start showing a profit. The two condensed income statement examples in Table 9-1 illustrate the point. In the first statement, the sales volume is at the break-even point and no profit is made. In the second statement for the same business, sales volume is beyond the break-even point and a profit is shown. In the two statements, the percentage factors are the same except for fixed expenses, total expenses, and operating profit.

As shown in the example in Table 9-1, once your sales volume reaches the break-even point, your fixed expenses are covered. Beyond the break-even point, every dollar of sales should earn you an equivalent additional profit percentage. Remember that once sales pass the break-even point, the fixed expenses percentage goes down as the sales volume goes up. Also, the operating profit percentage increases at the same rate as the fixed expenses percentage decreases—provided that variable expenses are kept in line.

Locate reducible expenses

Your income statement provides a summary of expense information and is the focal point in locating expenses that can be cut. For this reason, the information on it should be as current as possible. As a report of what has already been spent, an income statement alerts you to expense items that you should watch in the present

EXPENSE REPORT

Attach Receipts

ABC Catering Service
123 Main Street, Yourtown USA 12345

| EXPENSE ACCOUNT OF: Bill Smith | | | For Period From: June 11,19xx | | To: June 17,19xx | |

DATE	TRAVELLED		MI/KM	TRANS-PORT.	HOTEL	MEALS			PHONE	PARKING	MISC. EXPLAIN BELOW *	DAILY TOTAL
	FROM	TO				BKFST.	LUNCH	DINNER				
SAT												
SUN	Yourtown	Theirtown	229		$58.60		$7.90	$11.40	$4.15			$82.05
MON	Convention				$58.60	$8.19	$9.14	$12.10	$7.55		$46.50	$142.08
TUES	Convention				$58.60		$6.44	$23.12	$3.18			$91.34
WED	Theirtown	Yourtown	229			$4.78	$6.55					$11.33
THURS												
FRI												
		TOTALS	458		175.80	12.97	30.03	46.62	14.88			$326.80

* EXPLANATION

MISC. June 16: Purchased management training tape at convention

ELAPSED BUSINESS MILES/KILOMETERS

Previous Total	
Current Week	458
Total to Date	458

CREDIT CARD BILLS

Bus. MI/KM	458 @ 0.2 =	$91.60
TOTAL EXPENSE		$418.40
Less Advance		$400.00
Balance		$18.40

☐ Claimed   ☐ Refunded

Signature of Claimant:

Approved by:

Date:

9-1 As you travel on business, make sure you keep track of all expenses. Your tax advisor can tell you which are currently deductible.

business period. If you get an income statement only at the end of the year, you should consider having one prepared more often. At the end of each quarter is usually sufficient for smaller firms. Larger catering services should receive the information monthly.

Regardless of the frequency, the best option is to prepare two income statements. One statement reports the sales, expenses, and profit or loss of your operations cumulatively for the current business year to date. The other statement reports on the same items for the last complete month or quarter. Each of the statements should also carry the following information:

- This year's figures and each item as a percentage of sales
- Last year's figures and the percentages
- The difference between last year and this year—over or under
- Budgeted figures and the respective percentages
- The difference between this year and the budgeted figures—over or under
- Average percentages for similar businesses (available from catering associations, the U.S. Department of Labor, and other sources)
- The difference between your annual percentages and the industry ratios—over or under

Monthly Summary Sheet

Date:	July 31, 19xx

123 Main Street, Yourtown USA 12345

AUTOMOBILE INFORMATION

Make of Auto: Ford

Year & Model: 1991 Ford Van

Vehicle I.D. Number: 1234567890-2345678901

Driver of Vehicle: Mack Smith

Odometer **End of month:** 37,283.00

Beginning of month: 35,421.00

Total Miles Driven: 1,862.00

Qualified Business Miles Driven: 1,219.00

Allowable Reimbursement Rate: 1,219.00 x $ 0.28 /mi

Total Expense $ $341.32

YEAR TO DATE - INFORMATION

	BUSINESS MILES	TOTAL MILES
Prior YTD	6,912	10,479
Current Month	1,219	1,862
New YTD	8,131	12,341

DATE: _____

SIGNATURE : _____

APPROVAL : _____

9-2 Use of your automobile for business is a legitimate expense. Keep accurate records of your trips and their purposes.

Table 9-1 Condensed income statements

	A		B	
	Break-even amount	**Percent of sales**	**Profit amount**	**Percent of sales**
Sales	$500,000	100	$600,000	100
Cost of sales	300,000	60	360,000	60
Gross profit	200,000	40	240,000	40
Operating Expenses				
Fixed	150,000	30	150,000	25
Variable	50,000	10	60,000	10
Total	200,000	40	210,000	35
Operating Profit	$ NONE	0	$ 30,000	5

This information allows you to locate expense variations in three ways:
- By comparing this year to last year
- By comparing expenses to your own budgeted figures
- By comparing your percentages to the operating ratios for similar businesses

The important basis for comparison is the percentage figure. It represents a common denominator for all three methods. When you have indicated the percentage variations, you should then study the dollar amounts to determine what kind of corrective action is needed.

Because your cost-cutting comes largely from variable expenses, make sure that they are indicated on your income statements. *Remember that variable expenses* fluctuate with the increase or decrease of sales volume. Some variable expenses are overtime, subcontractors, advertising, sales salaries, commissions, and payroll taxes. *Fixed expenses* stay the same regardless of sales volume. Among them are your salary, salaries for permanent employees, depreciation, rent, and utilities.

When you have located a problem expense area, the next step is to reduce that cost so as to increase your profit. A key to the effectiveness of your cost-cutting action is the worth of the various expenditures. As long as you know the worth of your expenditures, you can profit by making small improvements in expenses. Keep an open eye and an open mind. It is better to do a spot analysis once a month than to wait several months and then do a detailed study.

Take action as soon as possible. You can refine your cost-cutting action as you go along. Be persistent. Results typically come slower than you might like. Keep in mind that only persistent analysis of your records and constant action can help keep expenses from eating up profit.

HOW CAN I REDUCE OVERHEAD?

Business overhead is simply the costs of keeping your doors open. If your catering business is located in your home or a portable commissary, overhead costs are probably small. If you have a separate commissary, an office, and office personnel, your overhead is greater. It's also large if you have high debt to banks, suppliers, and investors.

The key to reducing overhead is to start out small and let your growing business force you into larger quarters. If you build a perception of quality in your customer's mind, you won't have to maintain impressive offices—just a clean and healthy kitchen. You can also reduce overhead by carefully watching the costs of supplies. Printed stationery is an excellent way to promote the quality of your business, but you don't need printed notepads unless the customer will see them. For the price of generic ink pens, you can often get ones that include your business name and telephone number, but don't buy so many that they wind up costing more because you've changed your address or telephone number. Buy supplies in quantity if you can, but don't buy more than you will use in three to six months unless you're certain that they won't become out-of-date.

Personnel costs are where the profits of a small catering business can quickly be eaten away. Don't hire an office manager or secretary until you absolutely must. It's more profitable to do the required filing and office functions yourself after normal business hours or on weekends. Alternatively, you can ask the help of a spouse or older child who can be put on the payroll as soon as your business can afford it.

Some small catering services use temporary help or outside services rather than hiring employees and dealing with all the taxes and records that come with it. They have records kept by a bookkeeping or accounting service, office cleaning done by a janitorial service, telephones answered by an answering service, and correspondence performed by a secretarial service. Catering jobs that the owner can't handle are subcontracted out to other catering services. Smart caterers know that the complexity of regulations and taxation is endlessly multiplied when the first employee is hired—so they avoid hiring anyone until their success requires them to do so.

Long-distance telephone calls can quickly add to your expenses and cut into your profits—especially when they are personal calls made by employees. Many successful catering services use a telephone call record such as the one in Fig. 9-3 to keep track of long-distance calls, then compare the report with the monthly phone bill. Calls not listed on the report are assumed to be personal calls and should be checked out.

HOW CAN I EARN DISCOUNTS?

Every businessperson wants to take advantage of discounts. If your gross profit is five percent of sales, a ten percent discount on materials can dramatically increase overall profits. So how do you ensure that you're getting the best price for the materials and equipment you buy? You ask!

Let's say that you order job materials through a specific materials supplier in your area. Do you know what discounts are available to you for cash in advance? Do you know what discounts can be earned by ordering all of your provisions through a single wholesaler? Or can you receive provisions at no charge because ordering a few more of an item will lower your per-unit charge enough to pay for the extra items? Can you receive higher discounts from the wholesaler's competitor for all provisions you buy from them? How about if you buy only provisions in which they specialize?

ABC Catering Service

123 Main Street, Yourtown USA 12345

| | | | | TIME PERIOD FROM: June 1 | | TO: June 30, 19xx |

Date	Caller	Call To	Company and Location	Code	Phone #	Charges
June 7	Bob	Phoenix	Phoenix Catering Services		555-678-9012	$6.37
June 12	Bob	Des Moines	Hyatt Hotel (for convention reservations)		555-123-4567	$9.25
June 14	Hank	Ottawa	Canadian Caterer's Association		555-987-6543	$11.67
June 23	Bob	Des Moines	Hyatt Hotel		555-123-4567	$8.22
June 28	Larry	Theirtown	Smith Wholesale Grocers		555-444-5555	$3.45

NOTES OR COMMENTS:

9-3 Telephone bills can escalate, especially if the telephone is misused by employees for personal calls. Your best insurance is to keep a telephone call record of long-distance calls.

Here are a few ways to ensure that you're earning the greatest available discounts:
- Pool your purchases with other friendly competitors in order to earn greater quantity discounts.
- Order through a single salesperson, especially one who works on commission, and always ask for "best pricing" and available discounts.
- Ask, "Are there any discounts or price breaks that I should be aware of?"
- If necessary, sign a contract with a single wholesaler to whom you will give all of your business in exchange for an additional three or five percent discount—as long as their standard prices are equal to or less than other wholesalers.
- Ask if members of any local or national catering or food-service associations earn additional discounts.
- Find out if your wholesaler allows a discount for "cash and carry."
- Even if you have a favorite wholesaler, always continue to shop around for better pricing, discounts, and terms.

Keep in mind when searching for discounts, though, that some wholesalers charge a little more because they offer services that are worth the difference in price.

For example, suppose a crosstown wholesaler can give you immediate delivery of hard-to-find ingredients that you often need but can't afford to stock in quantity. The loss of a five-percent discount might be less than the cost of stocking them or having to stop what you're doing to pick them up. Remember, you don't want the lowest price, you want the one that's most profitable to you in the long term. You don't want "cheap," you want quality at the best price.

CAN I REDUCE EXPENSES THROUGH DEPRECIATION?

You can reduce your annual tax obligation for a major expense over more than one tax year by using *depreciation*. Depreciation is simply a method of spreading out the expense of a purchase over time. In order to depreciate, or slowly charge off the cost, the purchase must be of a fixed asset (other than land) that you use in your business, and must meet other requirements. Depreciable assets include those purchased to be used in your business for more than a year: buildings, vehicles, equipment, tools, furniture, and fixtures.

Most small businesses don't have enough fixed assets to worry about depreciation more than once a year, typically as the year's books are being closed. So what do you need to know about depreciation? First, keep in mind that nothing is certain while Congress is in session. Any rules of depreciation current as this book is written might be invalid as Congress and the IRS make changes to tax law. Check with your accountant about setting up a depreciation system for your business based on current rules and guidelines.

At the time this book is written, *MACRS (modified accelerated cost recovery system) depreciation* allows all fixed assets placed in service after 1986 to be assigned a "recovery period" over which the expense can be spread. The length of the recovery period depends on the type of fixed asset. The current schedule allows for 3-, 5-, 7-, 10-, 15-, 20-, 27.5-, and 31.5-year recovery periods. Under the MACRS rules, the entire cost of an item is recovered. There is no "salvage value" at the end of the recovery period as there was with prior depreciation methods.

To make things somewhat more confusing, three methods of depreciation are allowed depending on the type of asset and its recovery period. Shorter recovery periods (10 years or less) use the "200% declining-balance" method, and 15- and 20-year recovery periods use the "150% declining-balance" method. Longer periods are used only for real estate and use the "straight-line" method.

Not to get too deep into depreciation, but to help you understand ways of reducing business costs, here are definitions for these three depreciation methods:

- *The straight-line method* is quite simple. A $10,000 fixed asset with a 5-year recovery rate is depreciated at $2000 (⅕ or 20%) per year.
- *The declining-balance method* accelerates the amount of depreciation taken in the early years and reduces the amount taken in the later years. The 200% declining (or double-declining) balance approach depreciates a $10,000 asset by $4000 (⅖ or 40%) the first year, then $2400 the second year ($10,000 − $4000 = $6000 × 40%), $1440 the third year ($6000 − $2400 = $3600 × 40%), $864 the fourth year ($3600 − $1440 = $2160 × 40%), and $518.40 the final year ($2160 − $864 = $1296 × 40%). In this example, the 150% declining-balance method depreciates 30 percent (150% of ⅕) of the remaining balance per year.

- *Expensing of depreciable assets* can be elected. Depending on your cash flow and tax liability, you might elect to "expense" the purchase of a fixed asset (up to $10,000) during the year in which it is purchased. In the case of a $10,000 purchase, you would write off the entire $10,000 as an expense during the year it was purchased, with no depreciation necessary. The only requirement is that your business must show a profit. That is, the expense must not force your business into a loss for the year. Many small businesses with few fixed assets, which typically show a profit and don't want to mess with depreciation, expense the purchase of fixed assets up to $10,000—or any lower limit they set for themselves. It helps lower their current-year taxes.

As this book is being written, Congress is considering increasing the limit of depreciable assets that can be expensed in a fiscal year. Check with your tax adviser or accountant for the latest information.

HOW CAN I INCREASE CASH FLOW?

Every time you purchase on credit, you add interest costs to your business. If you had more cash, you would be able to save more on interest expense. For this and other reasons, you can reduce your costs by increasing cash flow.

The cash-flow forecast shown in Fig. 9-4 identifies when cash is expected to be received and when it must be spent to pay bills and debts. It shows how much cash will be needed to pay expenses and when it will be needed. It also allows the owner to identify where the necessary cash will come from. For example, it helps you determine whether the funds needed for the purchase of new tools can come from the collection of accounts receivable or must be borrowed.

The cash-flow statement

The cash-flow statement, based on estimates of sales and expenses, indicates when money will be flowing into and out of the business. It enables you to plan for shortfalls in cash resources so short-term working capital loans—or a line of credit—can be arranged in advance. It allows you to schedule purchases and payments so you can borrow as little as possible. Because not all sales are cash sales, you must be able to forecast when accounts receivable will be cash in the bank, as well as when regular and seasonal expenses must be paid.

The cash-flow statement can also be used as a budget, helping you increase your control of the business through comparing actual receipts and payments against forecasted amounts. This comparison helps you identify areas where you can manage your finances even better.

By closely watching the timing of cash receipts and payments, cash on hand, and loan balances, you can readily identify potential shortages in collecting receivables, unrealistic catering credit, or loan repayment schedules. You can also identify surplus cash that can be invested for a greater return on your investment. In addition, the cash-flow statement will help you convince your banker why you need a certain loan and how you expect to pay it off.

A cash-flow statement or budget can be prepared for any period of time, but a one-year budget matching the fiscal year of your business is the most useful. Many successful catering services prepare their cash-flow statements on a monthly basis

		Cash Flow Forecast

ABC Catering Service

123 Main Street, Yourtown USA 12345

DATE: June 30, 19xx

FOR TIME PERIOD: Second Quarter

APPROVED BY:

PREPARED BY:

	Date: April 30		Date: May 30		Date: June 30	
	ESTIMATE	ACTUAL	ESTIMATE	ACTUAL	ESTIMATE	ACTUAL
Opening Balance	11,234.00	10,934.00	11,531.00	11,731.00	12,225.00	12,334.00
Collections From Trade	5,280.00	4,921.00	5,667.00	5,822.00	5,950.00	5,123.00
Misc. Cash Receipts	1,258.00	1,715.00	1,520.00	1,433.00	1,620.00	1,559.00
TOTAL CASH AVAILABLE	**$17,772.00**	**$17,570.00**	**$18,718.00**	**$18,986.00**	**$19,795.00**	**$19,016.00**
DISBURSEMENTS						
Payroll	1,945.00	1,955.00	1,945.00	1,936.00	1,945.00	1,989.00
Trade Payables	2,111.00	1,945.00	2,200.00	2,111.00	2,300.00	1,980.00
Other	786.00	765.00	822.00	754.00	833.00	875.00
Capital Expenses	789.00	899.00	800.00	812.00	820.00	844.00
Income Tax	2,123.00	2,192.00	2,123.00	2,146.00	2,123.00	2,111.00
Bank Loan Payment	567.00	567.00	567.00	567.00	567.00	567.00
TOTAL DISBURSEMENTS	**$8,321.00**	**$8,323.00**	**$8,457.00**	**$8,326.00**	**$8,588.00**	**$8,366.00**
Ending Balance	$9,451.00	$9,247.00	$10,261.00	$10,660.00	$11,207.00	$10,650.00
Less Minimum Balance	$10,000.00	$10,000.00	$10,000.00	$10,000.00	$10,000.00	$10,000.00
CASH AVAILABLE	**($549.00)**	**($753.00)**	**$261.00**	**$660.00**	**$1,207.00**	**$650.00**

FOR INTERNAL USE ONLY

9-4 Make sure you keep accurate forecasts of cash flow to ensure that your catering business doesn't run out of money or needlessly pay interest on borrowed money.

for the next year. Your cash-flow statement should be revised no less than quarterly to reflect actual performance in the previous three months of operations to verify projections. A cash-flow statement includes sales budgets, selling expenses, direct labor expenses, and other vital components. The result of all this budgeting is the cash budget.

Paying bills

Another way of increasing cash flow is by reviewing every invoice you receive to ensure its accuracy before paying it. Some invoices inadvertently include misdirected charges. Others incorporate service charges that are unearned. A few dishonest people make a living by sending bogus invoices to thousands of businesses each month, hoping that a few will pay without reviewing them.

Set aside a time each week when you review all invoices received against your records. As you incur any charges, write them in a notebook or slip a note into a box so each one can be verified. If you have a staff that prepares your bills for payment, you'll need more complete records so that they or you can verify each invoice or statement received against your records.

Some businesses use a rubber stamp for invoices that requires a checkoff for charge created, invoice checked, and invoice paid. Larger firms use formal "purchase orders" that are required for every charge created, other than those that use petty cash.

As an additional benefit, when you call your suppliers with questions regarding their invoices, you will find that many will attempt to be even more accurate on future invoices. They know that you review your invoices. They might be perfectly honest but still make honest mistakes—unless they know that you will probably call them to ask about any questionable charges. They will be especially careful if you tell them that you will set the invoice aside for later payment if you find any questionable charges.

HOW CAN I REDUCE BAD DEBTS?

A primary cause for bad-debt loss is a credit decision based on an inadequate credit investigation. Your credit-checking method should be geared for speed and efficiency to enhance the flow of catering jobs while reducing bad debts.

The depth of your investigation into a customer's credit depends on many factors: the size of the order and the potential for future orders, the length of time the customer has been in business, the status of the present account, whether the account is seasonal, the amount of time until delivery, the relationship of the order to the total credit exposure of the customer, and whether a deposit is required.

Sources for credit information include local credit research services, Dun & Bradstreet Reports, and NACM Credit Interchange and Industry Credit Reports. If you need to extend credit to customers, test the services of credit research and reporting firms listed in your local telephone book's yellow pages. The right vendor for you is the one who can give you both accurate and prompt reports at a reasonable cost.

Accepting credit cards such as Visa, MasterCard, American Express, and Discover can transfer bad-debts problems to others and increase cash flow for your business. However, credit cards involve an initial setup cost and ongoing service charges. Talk with your banker about offering your customers the option of paying for services with their credit card.

If you don't get your money when it is expected, make sure the customer is notified of the payment past due, as shown in Fig. 9-5. This record makes it easier to take future legal action or sell the account to a collection agency, if necessary.

HOW CAN I EFFECTIVELY SCHEDULE MY TIME?

How does scheduling your work have anything to do with reducing the costs of doing business? In many ways. By prioritizing your catering jobs into most-important, less-important, and least-important, you can make sure that you're always doing what's most valuable to your business. A "most-important" job is one with the shortest deadline, the quickest payout, the most important customer, and the greatest opportunity for your catering firm.

Of course, none of your customers are less important than any others. All have equal potential for helping your business succeed, either through jobs they hire you to complete or through other customers they bring you. Nevertheless, the cash cus-

PAYMENT PAST DUE

123 Main Street, Yourtown USA

Dick Jones
777 Mountain Road
Yourtown USA 12345

| DATE: | June 30, 19xx |

Comments: We appreciate your business, Mr. Jones, and want to continue your good credit. To do so, we must have a payment of at least %200 on this account by July 15.

Bill Smith

Statement of Account

Date	Invoice Number	Description	Amount	Total
April 14	92111	Wedding Reception Catering	$947.56	$947.56
April 14	Payment on Account		($200.00)	($200.00)
May 30	Payment on Account		($125.00)	($125.00)
June 25	Payment on Account		($75.00)	($75.00)
Amount Due Now			**Amount Remitted**	
$547.56				

Thank you for your prompt attention

In reviewing your account, we have determined that the above invoices have not been paid and are now past due. We would be most grateful for your prompt attention and remittance. If you have any questions or problems with this billing, please contact us immediately. If your remittance has already been sent out, please disregard this notice.

9-5 Notify past-due accounts of their status as soon as possible.

tomer who must feed 28 wedding guests this weekend has a greater need for your services than does the customer who needs you to quote on a banquet scheduled in four months. Prioritize your work based on the customer's need as well as your own.

Many successful catering services reduce costs through scheduling by balancing the customer's need and their own for each job. They do this balancing by following these guidelines:

- Take care of the jobs first that require preparation or delivery the soonest.
- If possible, group similar jobs, such as baking breads, together during the same time period to reduce preparation and clean-up time.
- As practical, group catering jobs regionally (such as valley jobs, dock jobs, and industrial park jobs) to reduce travel time between jobs.
- Give highest priority to jobs that provide your business with the greatest cash flow (cash, net 15 days, etc.) rather than slow-pay jobs (such as long-term contracts or net 90 days).
- If workable, give high priority to those jobs that improve your relations with customers (such as special favors or offering no-charge consulting).
- Plan for problems. We all know that problems arise—unexpected party guests, food shortages—so assume that they will happen and plan for them

ABC Catering Service

Monthly Activity Planner

123 Main Street, Yourtown USA 12345

PERSON: Bill Smith
FROM: July 1, 19xx
TO: July 31, 19xx

PRIORITIES	Monday	Tuesday	Wednesday	Thursday	Friday	Saturday	Sunday
1 Orient new employee	Introduce Bob	Staff mtg @ 9am	Review resources	Call suppliers	Meet with Bob	Golf with Frank	
	Review job						
2 Increase business with additional proposals	Write proposals		Mrs. Johnson	Fred Smith	Carter Co.		
			@ 3pm	@ 11am	@ 2pm		
3 Train employees on new buffet service		Buffet Service	Buffet Service	Buffet Service		Theirtown	Theirtown
		9-10am	1-2pm	3-4pm			
4 Market new buffet services	Theirtown		Shopper ad mgr	Newspaper ad			
			@ 10am	mgr @ 11am			
5							

9-6 A monthly activity planner helps you manage your greatest asset: your time.

123 Main Street, Yourtown USA 12345

DAY OF THE WEEK:
Tuesday, 17th
MONTH AND YEAR:
June, 19xx

TIME	TO DO	NOTES
8:00- 9:00	Training Session–New Servers	
9:00- 10:00	Pick up groceries for Hastings Banquet	
10:00- 11:00		
11:00- 12:00	Write Franklin Proposal	
12:00- 1:00	Lunch–Kiwanis	
1:00- 2:00	Present Proposal to Franklin Stereo Systems	Will see Larry at Kiwanis meeting
2:00- 3:00	Begin preparation for Harris Dinner Tonight	Don't forget to pick up centerpiece
3:00- 4:00		
4:00- 5:00		
5:00- 6:00	Early dinner with family	
6:00- 7:00	Deliver food for Harris Dinner	
7:00- 8:00	Serve Harris Dinner	
8:00- 9:00		
9:00- 10:00	Clean up Harris Dinner	
10:00- 11:00		
11:00- 12:00		

9-7 Depending on how you work, a daily planner can save you time.

as part of every job. Make sure that you have sufficient food items as well as a quick source for more, that plans have been checked in advance for accuracy, and that backups are available for your most critical equipment.

A monthly planner such as the one in Fig. 9-6 can help with long-term planning and help you develop your daily planner (Fig. 9-7) or list of things to do.

SUCCESS ACTION PLAN

Whether your catering business is one month old or ten years old, the ideas in this chapter can help you reduce business costs and, thus, increase profits. Here are some things you can do right now to put these ideas into action:

❏ Gather your latest records and analyze your expenses. If your business has a history, compare the percentage of these expenses to percentages of prior months and years. Are there any patterns or movements that point to reducible expenses?

❏ If you haven't done so already, calculate your catering business' break-even point.

❏ Review your fixed costs, or overhead, for expenses that can be reduced. Remember, every investment (reflected in an expense) should earn a profit. Is your telephone profitable? How about your rent? If not, reduce these expenses—or increase their profitability.

❏ Search for discounts. Talk with suppliers, lease holders, or others to whom you pay money. Ask them about available discounts and prepayment options. Some will offer a two-percent discount or more if you pay cash rather than wait for the bill. That's 24 percent a year!

❏ Determine whether you can take advantage of depreciation laws to reduce your tax obligation. Or is your catering service better served by expensing depreciable assets?

❏ Develop a cash-flow statement for your catering service on a regular basis and use it as a barometer for the success of your business.

❏ Review the options for reducing bad debts in your business and select ones that fit your situation.

❏ Use the worksheets and forms in this chapter to better manage your time. Copies are included in the appendix of this book.

10

How can
I reduce risk?

You've learned how to increase sales and reduce expenses for your catering business, but even as your business grows and profits, you can still lose money. An otherwise profitable business can quickly be thrown into many situations in which the future of the business is in jeopardy, including the following:

- An employee is injured on the job and sues you.
- An employee runs off with money stolen from your business.
- A fire or flood wipes out your office, tools, machinery, and important records.
- A partner in your business files bankruptcy and the courts attach your business.
- The local economy goes sour and you can't find any profitable catering jobs for six months or more.
- A business for which you cater files bankruptcy and you don't get paid what's owed to you.
- A business partner is involved in a divorce settlement and business assets must be sold to meet a court order.
- The IRS comes after you for a large tax bill they think you owe them and takes over your bank account until everything is resolved.

The list goes on. What can you do about these calamities? First, make sure you understand the risks involved in your business. Second, take precautions to ensure that the risks are minimal. They will never go away, but, through smart risk management, you can minimize them and prepare for the worst.

WHAT RISKS DOES MY CATERING BUSINESS FACE?

The best time to minimize the risk of business disasters is before they happen. And the first step to minimizing risk is identifying the risks that can occur. Business risks that catering services typically face include the following:

- Acts of nature (fire, flood)
- Acts of people (theft, vandalism, vehicle accidents)
- Personal injury (of employee or user)
- Legal problems (liens, unfair catering practices, torts)
- Financial (loss of income, funding, or assets)
- Taxation (judgments, tax liens)
- Management (loss of partner's or owner's capacity to manage)

Of course, every method of reducing risk—attorneys, bonds, insurance, binding agreements, security systems, fire alarms, and so on—cost money. So when is it more cost-effective to accept the risk rather than pay for products or services that eliminate the risk? It's a simple question with a simple answer: It all depends.

Actually, the best time to minimize risk in your business is right now. The real answer lies in balancing the cost of loss against the cost of security. For example, if your catering vehicle is an older van, collision insurance that costs an extra $300 a year is more expensive than absorbing the cost of body damage to the van from minor accidents.

In this chapter, you learn how to minimize risks to your business from the sources just mentioned. You do so with the help of others: insurance agents, attorneys, and other professionals.

HOW CAN I MINIMIZE RISK?

You can reduce the risks involved in owning and operating your catering business by using the knowledge and skills of others. You can select an insurance agent, an attorney, and an accountant whom you trust and let them guide you toward cost-effectively minimizing risks without spending too much time and money doing so.

Insurance agent

A good insurance agent is as valuable to your success as any other professional consultant. A good insurance agent can both ensure that you're exposure to risk and keep your insurance costs at a minimum.

As when selecting other advisers, ask around among other catering services and professionals for recommendations of a good insurance agent. If possible, search for one who primarily serves the business community rather than the family or individuals. They will better understand your problems and concerns.

Ask prospective agents for some advice on a specific problem. Don't tell them what you think the solution is. Their responses can help you determine which are the best at cost-effective problem-solving.

You can do certain specific things to reduce insurance costs. For example, you can save money over the long term by increasing your vehicles' deductible. In fact, the best way to save on all insurance costs—auto, fire, theft, health—is to increase your deductible to an amount that's manageable. Ask yourself whether paying the higher deductible annually would significantly change your premiums. That is, if your deductible was increased from $50 to $200, would you save the $150 in annual premiums?

Finding an attorney

To find an attorney who is familiar with your size and type of business, ask for a referral from a business colleague, your accountant, your banker, your local chamber of commerce, or other catering or food services in your area. Some local bar associations run an attorney referral and information service; check your local telephone book's yellow pages under "Attorneys' Referral & Information Services." Some referral services give you only names and telephone numbers; others actually give information on experience and fees to help you match your needs to the attorney's background and charges.

As discussed earlier, an attorney can help you decide which is the most advantageous business structure to reduce risks. He or she can also help you with zoning, permit, or licensing problems, unpaid bills, contracts and agreements, trademarks, and some tax problems.

Because a lawsuit, claim, or other legal action against your business is always possible, it is wise to have an attorney who is already familiar with your business lined up before a crisis arises. An attorney with experience serving catering businesses can also advise you on federal, state, and local laws, programs, and agencies to help you through loans, grants, procurement set-asides, and tax problems. Your attorney might be able to advise you about unexpected legal opportunities and pitfalls that might affect your business.

In choosing an attorney, experience and fee should be related. One attorney might charge an hourly rate that, at first glance, looks cheaper than another attorney's. However, because of a lack of experience in solving legal problems for food-service businesses, the less-expensive attorney might actually cost more to solve the same problem. If you feel overwhelmed with the selection process, take a trusted friend to your initial meeting with the attorney to help you keep on track as you interview the attorney about services and fees.

If you retain a law firm, be sure you understand who will work on your projects and who will supervise the work. If "junior attorneys" handle your work, the fees should be lower. That's okay as long as you know that an experienced attorney will review and be ultimately responsible for the work done.

Let your attorney know that you expect to be informed of all developments and consulted before any decisions are made on your behalf. You will also want to receive copies of all documents, letters, and memos written and received regarding your project. If this isn't practical, you should at least have the opportunity to read such correspondence at your attorney's office.

Whenever giving your attorney a project—defending a lawsuit, reviewing a contract, consulting on tax matters—ask him or her to estimate the costs and time required to adequately complete the project. You might want to place a periodic ceiling on fees, after which your attorney needs to call you before proceeding with work that will add to your bill. Finally, if you hire an attorney on retainer, make sure that you have a written agreement between you that clearly describes just what you and the attorney expect from each other.

Saving attorney fees

Everybody loves to save money! Especially when the money saved is significant. Here are some ideas on how you can save money as you work with your attorney:

- Talk about fees up front, making sure that you're clear on what will be charged and when. The fees could be established by the hour, by the job (flat fee), or on a contingency fee (ranging from 25 to 50 percent). In most cases, out-of-pocket expenses such as long-distance telephone calls, filing fees, and transcripts are paid by the client unless agreed upon in advance.
- Reduce your lawyer's research charges by bringing all pertinent information and documents with you for your meeting.

- If you expect to use a specific number of hours of your attorney's time during the coming year, try to contract for that minimum at a lower rate.
- Negotiate each transaction separately. Some legal matters can be handled with just a few hours of your attorney's time, while others require extensive time and research. Obviously, the first type should be negotiated as an hourly or flat fee, while the large job should be negotiated as a flat fee or a contingency project. Make sure you get a monthly itemized bill.
- If possible, settle a case rather than go through litigation. Even litigation will typically not get you "every last dollar"; it will be negotiated. Besides, the legal system might take years to resolve your dispute.
- Treat your attorney as a professional counselor who works for you. If your budget is tight, inform him or her. If you're not clear on why you should take your lawyer's advice, ask. In other words, keep the lines of communication open.

HOW CAN I MANAGE RISK?

Risk management consists of identifying and analyzing the things that might cause loss, and choosing the best way to deal with each of these possibilities. You've worked hard to build your catering business, and you've poured a lot of time, effort, and money into building it up. Spend some time looking at the best ways of reducing risk.

The best way to reduce risk in your growing catering business is to continue the learning process. You've been a student for all of the years you've worked in food service, learning how to do your job better, faster, and more efficiently. Now you're starting your own business and have learned about dozens of new topics. Here are three things you can do to continue the learning process, increase your knowledge, reduce risks, and make your business grow:

- Work closely and creatively with your professional advisers—your attorney, your accountant, and your insurance agent. As you periodically review your business records, you will see ways that you can do things better the next time. You will begin to develop your skills in planning and managing your business.
- Continue to learn about all aspects of business operations, constantly acquiring new ideas and new skills. Sign up for intermediate and advanced business courses at your local community college or for seminars sponsored by regional business development centers. Also, continue to learn more about the catering trade through association books, tapes, seminars, courses, and conventions.
- Get to know other business owners with similar needs or problems. Your business has little in common with retailers, but you have much in common with other food-service businesses. Talking with others can help you avoid repeating mistakes they have made; you will benefit from their experiences and they from yours. As mentioned earlier in this book, local and national associations offer membership, social events, networking opportunities, newsletters, and seminars for catering services. They also provide a way to learn about services you might need, such as lawyers and accountants.

Exposures to loss

Identifying exposures to loss is a vital step to reducing your risks. Until you know the scope of all possible losses, you won't be able to develop a realistic, cost-effective strategy for dealing with them. The last thing you want to do is come up with a superficial "Band-Aid" approach that might cause more problems than it solves.

It's not easy to recognize the hundreds of hazards or perils that can lead to an unexpected loss. Unless you've experienced a fire, for example, you might not realize how extensive fire loss can be. Damage to your building and commissary are obvious exposures, but related losses include damage or destruction caused by smoke and water, damage to employees' personal property, damage to customers' or suppliers' property, the loss of income during the time it takes to get the business back to normal, and the loss to competitors of customers who might not return when you reopen for business.

What's the solution? Begin the process of identifying exposures by taking a close look at each of your business operations, and asking yourself two important questions:

- What could cause a loss to my business operation?
- How serious is that loss to the continuation of my business?

Many business owners use a "risk analysis" questionnaire or survey as a checklist. These are available from insurance agents, most of whom will provide the expertise to help you with your analysis. With their knowledge and experience, you're less likely to overlook any exposures.

Most risk-analysis questionnaires and surveys look at potential for property losses, business-interruption losses, liability losses, key person losses, and automobile losses.

Property losses

Property losses stem from physical damage to property, loss of use of property, or criminal activity. Property damage can be caused by many common perils; fire, windstorm, lightning, and vandalism are typically the first that come to mind. It's a rare business that doesn't buy insurance to protect against these, but to cope effectively with the possibility of physical damage to property, you should consider more than just damage to or destruction of a building.

Contents might be even more susceptible to loss than property is. Your catering business could lose valuable accounting records, making it difficult to bill customers or to collect from customers who owe money. Vital food-preparation equipment might become inoperable because of fire and, if replacements can't be found and installed immediately, your business might be forced into a temporary shutdown. Unless you continue to pay them, a shutdown might force experienced employees to find work elsewhere—maybe with a competitor.

Your business could lose the use of property without suffering any physical damage. For example, a government agency can close your landlord's properties down as part of a lawsuit, for delinquent taxes, or other causes. Or, if your catering business is all in your work vehicle, a mechanical malfunction can virtually place your business in the repair shop.

Small businesses are very susceptible to crimes committed by others. Burglary and robbery are obvious perils, but don't overlook possible exposure to "white collar" crime: employee theft, embezzlement, or forgery. An experienced insurance agent can help you define the types of risks your catering business faces in your locality.

Business-interruption losses

You've already seen how a direct loss from a fire can temporarily shut down your business. Although property insurance provides money for repairing or rebuilding physical damage that's a direct result from a fire, most property policies don't cover indirect losses such as the income lost while your business is interrupted for repairs.

A special kind of insurance called *business-interruption insurance* covers indirect losses that occur when a direct loss forces a temporary interruption of business. This kind of policy would help, for example, in the case of an industrial caterer whose sole truck was stolen during the height of her busiest season. She lost nearly a month's income because it wasn't available to her.

Not only is income reduced or cut off completely during such interruptions, but many business expenses continue, such as taxes, loan payments, salaries to key employees, interest, depreciation, and utilities. Without income to pay for these expenses, your business is forced to dip into reserves.

In addition, business interruption often triggers extra expenses. For example, you might have to authorize overtime to shorten the interruption period, or rent a commissary or equipment to perform your services. These extra expenses put an additional strain on finances at a time when little, if any, income is being produced.

Business-interruption insurance reimburses policyholders for the difference between normal income and the reduced income earned during the enforced shutdown period.

Key persons losses

What would happen to your business if an accident or illness made it impossible for you to work? What if one of your partners or your renowned chef were to die suddenly? Most of us would rather not think about such "what ifs." Nevertheless, you must prepare your business for survival, long before a key person dies or is disabled. Unfortunately, it is a step that's often overlooked.

Here are some of the questions you should consider regarding the loss of key people to your catering business:
- How will the business survive if you become seriously ill or disabled?
- What will your source of income be?
- Who would take over your job so the business can continue?
- What if your heir is not qualified or is a minor?
- What will happen to the business if you die?
- If a will is not in place before your death, what happens to the business?
- If your life savings has been invested in the business, will the surviving family receive any cash to help them continue?
- What will the surviving family's source of income be while the future of the business is being decided?

- If the business is to be sold, where will working capital come from for the transition period?
- How is the fair market value of the business to be determined?
- Would the business's fair market value be apt to change because of the loss of a key person?
- If the business forms the bulk of the estate, what are the income and inheritance tax implications for the surviving spouse and heirs?
- Is there some strategy you could pursue now that could minimize that tax liability?
- If the business is a partnership, is a binding agreement in place that will allow a continuation of the business?
- What are the duties of the surviving partner regarding winding up the affairs of the partnership?
- Will the surviving partner be personally liable for losses that the business's assets are insufficient to cover?
- If your business is a corporation, how does the death or disability of a major stockholder affect your business?

Once again, planning is essential. Your attorney, accountant, and insurance agent can develop a legally binding strategy to reduce losses and to prevent outsiders from taking over your business during a catastrophe.

Loss control

You can keep your losses to a minimum in a number of ways. They include the following strategies:
- Preventing or limiting exposure to loss
- Risk retention
- Transferring risk
- Insurance

One principle of loss prevention and control is the same in business as it is in your personal life: Avoid activities that are too financially hazardous.

You might decide that your catering firm can afford to absorb some losses, either because the frequency and probability of the loss is low or because the dollar value of the loss is manageable. For example, suppose your catering business owns several older vehicles, and their drivers have excellent safety records. You might decide to drop the collision insurance on these vehicles, but retain it on newer vehicles.

HOW MUCH INSURANCE DO I NEED?

Another method of managing exposure to loss is by transferring the risk. The most common method of transferring risk is purchasing insurance. By insuring your business and equipment, you have transferred much of the risk of loss to the insurance company. You pay a relatively small amount in premium rather than run the risk of a much larger financial loss. That's why it's so important to select a reputable and professional insurance agent for your catering business, as discussed earlier.

Of course, you can be overinsured or pay more than is necessary for the amount of risk that you transfer. In business insurance, only you can decide which exposures you absolutely must insure against. Some decisions, however, are already made for you: those required by law and those required by others as a part of doing business with them. Workers' compensation insurance is an example of insurance that's required by law. Your bank probably won't lend you money for equipment, real estate, or other assets unless you insure them against loss.

Today, very few businesses—especially catering services—have sufficient financial reserves to protect themselves against the hundreds of property and liability exposures that they face. What those exposures are, what their dollar value is, and how much is enough, are difficult questions. That's why, as you build a team of business professionals to help you effectively manage your business, you should hire an insurance professional.

The insurance agent is the insurance industry's primary client representative. Typically, the independent agent is a small-business owner and manager. By using this distribution system, insurance companies are represented by agents who receive a commission for selling the companies' products and services. An independent agent may represent more than one insurance company.

The professional insurance agent has been trained in risk analysis. He or she is familiar with the insurance coverages and financial strategies available in your state and the regulations that govern them. With this experience, the agent can point out exposures that you might otherwise overlook and help you develop possible solutions. You make the final decisions, but your agent can suggest options from a vast menu of risk-management strategies. He or she has the technical knowledge to amend a basic policy by adding special coverages and endorsements. The resulting policy will be custom-tailored to your business' unique protection needs.

Insurance companies provide a number of related services to policyholders. As a small businessperson who wants to reduce both risk and costs, you should consider these services. For example, liability insurance coverages, particularly for property damage and bodily injury, usually include legal defense at no additional charge when the policyholder is named a party to the lawsuit that involves a claim covered by the policy. Litigation is costly, whether the claimant's suit is valid or frivolous. The legal-defense provision greatly reduces these costs to you.

Similarly, insurance companies that write a lot of workers' compensation insurance often have extensive rehabilitation services available. Generally, these services help injured workers return to useful employment and, in some cases, even help train the worker for a different job.

Essential insurance coverage

Four kinds of insurance are essential to your business: fire, liability, automobile, and workers' compensation insurance. Selecting from among the dozens of available policies and options can be somewhat confusing to most businesspeople. Use the following information to help guide you in making the right decisions for the right reasons:

- When buying fire insurance coverage, remember that you can add other perils—such as windstorm, hail, smoke, explosion, vandalism, and malicious mischief—to your basic policy at a relatively small additional fee.
- If you need comprehensive coverage, your best buy might be one of the all-risk contracts—such as the $1 million umbrella policy—that offer the broadest available protection for the money.

- Remember that the insurance company might compensate your losses by paying actual cash value of the property at the time of the loss, or it might repair or replace the property with material of like kind and quality, or take all the property at the agreed or appraised value and reimburse you for your loss.
- You can insure property that you don't own, such as a job site, for potential loss of assets at that site.
- You cannot assign an insurance policy along with property you sell unless you have the permission of the insurance company.
- Even if you have several policies on your property, you can still collect only the amount of your actual cash loss. All the insurers share the payment proportionately.
- Special protection other than the standard fire insurance policy is needed to cover the loss by fire of accounts, bills, currency, deeds, evidence of debt, and securities.
- After a loss, you must use all reasonable means to protect the property from further loss or run the risk of having your coverage canceled.
- In most cases, to recover your loss you must furnish within 60 days a complete inventory of the damaged, destroyed, and undamaged property showing in detail quantities, costs, actual cash value, and amount of loss claimed.
- If you and your insurer disagree on the amount of the loss, the question may be resolved through special appraisal procedures provided for in the fire insurance policy.
- You may cancel your policy without notice at any time and get part of the premium returned. The insurance company also may cancel at any time within a specified period, usually five days, with a written notice to you.
- You can get a substantial reduction in premiums by accepting a coinsurance clause in your fire insurance policy. A coinsurance clause states that you must carry insurance equal to 80 or 90 percent of the value of the insured property. If you carry less than this, you cannot collect the full amount of your loss, even if the loss is small. What percent of your loss you can collect depends on what percent of the full value of the property you have insured it for.
- If your loss is caused by someone else's negligence, the insurer has the right to sue this negligent third party for the amount it has paid you under the policy. This right is known as the insurer's right to *subrogation*. However, the insurer will usually waive this right upon request. For example, if you have leased your insured building to someone and have waived your right to recover from the tenant for any insured damages to your property, you should have your agent request the insurer waive the subrogation clause in the fire policy on your leased building.

Here are some important considerations when purchasing liability insurance:

- You might be legally liable for damages even in cases where you used "reasonable care."
- Under certain conditions, your business might be subject to damage claims even from trespassers.
- Most liability policies require you to notify the insurer immediately after an incident on your property that might cause a future claim. It holds true no matter how unimportant the incident might seem at the time it happens.

- Even if the suit against you is false or fraudulent, the liability insurer pays court costs, legal fees, and interest on judgments in addition to the liability judgments themselves.
- You can be liable for the acts of others under contracts you have signed with them, such as independent contractors. This liability is insurable.

One of the most common types of risk transference is purchasing automobile or vehicle insurance. Here are some pointers on making an informed decision about car insurance:

- When an employee or a subcontractor uses a car on your behalf, you can be legally liable even though you don't own the car or truck.
- Five or more automobiles, trucks, or motorcycles under one ownership and operated as a fleet for business purposes can generally be insured under a low-cost fleet policy against both material damage to your vehicles and liability to others for property damage or personal injury.
- You can often get deductibles of almost any amount—$250, $500, $1000— thereby reducing your premiums.
- Automobile medical-payments insurance pays for medical claims, including your own, arising from vehicular accidents regardless of the question of negligence.
- In most states, you must carry liability insurance or be prepared to provide a surety bond or other proof of financial responsibility when you're involved in an accident.
- You can purchase uninsured motorist protection to cover your own bodily injury claims from someone who has no insurance.
- Personal property stored in a car or truck and not attached to it (such as food-service supplies in your catering truck) is not covered under an automobile policy.

Workers' compensation insurance is required in most states if you have employees. You can reduce the cost of this mandatory insurance by knowing the following:

- Federal laws require that an employer provide employees a safe place to work, hire competent fellow employees, provide safe tools, and warn employees of existing danger. Whether or not you provide these things, you are liable for damage suits brought by an employee and possible fines or prosecution.
- State law determines the level or type of benefits payable under workers' compensation insurance policies.
- Not all employees are covered by workers' compensation insurance laws. The exceptions are determined by state law and therefore vary from state to state.
- You can save money on workers' compensation insurance by seeing that your employees are properly classified. Rates for workers' compensation insurance vary from 0.1 percent of the payroll for "safe" occupations to about 25 percent or more of the payroll for very hazardous occupations.
- Most employers can reduce their workers' compensation insurance premium cost by reducing their accident rates below the average. To do so, they use safety and loss-prevention measures established by the individual state.

Desirable insurance coverage

Some types of insurance coverage, while not absolutely essential, add greatly to the security of your business. These coverages include business-interruption insurance and crime insurance. Whether these coverages are vital to your business depends largely on how and where your business operates. A small firm with two partners who have identical skills might not require business-interruption insurance. A multimillion dollar "one-woman-band," on the other hand, might need extensive insurance against business interruption. The same applies to crime insurance: Some business locations require it, while others might not.

As mentioned earlier in this chapter, business-interruption insurance covers fixed expenses (such as salaries to key employees, taxes, interest, mortgage, and utilities) that will continue if a disaster shuts down your business, as well as reimbursing the profits you will lose. The business-interruption policy provides payments for amounts you spend to hasten the reopening of your business after a fire or other insured peril. You can also get coverage for the extra expenses you suffer if an insured peril seriously disrupts your business rather than closes it down.

Under *contingent business-interruption insurance*, you can also collect if fire or other peril closes down the business of a supplier or customer, and it interrupts your business. Some business-interruption policies even indemnify you if your operations are suspended because of failure or interruption of the supply of power by a public utility company.

Crime insurance is a cost of doing business nearly everywhere in the country. Unfortunately, in some areas it is a major expense. Here are some facts to consider when purchasing crime insurance for your catering business:

- Burglary insurance excludes such property as accounts receivable files. If you lose them to a burglary, you will have problems collecting from your accounts or from your insurance company.
- With many policies, coverage is granted under burglary insurance only if there are visible marks of the burglar's forced entry. If a burglar somehow found your keys, you might not be protected.
- Burglary insurance can be written to cover damage incurred in the course of a burglary, in addition to valuables stolen.
- *Burglary insurance* covers theft on your property. *Robbery insurance* protects you from loss of property, money, and other assets by force, trickery, or threat of violence on or off your premises.

Consider purchasing a comprehensive crime policy written specifically for small business owners. In addition to burglary and robbery, it covers other types of loss by theft; destruction and disappearance of money and securities; and theft by employees.

If your business is located in a high-risk area and cannot get insurance through normal channels without paying excessive rates, you might be able to get help through the federal crime insurance plan. Your insurance agent or state insurance commissioner can tell you where to get information about these plans.

SUCCESS ACTION PLAN

Risk is a part of life, and of business. You cannot eliminate all risk in your catering business, but you can manage it. Here are a few things you can do to reduce the risks in your catering business:

❏ Make a list of the risks that your business faces and rate the possibility of occurrence within the five years as low, moderate, or high.

❏ For each of the identified risks, identify the results of the loss (such as loss of six months' income, loss of all assets, or loss of business).

❏ For each identified risk, list actions you can take now to reduce the risk to an acceptable level (install a security system, establish a cash-handling system, purchase insurance, move the business to a lower-crime area, and so on).

❏ Find an insurance agent who has the knowledge and resources to help you reduce your risk exposure to an acceptable level.

❏ Periodically review your exposure to risk and what it costs you to reduce it. You might decide to increase or reduce risk exposure to enhance long-term profits.

11
How do I solve business problems?

As the owner of your own catering business, you deal with problems on a daily basis. Learning how to effectively solve problems can dramatically affect the growth and success of your business. Most business owners solve problems by intuition. By learning the "skill" of problem-solving—just as you learned the skill of food preparation—you become more comfortable with solving problems and reduce the inherent stress of your job. This is true for the new caterer as well as those who have operated their businesses for many years but feel that "something" is standing in the way of their business's growth.

What is a problem? A problem is a situation that presents difficulty to your desire to move ahead. Here are a few examples:

- A food warmer doesn't function as it should.
- A vital ingredient to your main dish is unavailable.
- An employee is undermining your authority.
- New-business income is down.
- A customer is complaining about poor service and threatens to criticize your business to influential friends.
- You're two payments behind on your lease and they've threatened to sue.

Where do problems come from? Problems arise from every facet of human and mechanical functions, as well as from nature. We cause some problems ourselves, through decisions such as hiring an untrainable employee. Other problems are caused by forces beyond our control, such as a primary provisioner going out of business without notice. Problems are a natural, everyday occurrence of life. However, if mismanaged, they cause tension and frustration that only compounds the problem. You must learn how to deal with the problems in your catering business in a logical, rational fashion.

STEPS TO SOLVING ANY PROBLEM

The solutions to some problems, such as how to plan next week's work schedule, are typically simple and require only a few moments of contemplation and planning. Other problems, such as how to increase income by $100,000 in the next six months, are more critical to your operation and require more time and effort. In fact, for critical problems, you might want to set aside a full day for analyzing the problem and finding the best solutions.

Before a problem can be solved, you must first recognize that a problem exists. Here is where your approach to problem-solving is crucial. You should not allow the problem to intimidate you. Don't take it personally. Approach it rationally and remind yourself that every problem is solvable.

Fear of failure can block your ability to think clearly. You can overcome this natural fear if you follow these guidelines:

- Follow a workable procedure for finding solutions.
- Accept the fact that you can't foresee everything.
- Assume that the solution you select is your best option at the time.
- Accept the possibility that things might change and your solution might fail.

Once you recognize that a problem exists, your next step is to identify or define the problem itself. You can do so by asking yourself questions like the following:

- What exactly happened?
- What started the problem?
- Did something occur that wasn't supposed to?
- Did something break that was suppose to operate?
- Were there unexpected results?

Then, ask questions like these that help you identify the nature of the problem:

- Is this a person, equipment, or operational problem?
- What product or service does it involve?
- Is the problem tangible or intangible?
- Is the problem internal or external to the firm?

Next, evaluate the significance of the problem. To determine how important this problem is to the scheme of things, ask yourself:

- Is this problem disrupting operations?
- Is this problem hampering sales?
- Is this problem causing conflict among people?
- Is this problem affecting employees and their productivity?
- Is this problem affecting business goals and, if so, which ones?
- Is this problem affecting customers, suppliers, subcontractors, or any other external people?

Realize that some problems are "100-year floods" that don't occur often enough to warrant extensive attention. To determine the frequency of a problem, ask these questions:

- Is it a problem that occurred in the past and in which the main concern is to make certain it doesn't occur again?
- Is it a problem that currently exists and in which the main concern is to clear up the situation?
- Is it a problem that might occur in the future and in which the basic concern is planning and taking action before the problem arises?

The answers to all of these questions will help you focus on the true problem. You can't effectively research the causes of a problem until you have a clear definition of what the problem is. Sometimes, managers spend many hours on what they perceive as the problem only to learn, after seeking the causes, that something else was really the problem.

To appropriately identify the problem and its causes, you might need to do some research. If the solution is worthwhile to the goals of your business, be willing to invest the required time and resources. If it isn't, don't.

Before beginning your search for a defined problem, consider what has previously been done by your firm (if anything) regarding this problem, what other firms have done, what knowledge you might need to acquire, what has been learned from past experience, and what do experts say about the problem. Also, make sure as you travel your road toward a solution that you don't trip on these common roadblocks:

- Bad habits
- Perceptions
- Fears
- Assumptions
- Affinity
- Procrastination
- Reactiveness
- Rashness
- Sensitivities

At this point you should have a clear understanding and definition or diagram of the problem. You understand what it is and maybe even why, but you have refrained from answering the next question: What should I do about it? It's now time to look for a solution.

HOW DO I FIND GOOD SOLUTIONS?

There are a number of methods for finding solutions:

- Analytical thinking
- Association
- Analogy
- Brainstorming
- Intuition

Try each of them out and select the best solution developed by these methods.

Analytical thinking

The analytical method of problem-solving is based on analysis. It is the most conventional and logical of all the methods and follows a step-by-step pattern:

1. Examine each cause of the problem.
2. For each cause, list the solutions that logically would seem to solve the problem, based on your direct knowledge and experience.
3. Check the possible solutions you arrive at with the research you have compiled on how the problem was solved by others.

Association

There are three types of associative thinking, a linking process either through similarity, difference, or contiguity. For example, *contiguity* finds solutions from things that are connected through proximity, sequence, and cause and effect. The process works as follows: List as many parts of the problem as you can think of. Then, giving yourself a short time limit, list as many ideas that have either proximity, sequence, or related cause and effect to the ones you have listed. For example, a contiguous association might be

- Misplaced recipes = cluttered desk (proximity)
- Misplaced recipes = rushing (sequence)
- Misplaced recipes = irate chef (cause and effect)

Associative thinking taps the resources of the mind. It brings into focus options you might not have considered if you stuck to ideas only directly related to the problem. As a result of associative thinking, you might find other relationships embedded in the problem that will lead to a better solution. For example, associative thinking might help you solve the problem of a shrinking marketplace by helping you discover related markets for your catering services.

Analogy

The analogical method of thinking is a way of finding solutions through comparisons. The process is based on comparing the different facets of the problem with other problems that might or might not have similar facets. An analogy might go like this:

"Employees have been coming in late to work quite often. How can I get them to be at work on time? This to me is like soldiers being late for a battle. Would soldiers come late to a battle? Why not? Because their future as a soldier depends upon being there, and because there are severe penalties for soldiers who are AWOL."

By comparing the situation of workers to the situation of soldiers, you might find a solution for a way to motivate employees to come to work on time.

Brainstorming

Brainstorming is based on a free, nonthreatening, anything-goes atmosphere. You can brainstorm alone or with a group of people. Most often a group of people from different departments of your firm or from diverse backgrounds is preferable. In brainstorming, the problem is explained to the group and each member is encouraged to throw out as many ideas for solutions as he or she can think of, no matter how ridiculous or far-fetched they might sound. All the ideas are written down on a large pad of paper, then discussed among the group, revised, tossed out, combined, and expanded. Based on the group's recognition of the effectiveness of each idea, the best ones are selected for closer review.

For example, in a brainstorming session, a group of all of your employees might mention for consideration any thoughts they have on how to increase sales or improve profits for the firm.

Intuition

Intuition is based on "hunches." It is not, as some think, irrational. Intuition or hunches are built on a strong foundation of facts and experiences that are buried somewhere in your subconscious. All the things you know and have experienced can lead you to believe that something might be true although you've never actually experienced that reality. Use your intuition as much as possible, but check it against the reality of the situation.

Selecting the best solution

You've now developed a list of possible solutions. Go through this list and cross out those that obviously won't work. These ideas aren't wasted, for they affect those ideas that remain. In other words, the best ideas you select might be revised using ideas that won't work.

Break the remaining solution down into its positive effects and negative effects. To do this, some catering business owners write each solution they are considering on a separate piece of paper. Below the solution, they draw a vertical line down the center of the sheet, labeling one column "Advantages" and the other column "Disadvantages." Then, they analyze each facet of the solution and its effect on the problem, listing each of the advantages and disadvantages they can think of.

One way to help you think of the advantages and disadvantages is to role-play each solution. Call in a few of your employees and play out each solution. Ask them for their reactions. Based on what you observe and on their feedback, you will have a better idea of the advantages and disadvantages of each solution you're considering.

After you complete this process for each primary solution, select those solutions that have the most advantages. At this point, you should be considering only two or three. In order to select the most appropriate solution from these, consider the following factors:

- Cost-effectiveness
- Time constraints
- Availability of personnel and materials
- Your own intuition

Before you actually implement the chosen solution, you should evaluate it. Ask yourself these questions:

- Are the objectives of the solution sound, clear, and simple?
- Will the solution achieve the objectives?
- What are the possibilities that it will fail and in what way?
- How can I reduce the possibility of failure?

Taking action

Finding the solution doesn't mean that the problem is solved. You still need to design a plan of action so that the solution gets carried out properly. Designing and implementing the plan of action is equally as important as finding the solution. The best solution can fail because it isn't well implemented.

When designing the plan of action, consider the following questions:

- Who will be involved in the solution?
- How will they participate?
- Who will be affected by the solution?
- How will they be affected?
- What course of action will be taken?
- How should this course of action be presented to employees, customers, suppliers, and others?
- When will the action start and be completed?
- Where will this action happen?
- How will this action happen?

- What's needed to make it happen?

Design a "plan of action" chart including all the details you need to consider to implement the plan and when each phase should happen. Keep in mind, though, that the best plans have setbacks for any number of reasons. A key person might be out for illness, a supplier might ship materials late, or a change at the customer's site might require that the timetable be changed.

As each phase of your plan of action is implemented, ask yourself whether your goals were achieved, how well they were achieved, and whether the action worked smoothly. To check your own perceptions of the results, get as much feedback as possible from your managers and employees. A solution that you consider successful might not be considered so by those closer to the action. Always remember that they are one of your most valuable tools in successfully carrying out your solution.

HOW DO I SOLVE COMMUNICATION PROBLEMS?

What does communication have to do with becoming a successful catering business owner? Plenty!

In fact, without good communication skills, you will soon not have your business. Your customers won't know what you can do for them or why your service is better than others, your banker won't know why you need the expansion loan, local regulators won't issue you required licenses and permits, employees won't know what you want them to do. Get the point? Communication is vital to the success of your business.

Of course, most caterers do communicate with customers, bankers, regulators, and employees. The problem is that many don't do it well enough to avoid the problems of incorrect specifications, hurt feelings, puzzling responses, inaccuracies, and delays that miscommunication causes.

On the other hand, powerful communications can
- Change prospects into long-time clients
- Appease disgruntled customers
- Clearly direct unproductive employees
- Gain support from powerful decision-makers
- Simplify training new employees
- Define independent contractors' responsibilities
- Encourage customers to pay their bills swiftly
- Help you negotiate better pricing from suppliers
- Acquire low-cost funding from lenders
- Improve community and media relations
- Improve the effectiveness of your advertising

Your catering business thoroughly depends on effective communications. It's actually the "secret" ingredient that separates experienced catering employees from successful catering service business owners. If you can communicate well with prospects, customers, suppliers, and employees, your business has a much better chance at success than if you are a poor communicator. So let's spend a few moments reviewing the basics of communications and how you can profit from them.

The concept of communication is very simple. Any communication requires three things:

- A thought: some information that you want someone else to have or that you want from them.
- A transmission: a method of getting this thought from you to someone else.
- A receiver: someone whom you want to acquire your thought.

It's that simple. And basic communication is used every day in your life in such situations as

- Telling an employee when and where to start a specific job.
- Asking a wholesaler when the next shipment of provisions will arrive.
- Reading a book about starting a successful catering business.
- Renting a video to take home after a long workday.
- Calling up an old friend to share some common experiences.

In each case, there is a thought (either a statement or a question), a transmission (oral speech, writing, or a graphic image), and a receiver (a subcontractor, supplier, reader, video clerk, or friend).

The thought you want to transmit to a receiver might be a fact, such as the status of a job, or an emotion, such as how you feel about the job. By its nature, business normally involves factual thoughts rather than emotions. The transmission might be conveyed in person, over the telephone, on a written fax, with a letter or invoice, with a diagram or drawing, or in a recorded message. The receiver might get your message instantaneously, in a few moments over a fax machine, in a few days via the mail, or months or even years from now in a published document.

In each case, you must decide who your receiver is, what the receiver needs to know, how best to present this information to the receiver, and how soon.

Clear communication requires clear thinking, asking yourself questions and then answering them. You can clarify your thinking by simply becoming more aware of the questions you ask yourself. The better the question, the better the answer. For example, ask yourself, "Do I want to know how to solve this specific problem, or all similar problems?" The key to clear thinking is simply asking questions of your questions, or redefining your question until it accurately states what you want to know. Then the answer comes easier.

HOW CAN I SAY WHAT I REALLY MEAN?

Every business day, you speak to many people in person or on the telephone. They are prospects, customers, suppliers, employees, subcontractors, health inspectors, bank employees, professionals, salespeople, and others. You might speak to each in a different way with a distinct vocabulary. For example, the words you use to explain how to make a special sauce are very different from those used to transact business at the bank.

So what's different? Why does a communicator speak differently to various people? Because each is a unique audience. Each audience needs different information and has a different vocabulary.

The first rule of saying what you mean is to consider your audience. That is, consider your listener. This rule is so obvious that you probably automatically follow it—most of the time. You walk into the bank and automatically switch to the jargon that is understood by the audience: the teller, loan officer, or banker. If, on the way out of the bank, you see a customer, you automatically return to food-service jargon—but only at the level the customer will probably understand. Then, seeing a friendly catering business owner in the parking lot, your vocabulary changes again, this time to highly technical terms. In each case, you have automatically considered our audience.

However, it is the exceptions to this "automatic" consideration that makes the most trouble. For example, suppose a prospect calls you. If you begin speaking with technical terms, the prospect might be impressed, but will more probably be confused (although he or she might never say so). If the prospect has extensive knowledge of foods and your specialty, however, he or she might feel insulted if you simplify your language.

How can you know the prospect's level of understanding? By asking. Don't, however, embarrass a prospect by asking, "How much of what I'm saying do you understand?" Instead, ask him or her to explain the problem that needs to be solved. By listening carefully to the response, you'll be able to determine the prospect's knowledge of catering and adjust your vocabulary accordingly.

Remember that you can always keep people talking by repeating their last few words in question form. Suppose a prospect says, "I really need someone to serve a Hungarian dinner." You respond, "Serve a Hungarian dinner?" and she will probably continue feeding you clues to help you determine her knowledge. "Yes, my husband's family will arrive from Hungary next month and . . ." Remember that a good communicator is first a good listener.

Need

Once you've determined your audience's understanding of the problem and its solution, you can start asking more questions to find out what they need. That is, is the audience looking for some technical information, for pricing, for an immediate solution, for a reason to buy from you, or for something else?

The best way to learn need is, again, to ask. Many catering services simply ask, "How can I help you?" and take their cue from the response. "Well, I'm not sure . . ." tells you to ask more questions until the problem is fully defined in the prospect's mind. "What I need is some pricing . . ." says that you need to review the benefits of your service and promise to work up an estimate. "I need someone to replace this evening's caterer who just walked out . . ." says you need to jump in your car and get over there.

In some cases, people will call you to pick your brain, saying things like, "I have this problem. How can I solve it?" If it's a problem to which you sell the solution, don't give it away. That might sound unfair, but, with some research and trial-and-error, the caller can find the solution on his own. What he would pay you for is to save him the time and trouble. Let him. You can simply explain, "I would have to see the situation before I could give you a comprehensive answer."

To summarize the point: Determine need. Ask yourself, what does this person need to know?

Presentation

After you've determined your audience's understanding and need, how can you best present the solution to this person? If the audience is a prospective customer who needs an estimate of catering costs for a specific event, your presentation is a quote or a bid. If your audience is a loan officer who needs information about your business, your presentation is a thorough loan application. If your audience is a disgruntled customer who wants a resolution to a problem he or she feels you caused, your presentation is an immediate and factual response and solution.

To present a solution, first define the problem. Once you've clearly defined the actual problem, the solution usually becomes obvious. For example, suppose an influential client calls to complain that the party you catered for him last weekend was a disaster because it ran out of food. He's going to tell all of his influential friends about this problem. Begin by asking questions: "Ran out of food?" "How many people were expected for the party?" "How many people actually came?" "Exactly what food was in short supply?" By probing, you learn that the client's wife had separately invited some of her coworkers to the party without telling him. There were 12 more guests at the party than had been expected. So the real problem is that the client's wife didn't communicate with him. The solution is to diplomatically explain the situation and offer to do whatever is necessary to please the customer.

Defining the problem doesn't blame anyone, it just makes sure that all the facts are used in developing a solution. It's nothing personal to you or to your client. The best way to communicate or present a solution to someone is to determine two things: what the audience already knows and what they need to know. By understanding these two things, you can easily present what the audience needs in a way that they will understand.

Measurement

Communications is a loop. There must be a return path of feedback in one of many forms. As you speak to someone in person, you can usually evaluate whether your audience is understanding what you say by watching their "body language": eye movement, hands and arms, smiles and frowns. On the telephone, it's more difficult to measure feedback. So you ask questions such as, "Does that make sense?" and, "Did I explain that clearly?" After such a clarifying question, leave a long pause for a response after the "yes" or "no." If you successfully communicated your thoughts, the listener will usually rephrase it in his or her own terms. If the listener doesn't, or if he or she repeats your own exact words back to you, consider that you might not have been sufficiently clear. Rephrase what you said, using such language as, "That's right. To put it another way . . ."

In summary, the four steps to saying what you mean are knowing your audience, knowing what they need to know, giving them what they need, and making sure they understand it.

HOW CAN I WRITE WHAT I MEAN?

In general, writing what you mean is the same as saying what you mean. The same four principles apply: audience, need, presentation, and measurement. Of course, they are applied somewhat differently.

The best and worst aspect of written communication is that it gives you time to come up with a response—and gives the reader time to ponder your response. So, even more than oral communications that drift away with the wind, written communications require time and thought. For many, what is so intimidating about writing is its permanence. However, this permanence is also what makes the written word so powerful: Write it once, clearly and accurately, and be done with it.

Writing secrets

Here are the three steps to writing guaranteed to make you more comfortable and more successful with written communications:

1. Prewrite.
2. Write.
3. Rewrite.

That's it! No successful document is written in a single draft. All successful writing evolves through these three stages once the audience, need, presentation, and measurement have been defined. The next several pages cover these three stages, with examples, until you're comfortable with them—even enjoy them.

Prewrite

Prewriting is simply preparing to write. You make notes about the topic you want to cover, put them in a logical order, and look for ways to make your ideas as clear as possible. For example, if you need to write a letter to a client diplomatically explaining why you ran out of food at her party last weekend, you would first list the topics you want to cover:

- The event was to serve 32 guests, as contracted.
- On learning of 12 extra guests, the caterer's chef stretched the food as far as possible, but still ran out of some popular foods.
- The client was evidently not aware of the additional guests nor of the actions by the chef.
- We're very sorry that a few of the guests were not able to taste some of the special delicacies.
- The client is an influential and valued customer and we apologize for the misunderstanding.
- We will be sure to allow for unexpected guests at her next event.
- We want to make all of our customers happy with our service.

Once you have all the topics written down, simply put them in a logical order in which the reader wants to see them. In this example, the order would be as follows:

1. The client is an influential and valued customer and we apologize for the misunderstanding.
2. We want to make all of our customers happy with our service.
3. We're very sorry that a few of the guests were not able to taste some of the special delicacies.
4. The event was to serve 32 guests, as contracted.
5. On learning of 12 extra guests, the chef stretched the food as far as possible, but still ran out of some popular foods.
6. The client was evidently not aware of the additional guests nor of the actions by the chef.
7. We will be sure to allow for unexpected guests at her next event.

Finally, look for ways to make your ideas as clear as possible. Help your reader visualize the problem and the solution.

To develop the list of topics that you want to cover in your written communication, think about questions to be answered. Typical questions would include the following:

- What's the purpose of this correspondence?
- What does the reader want to know?
- What are the facts of this situation, in random order?
- What's the most logical order for these facts?
- What does the reader want to know first?
- What single point do I want to leave in the reader's mind?

Find the answers to these and related questions, and you will have prewritten your correspondence.

Write

Now that you've prewritten what you want to say, the writing comes much easier. You simply elaborate on each point, in order. For example, the first topic to cover from the outline in the previous section is, "You're an influential and valued customer and we apologize for the misunderstanding." You can amplify it like this:

"Mr. or Ms. Client, you are an influential and valued customer. We certainly apologize for having run out of food at your recent dinner party. Our reputation is important to us and we don't want to jeopardize it."

Then you lead into the second point of the prewrite outline, which states that you want to make all of your customers happy with your service. You continue the correspondence, therefore, with something like, "We will do anything necessary to keep our good relationship with you and with your friends. If you're not happy with our service, then we're not happy."

Then you bring the third point, that you're sorry some guests did not get to taste everything, into your correspondence. However, you say it more positively, like this:

"I remember, Mr. or Ms. Client, how important the selection of the main dish was to you. It's preparation was also important to us. It is our chef's specialty and she was sad not to be able to allow each of your guests the opportunity to try it."

Then the fourth and fifth points are developed. In your prewrite outline, these stated that the event was to serve 32 guests, as contracted and on learning of 12 extra guests, the staff stretched the food as far as possible, but still ran out of some popular foods. In your actual letter, make these points as follows:

"In fact, learning that 12 extra guests had shown up for the party, our staff immediately went to work to stretch the food without compromising the quality you desire. Our master chef quickly prepared additional appetizers and desserts. The main course, which had been prepared earlier in the day, was the only food that we could not stretch."

Get the point? Once you've prewritten your correspondence, the writing is very easy. It's simply a matter of turning independent thoughts into smooth sentences. Don't worry about spelling, punctuation, or sentence structure at this point. Just develop each thought into a sentence or two.

Rewrite

After you've got the first draft written, you're ready for the cleanup stage. If you're not a adept speller, refer to a dictionary or a spell-checker in your computer's word processing system. Don't worry too much about "proper English." Simply read your sentences out loud and you will probably hear any major errors. If you're still uncomfortable with tenses and phrasing, ask someone with grammatical skills to review your draft before you complete it.

You can also dress up your writing by adding transitions such as "however," "in addition," "by the way," and "as we discussed." They make your correspondence sound more like conversation as well as signaling the reader that you're changing thoughts or want to emphasize a specific point.

One more point about writing: If you've decided to purchase and use a computer in your business, consider a word processing program such as WordPerfect, Microsoft Write or Word, XyWrite, AmiPro, WordStar, or others. Writing on a word processor allows you to prewrite, write, and rewrite quickly and easily. You can readily move words, sentences, and paragraphs around until you're satisfied with them. Then, you can store your finished documents on your computer so that future correspondence can reuse these well-written thoughts.

Some word processors include outliners, spell-checkers, thesauruses, and even grammar checkers. If yours doesn't include these features, they can be purchased separately and added to your system. A word processor lets you continually improve your written communications until they say exactly what you want them to say.

SUCCESS ACTION PLAN

As the owner of any business, you are paid in direct proportion to the problems that you solve for others. The problem you solve might be how Mr. Host can feed and impress 25 guests, or it might be how to get your employees to work more efficiently. Here are some proven ways that you can put your problem-solving skills into action:

- ❏ Take a problem—any problem—and apply the steps to problem-solving. Make these steps a part of your thinking.
- ❏ Apply analytical thinking, association, analogy, brainstorming, and intuition to develop options to solve your selected problem.
- ❏ From these options, select the most appropriate solution and take action.
- ❏ Determine how best to communicate your solution to others: in writing, speaking, or action.
- ❏ If your solution requires writing, use the prewrite-write-rewrite procedure to communicate your solution.
- ❏ Measure the success of your solution and learn how to improve it.
- ❏ Apply problem-solving and communication skills to other "opportunities" in your catering business and your life.

12

How can I ensure long-term success?

Success is not a destination, it's a journey. Hopefully, it is a long journey that will last your lifetime. But, of course, there are no guarantees in life, and certainly not in business. So how can you ensure the long-term success of your catering business? By developing advanced management skills as well as by keeping your business in perspective.

This final chapter is just the beginning of your future as a successful caterer. In it you learn negotiating skills, find the most effective management methods for you, learn how to weather business storms, and develop planning skills used by big business. It also discusses how to manage time and stress to improve the quality of your life.

HOW CAN I LEARN TO ENJOY NEGOTIATING?

Many people fear the face-to-face confrontation of negotiating. For example, they don't like to buy cars because they know that not negotiating the price is considered un-American. In fact, it is. Very few things in our economy are nonnegotiable. With just a little practice, you can actually enjoy negotiating with others.

The game

To remove any fear of negotiating, remember that it's just a game. You wouldn't be fearful of playing a checkers game or a softball game. In fact, many products and services you purchase include a percentage of the price set aside for those who negotiate. It ranges from a couple of percent to 20 percent or more of the price. In most cases, the higher the price, the higher the available discount. Many larger-ticket items, such as cars and houses, can be negotiated to a discount of 10 to 20 percent—even if the owner says "my price is firm."

You're not fearful of chess or many sports games once you understand the rules. There will always be unsportsmanlike players who break these rules, but the majority of players follow them. Negotiation, like any other game, has its own rules. Here are a few of them:
- Don't negotiate unless you're willing to buy. If you're looking at a $500 item and you offer $450, the seller might accept and you're stuck with something you didn't want—or you have to explain that you weren't serious.
- Don't fall in love. There are few unique items in this world. If you can find it

once, you can probably find it again. If you tell yourself that you must have this item, then you must have it—at any price.

- Don't be afraid to walk away. Once you've determined what the product or service is worth to you, set the realistic limit that you will pay. If it isn't met, walk away. Some sellers will call you back and reopen negotiations, others will let you go. Of course, you can always come back later and reopen negotiations yourself.

What products and services can you negotiate? Just about any of them. Suppliers often negotiate prices or terms on items or orders valued over a few hundred dollars. Some independent contractors negotiate their hourly fees if you can keep them busy during normally slow times. Car and truck dealers are notoriously adept negotiators, but you can often get the best deal by determining wholesale value (what they probably paid for the vehicle) and adding a standard commission and sales costs plus a little profit. Ask your banker for the wholesale blue-book value for the vehicle you're considering.

The other side of the table

Learning how to negotiate with sellers also helps as you face customers who want to negotiate. Set up your own pricing structure with this in mind, but always ask for a trade. That is, if a customer asks for a 5-percent discount, you might want to give it if the customer pays cash in advance. For a 10 percent discount, you might ask for cash in advance and a letter of recommendation when the job is done. The rule is: never give away a discount; trade it for something you want—even a token. Most important, never sell your services for less than they cost you to furnish.

WHAT ARE THE BEST BUSINESS TECHNIQUES?

Even though there are hundreds of worthwhile tips for growing your catering business in this book, one primary rule supersedes all others: Do what works best for you. That is, if your business is growing through telephone marketing while other catering services are using direct mail, do what works for you. You're certainly wise to at least try the other methods, but there are so many variables among local markets, customer types, client needs, and your own skills and personality, that the "best" way to do something is relative. What works well for you might not work at all for someone else.

Doing what works best doesn't mean always following the easiest path. A good business manager continually looks for new and better ways to complete the "process," discussed in the last chapter. This new and better way might be a new computer program that automates recipe and menu development, or developing a niche market that isn't being served. Remember, however, that just because something is new doesn't always mean that it is better. Be aggressive in your learning and conservative in your changing. Know what works for you.

One way to know what works is to continually rethink how you manage your business and serve your customers. Remember that to think is simply to ask yourself questions, then answer them. And the better the question, the better the answer. So, as you go about your daily business, ask yourself, "How can I do this job better, more efficiently, faster, more profitably, safer, or with more quality?" Here are some specific questions you might ask:

- How can I better handle incoming calls from prospects who want information and pricing in a hurry?
- How can I get more prospects to call me for a quote without spending too much money on advertising and promotion?
- How can I get my employees to stop spending so much time on break and more time at their jobs?
- How can I encourage my banker to extend me more credit during the slower business months?
- How can I find out if customers are happy or unhappy with my service?
- How can I get my customers to tell others about my service in a positive way?
- How can I ensure that my employees are working as safely as possible?
- How can I reduce my insurance costs without increasing my risk?
- How can I cut costs without cutting my quality of service?

A successful caterer is always rethinking the way to do everything from managing a kitchen to purchasing equipment to serving customers. To make your business grow, you must continually rethink your business.

One more tip: if you are better at catering than you are at business management, hire a manager. If you become a better business manager, hire a caterer to do the work. Do what you do best—and what you enjoy most.

HOW CAN I MAKE SURE MY BUSINESS TECHNIQUES WORK?

Making sure that your business techniques are effective involves a seeming contradiction to the rule of doing what you do best: If it ain't broke, break it!

Actually, the two rules work together. Do what works for you, but make sure it's really working. And to test its strength, try to break it from time to time. For example, suppose new customers are coming to you faster than you can handle them—take some time to plan what you'll do when the customers aren't coming at all. Or, if you've set up a kitchen staff that smoothly handles food preparation and service, consider what you'll do if your chef or staff decides to move to the competition or to leave the area. What would you do to ensure that valuable recipes aren't lost, that proven procedures are documented, that your next chef or kitchen manager is as efficient as the one you have? Plan now as if it already happened, because it will.

Murphy owned a catering business!

HOW CAN I HANDLE BUSINESS RECESSIONS?

No businesses are truly recession-proof. All businesses have cycles where sales become easier or harder to make. Catering services are subject to the same business cycles that most businesses face. Even so, you can take steps to minimize your market's downswing and extend its upswing.

First, determine the business cycle for your market. Review income and financial records from prior years, or check with regional restaurant associations, then draw a chart illustrating the local business cycle. In your region, it might be that most of the market for your service occurs in the spring and summer—or maybe in the winter and fall. Or the cycle might be fairly steady across a particular year, but alternate years fluctuate up or down. The first step to coping with recessions in the local business cycle is to determine exactly what and when that cycle is.

Once you know what your business cycle is, the next step is to begin planning for it. If you're coming up to a typically slower period, determine what you need to do right now. In past years, how much has income dropped? For how long? Can you find income sources in other specialities where the cycle is moving up? What expenses can you cut back? Do you have an employee who would like a seasonal lay-off to catch up on other interests? Maybe you need to dramatically cut back on your expenses and debts for this period. If so, list them now and determine which ones will naturally diminish and which will need to be reduced.

One successful catering service owner, while in a busy period, decided that times would be much slower six months later. So she talked with her bank and other creditors, offering to prepay debts and expenses now so she could cut back payments later. It worked. When times got rougher, she reduced her expenses and wintered the problem. If you aren't into your slow season yet, you can also talk to your banker about building a line of credit now that will help you get through the tougher times ahead.

One more option when you are facing a downturn in catering business is to trade out your services. That is, if your bank or a major creditor is beginning to pressure you, offer to perform catering services for them in lieu of partial or complete payment. Even if they don't require your services now, you can promise future services as required or learn if they have other customers who might wish to hire or trade. Many creditors would rather work out a trade than absorb a bad debt. Of course, much depends on your relationship with them.

Some creditors, such as the Internal Revenue Service and other governmental agencies, will not consider service trades. However, they can sometimes develop terms for a businessperson who has an otherwise good financial record and the opportunity for growth once the local economy turns around. But don't expect compassion; it's purely business.

Another source for cash to tide you through a recession is available from a first or second mortgage on your building, your home, or other large asset. Speak with your lender about this opportunity. Even if you decide not to take out a mortgage, you will be ready if and when you need to do so.

Finally, consider widening your market. Travel to a nearby metropolitan area and study whether you can expand your services to reach it. If so, you can pick up additional sales by either subcontracting your services or by promoting your services in the expanded market. It certainly beats starving at home.

HOW DOES BIG BUSINESS GET BIG?

Your larger competitors probably got that way with the help of *strategic planning*. Strategic planning is a process that helps you assess the current business environment, redefine your company's mission or purpose, decide where you want your business to be in three to five years, recognize your firm's strengths and weaknesses, and map out the course that will take your firm where you want to be. A business plan defines your business, a marketing plan defines your market, and a strategic plan defines your future.

Strategic planning

Why should you spend the many hours it takes to develop a strategic plan for your business? Because you want to succeed in business. Technology and the fast pace of change are making business management more complex. Strategic planning helps you foresee and react quickly to market changes and opportunities, and identify areas in which your business is lagging behind. Also, competition is becoming tougher. In most cases, small businesses find themselves competing with much larger companies—ones that know the benefits of strategic planning and practice it. The strategic planning process involves your employees, your lender, your accountant, and possibly your attorney, helping each to feel more a part of your team.

The strategic planning process begins with an assessment of the current economic situation. First, examine factors outside of your company that can affect its performance, looking for forecasts on the national, regional, local, and your industry's business economy. Sources for this information include business trade publications such as the *Wall Street Journal*, trade journals, the U.S. Department of Commerce (for their 12 leading economic indicators and other figures), local and regional chambers of commerce, and food-service associations.

Next, conduct a planning session with key employees and independent advisers. Present your written summary of economic forecasts, then ask everyone to put on their "creativity caps." Have lots of writing pads, flip charts, or a large writing board for recording any ideas. All ideas are equally important and valid.

This group of people is your "SWOT team." That is, together you will be listing your firm's strengths, weaknesses, opportunities, and threats. Try to list at least 10 items in each category. Here are some idea-starting examples:

Strengths
- Our catering service is well-known in the community.
- We have developed excellent suppliers.
- Our financial credit rating is good.
- We have a highly qualified and efficient staff.

Weaknesses
- Our regional economy is in a recession.
- Some employees don't work as part of a team.
- Our recordkeeping system is too cumbersome.
- We cannot always respond quickly to market changes.

Opportunities
- Our major competitor will probably be out of business within a year.
- Our major supplier is offering discounts for which we can easily qualify.
- Most of our customers can purchase additional services from us if we let them know of availability.
- Installing a new telephone system would improve sales and enhance relations with our current customers.

Threats
- A new competitor is cutting prices to attract market share.
- The new competitor lured away two employees by offering better pay.

Get the picture? Before you decide where you want the company to be in a few years, you must know where it has been, where it is now, and what obstacles you should expect. Make sure that everything is down in writing—even the "dumb" ideas—before you leave your meeting.

Mission statement and objectives

An organization's mission statement describes its purpose. You developed a preliminary mission statement earlier in this book when you set up your business notebook. Now is the time to look at how it can be refined to clarify where you want the firm to go and why.

A mission statement is typically short, a single sentence or paragraph. It can include any or all of the following: reason for the firm, the products or services offered, the market and clients served, and the intended direction of the firm. Here are some samples:

- "The ABC Catering Service provides economical catering in the northeast section of Yourtown."
- "Our goal is simple: we want to be the best ethnic catering service in this part of the state."
- "ABC Catering Service's goal is to provide the highest quality catering to high-income clients in Smith County. We intend to capitalize on our reputation for quality by expanding into related food services within three years."

From the mission statement and your strategic planning sessions comes a list of five to ten key results areas, or *KRAs*. Typical KRAs include the following:

- Increase revenues.
- Improve profitability.
- Enhance credit and collections policies.
- Keep pace or outdistance our competition.
- Improve efficiency.
- Increase the level of service offered to customers.
- Capitalize on emerging trends.
- Utilize newer technology to improve operations.
- Improve labor relations.
- Improve internal relations.
- Improve relations with suppliers.
- Enhance our image through publicity and advertising.
- Capitalize on our physical facilities.
- Improve organizational structure.
- Arrange for sale or transfer of business.

Obviously, this list is not complete. Nor should you include all of these noble KRAs in your list. Pick a few that are most appropriate to your mission statement and make them your goals.

The next step in strategic planning is to define specific strategic and tactical objectives for each of your key results areas. A strategic objective indicates what you want to accomplish in measurable terms, such as "increase revenues from existing customers by $6000 per month by December 31." The tactical objective then lists the short-term objectives or steps needed to meet the strategic objective. In the case of increasing sales by $6000 per month, tactical objectives could include these:

- Identify services now offered that could be cross-sold to existing customers.
- Determine which service can most easily be cross-sold.
- Determine the best method of selling these services to existing customers: telemarketing, direct mail, or automatic reorder services.

Next, establish a budget for accomplishing these objectives. If you're expecting to earn $6000 in additional sales and you typically allocate 20 percent of your costs to sales, your budget could be up to $1200 per month. Or you might need to establish a budget for setting up the process without expecting to receive offsetting income for a short period of time.

Finally—and just as important—set up a monitoring system to ensure that your strategic plan is on target for reaching its goals. Many successful catering businesses dedicate a portion of scheduled management meetings to reviewing progress on the firm's strategic plan.

Establishing a strategic plan for your catering business might seem like a lot of work, but remember that it actually saves you time and makes you money by keeping you focused. Big businesses use strategic planning because, in many cases, it is a major reason why they became big.

HOW CAN I MAKE SURE MY BUSINESS WILL CONTINUE?

The catering business you've started, nourished, managed, and expanded has become a part of you. For many firms, the owner is the business and vise versa. So what happens to your catering business when you or your partner dies or is disabled? That's up to you.

Life insurance and good planning can provide significant amounts of cash to help employees and family members cushion the financial impact of the death or retirement of the owner/manager of a sole proprietorship, partnership, or a closely held corporation. It can also help attract and retain valuable employees.

Sole proprietorships

The personal skills, reputation, and management ability of the sole proprietor helps to make the business successful. Without these human values, the business is worth only the liquidation value of the tangible assets. The sole proprietor's personal and business assets are one and the same. When death occurs, the loss can become a financial disaster to the proprietor's estate and fatal to the business. The business that was producing a good living for the owner and family will become defunct. What are the options?

Family continuation

The business may be transferred to a capable family member as a gift through provisions in the proprietor's will or by a sale provided through a prearranged purchase agreement effective at death. However, cash is needed to offset losses to the business caused by the owner's death, to equalize the value of bequests made to other family members if the transfer is a gift, and to provide the sale price if the transfer is through sale.

New owner

If the buyer is a key employee, competitor, or other person, the business may be transferred at death based on a prearranged sale agreement. Cash is needed to provide a "business continuation fund" to meet expenses and perhaps to offset losses until the business adjusts to the new management.

Liquidation

If future management is not available, the business must be liquidated. Cash is needed to offset the difference between the business's going-concern value and its auction-block liquidation value, to provide a fund for income replacement to the family, and to pay outstanding business debts.

Partnerships

Unless there is a written agreement to the contrary, the death of a partner automatically dissolves the firm. In the absence of such an agreement, surviving partners have no right to buy the deceased's partnership interest. Surviving partners cannot assume the goodwill or take over the assets without consent of the deceased's estate. If the deceased was in debt to the partnership, the estate must settle the account in full and in cash.

The options to a business upon the death of a partner are liquidation and reorganization. The surviving partners have exclusive possession of firm property, but no right to carry on the business. If the business is continued, the surviving partners must share all profits with the deceased's estate and are liable for all losses.

Liquidation

If the surviving partner and deceased's heirs do nothing, the business is liquidated, resulting in "auction price" value for the salable assets. In a liquidation, the surviving partners act as liquidating trustees. They must convert everything into cash at the best price obtainable. They must also make an accounting to the deceased's estate, divide the proceeds with the estate, and liquidate themselves out of their business and income. The business may receive nothing for goodwill.

This solution is disastrous for both the dead partner's family and the surviving partners. It also means termination of jobs for the surviving partners and employees.

Reorganization

As an alternative to liquidation, the surviving partners may attempt to reorganize the partnership by taking the heirs into the partnership. But if heirs are incapable of working, the survivors must do all the work and still share the profits, unless they accept a new partner picked by the heirs. The surviving partners can also sell their interest in the business to the heirs or buy out the interest controlled by the deceased partner's heirs.

Some preparations can be made prior to the death of a partner that will make a reorganization smoother. A *buy and sell agreement* funded with life insurance should be entered into while all partners are alive. Such an agreement, drafted by an attorney, typically includes a commitment by each partner not to dispose of his or her interest without first offering it at an agreed sale price to the partnership. The agreement also includes a provision for the partnership to buy a deceased partner's interest. The funding of the purchase is typically from the proceeds of a life insurance policy written for that specific purpose.

Corporations

The death of a stockholder who has been active in the operation of a closely held corporation allows the business entity to continue its legal structure, but not its personal structure. The interests of the heirs of the deceased inevitably come in conflict with the interests of the surviving associates. Two options are available in this situation, retention of stock by the heirs or the sale of stock by the heirs.

Retention of stock by heirs

The deceased's family may retain the stock interest. If the heirs have a majority interest, they may choose to become personally involved in management in order to receive income. Alternatively, they may choose to remain inactive, elect a new board of directors, and force the company to pay dividends. In either case, the surviving stockholders might lose a voice in management and possibly their jobs, while the deceased's family might become heirs to a business on the brink of failure. If the heirs have a minority interest and are not employed by the surviving associates, their only means of receiving an income from the corporation is through dividends.

Sale of stock by heirs

After the death of a stockholder, the deceased's heirs or estate may offer to sell the stock interest to the surviving stockholders or to an outside buyer interested in purchasing stock in the corporation.

While all of the interested parties are alive, they can enter into a binding buy and sell agreement funded with life insurance, similar to the one for a partnership. It is done with a "Stockholder's Buy and Sell Agreement," drawn up with the assistance of a corporate attorney and accountant.

Key employees

Many growing firms develop key employees who are assets that the firm cannot afford to be without. Although these key employees might not own an interest in the firm, they are nonetheless valuable to its continuation. So what happens if a key employee dies?

Catering services who have key employees should consider life insurance payable to the firm on the death or disability of one of these human assets. The amount of life insurance should be sufficient to offset financial losses during the readjustment period, retain good credit standing, and assure customers and suppliers that the company will continue as usual. In addition, key-employee insurance could retire loans, mortgages, or bonds, attract and train a successor, or carry out ongoing plans for expansion and new developments.

Talk to your insurance agent about the appropriate policy for insuring your business against the loss of a proprietor, a partner, a stockholder, or a key employee. It's one of the costs of growth.

HOW CAN I MANAGE TIME AND STRESS?

A growing catering business seems to take up at least 24 hours of your day—maybe more. Don't let it! Some catering business owners spend most of their day "fighting fires," while others let the fires burn each other out. The smart catering owner manages available time by prioritizing the jobs to be done. Those that are vital to the success of the business get done first. Important jobs come next. Those that are of limited value fill up the remainder of your time, if there is any.

Many successful catering service owners start their day with a planning session of up to a half hour. In this time, you plan out the events of the day to ensure that the vital jobs get done and the important jobs are handled as time is available. You might also want to schedule "chat" time with employees or customers, but make sure that the discussion stays mostly on business, or at least on personal topics that will help forge a better business relationship.

To ensure that your time is well-managed, first organize your workspace so that important papers don't get lost and unimportant papers do. You can also make a rule that you will avoid handling papers more than once. If you pick up a piece paper, make a decision regarding it right then, if possible.

Set up a regular work schedule. It might be from 7 a.m. to 6 p.m., or 8 a.m. to 5 p.m., or noon to midnight. Whatever it is, try to stick to it. If you manage your time well, you will usually be able to do so. If you have one time of the day that seems more productive for you than others, plan your most important functions around it.

To make the most of travel and waiting time, take work with you in a briefcase, or purchase a cellular phone or laptop computer that you can use to keep productive every minute. As your time-management skills improve, you'll learn how to do more than one thing at a time. For example, while you're waiting to talk with a customer or supplier, you could make job notes, or talk with a key employee, or gather information on an upcoming bid.

Meetings seem to be one of the biggest time-wasters. To avoid wasting time, organize all of your meetings. Meetings, to be productive, must have a purpose or agenda and a time limit. Even if you didn't call the meeting, if you see that it has no focus or structure, you can step in and say, "I have another appointment in an hour. What topics do we have to cover in that hour?" List those topics as the agenda.

One more time management tip: use one of the popular time-management planning systems available at stationery and office-supply stores to help you get the most out of your day. They include Day Timer, Day Runner, and Planner Pad. These and other systems give you a place to record appointments, daily to-do lists, special projects and their steps, as well as keep a contact book for names and addresses. If you spend most of your time in the office at a computer, one of the many contact-management and scheduling programs will help you manage your time. If you use a portable computer, you can install these programs on it and carry this information wherever you go.

Time and stress are closely related. The lack of time to do what you need to do often increases personal stress. How do you manage both? Here are some ideas from successful catering services:

- Plan your time and establish priorities on a daily to-do list. Decide what your prime time is, and do your most important or difficult tasks then. Set business hours, specific times when you're at work, and times when you turn on the answering machine because you're on-duty, but off-call. You, your customers, and your family appreciate knowing your set routine, even though you know that for special events or emergencies you can break that schedule.

- Notice what your four or five big time-wasters are and learn techniques to eliminate them or compensate for them. Some common ones are telephone interruptions, visitors, socializing, excessive paperwork, lack of policies and procedures, procrastination, failure to delegate, unclear objectives, poor scheduling, lack of self-discipline, and lack of skill in a needed area.

- Stay in contact with people. As you move from a catering service employee to a catering business owner, you will naturally spend more time at "the office." Make sure that you get out to talk with your customers, your employees, and for social events. Staying in contact helps your morale if you feel isolated. Just as important, your contacts appreciate your visibility and your interest in sharing time with them.

- Build a fitness program into your day. As an active catering service employee, you might have gotten plenty of exercise doing your daily job. However, as a business manager you might not—unless you take time for fitness. Many successful businesspeople exercise in order to think creatively because physical activity sends oxygen to the brain and helps the mind function better. With regular exercise your health will improve, your stress level will go down, and your trim look will inspire people to have confidence in your abilities.

- If you're working from your home, give your business as much of a separate and distinct identity as possible. Although you might save a few dollars by using the dining room table as a desk and a cardboard box as a file cabinet, the stress and strain of operating without proper space and supplies will take its toll. Have a separate room or area for your business, with a separate entrance if customers or suppliers visit. Consider soundproofing so your family won't be bothered by your noise and vice versa. In addition to the psychological and physical comfort of having a separate room for your home office, the IRS requires it in order for you to make a legitimate claim for tax deductions.

- Take care of your major business asset: *you*. Being the boss can be exciting, fulfilling, and rewarding, but it can also be lonely, stressful, and demanding. Learn to balance your professional and personal life. Go on vacation. Get a weekly massage. Join a health club. Take a class in meditation or spiritual studies. Attend a business owner's breakfast club. Your business depends on you to be at your best.

WHAT ABOUT RETIREMENT?

When should you retire from your profitable catering business? When you want to. Some catering services hold off retiring until they are no longer physically able to work their trade. Others make plans to retire when they are 65 or even 62 years old. Still others give their business ten or 20 years to grow, then sell it to semi-retire or to move to a different trade. Some work their children into the business, then gradually turn it over to them.

Some successful catering business owners sell their shares to a partner or to another corporation. Others sell or give their equity in the business to a daughter or son. A few simply liquidate their assets and keep the proceeds. Some sell out to key employees or to competitors.

The business can be sold outright for cash, earning you a cash settlement for your equity. Alternatively, you can "carry the paper," selling it on a contract with a down payment and monthly payments for a specified term. In this case, buyers often require a noncompetition contract that says you can't go to work for a competing catering service or start another catering firm in the same market.

HOW CAN I IMPROVE THE QUALITY OF MY LIFE?

The primary reason you started your own business is to increase your opportunities to enjoy life. You wanted to offer a needed service, help others, extend your skills in catering and in business, and be able to afford the better things of life. However, you didn't want to spend your entire waking time working. In fact, you might get so caught up in the chase for success that you miss the opportunities that success brings along the way.

Those who have found success in catering and other fields will tell you that success is often empty if isn't shared with others. And that doesn't mean waiting until a successful destination—say $1 million net worth—is reached. It means sharing success with others along the way, on a day-to-day basis. Maybe, for you, it means sharing your success with your close family, a few close friends, your employees, or even some humanity-serving organization in which you believe. In any case, consider that your financial success will mean much more to you if you can use it to bring physical, emotional, or spiritual success to others.

Manage your life outside your business as you do your time at the business. Look for ways to help others. Find methods of giving yourself the things you most enjoy, whether they are time with friends, time with hobbies, time with competitive sports, or time alone. Especially, take time to recharge your "batteries." You will use lots of personal energy in starting, managing, and growing your catering business. Make sure you take the time to re-energize yourself.

SUCCESS ACTION PLAN

Your road of success continues to widen ahead of you. To ensure that it extends beyond the horizon, here are some actions you can take now to ensure long-term success:

❑ Find ways in which you can use your negotiating skills to develop win-win situations.

❑ Determine what business methods and techniques work best for you and apply them to other areas of your business and your life.

❑ Periodically review your business methods to ensure that they are truly effective. If they are not, change them.

❑ Plan now for the inevitable business recession. Define your action plan in advance. What will you do if business falls off 25 percent over the next six months? Be specific.

❏ Test "strategic planning" in your business. Review your catering service's strengths, weaknesses, opportunities, and threats. How can you revise your mission statement and your business to better reflect the way you want to do business?

❏ Take steps now to ensure that your business will continue if faced with the loss of an owner, a key employee, or a key client.

❏ Determine how you can best manage your time and reduce the stress that is inevitable with business ownership. Enjoy!

❏ Whether you're 25 or 65, plan for the day when you will release your business and move to retirement.

❏ Remember why you wanted to start a catering business in the first place: to improve the quality of your life.

Appendix

Forms and worksheets for catering services

Publication	Frequency of Publication	Contact Phone	No. of Inserts	Our Contract	Size	No. of Colors	Placement	Artwork Due	Authorized By	Ad Title Headline

ADVERTISING PLANNING SCHEDULE

For the Month of:

A-1 Advertising planning schedule.

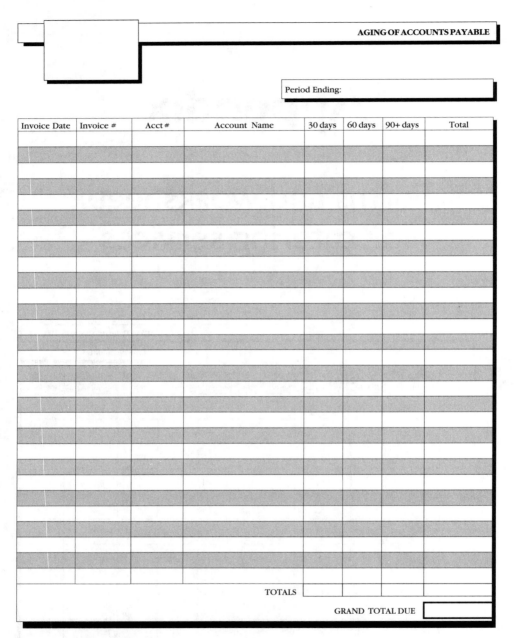

AGING OF ACCOUNTS PAYABLE

Period Ending:

Invoice Date	Invoice #	Acct #	Account Name	30 days	60 days	90+ days	Total
			TOTALS				

GRAND TOTAL DUE

A-2 Aging of accounts payable.

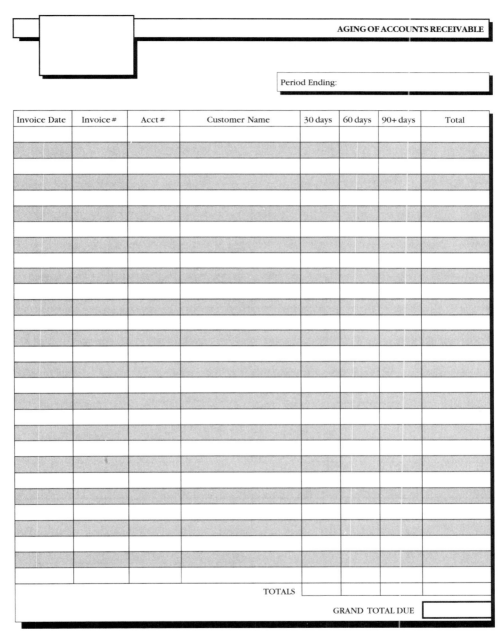

AGING OF ACCOUNTS RECEIVABLE

Period Ending:

Invoice Date	Invoice #	Acct #	Customer Name	30 days	60 days	90+ days	Total
			TOTALS				
			GRAND TOTAL DUE				

A-3 Aging of accounts receivable.

BID CONTROL SHEET

DATE: _____

☐ PRE-BID

ITEM NUMBER: _____
REQ TYPE: _____

CLOSE DATE: _____
REVISED CLOSE DATE: _____

☐ PHONE BIDS

REQ NUMBER: _____
QUANTITY: _____

DATE REQUIRED _____
MAILING DATE _____

☐ SEND SAMPLES

DESTINATION: _____

BUYER'S NAME _____

SPECIAL INSTRUCTIONS TO DATA ENTRY OPERATOR:
_____

VENDOR CODE	VENDOR NAME	BID PRICE 1	BID PRICE 2

CANCEL BID: _____   REASON CLOSE DATE REVISED: _____

RECOMMENDED BYPASS BID OR ACCEPTED OTHER THAN LOW BID FOR FOLLOWING REASON:
_____
_____
_____
_____
_____
_____

NEW VENDOR ADDRESS:

_____   _____
_____   _____
_____   _____
_____   _____

RECOMMENDED BY _____   APPROVED BY _____

A-4 Bid control sheet.

Cash Disbursements Register

PERIOD ENDING:

Date	Check Number	Account Number	Amount	Name

A-5 Cash disbursements register.

Cash Flow Forecast

DATE:

FOR TIME PERIOD:

APPROVED BY:

PREPARED BY:

	Date:		Date:		Date:	
	ESTIMATE	ACTUAL	ESTIMATE	ACTUAL	ESTIMATE	ACTUAL
Opening Balance						
Collections From Trade						
Misc. Cash Receipts						
TOTAL CASH AVAILABLE						
DISBURSEMENTS						
Payroll						
Trade Payables						
Other						
Capital Expenses						
Income Tax						
Bank Loan Payment						
TOTAL DISBURSEMENTS						
Ending Balance						
Less Minimum Balance						
CASH AVAILABLE						

FOR INTERNAL USE ONLY

A-6 Cash flow forecast.

Cash Receipts Register

PERIOD ENDING:

Date	Check Number	Account Number	Amount	Name

A-7 Cash receipts register.

CREDIT APPLICATION

DATE:

BUSINESS INFORMATION	DESCRIPTION OF BUSINESS		
NAME OF BUSINESS	NO. OF EMPLOYEES	CREDIT REQUESTED	TYPE OF BUSINESS
LEGAL (IF DIFFERENT)	IN BUSINESS SINCE		
ADDRESS	BUSINESS STRUCTURE		
CITY	☐ CORPORATION ☐ PARTNERSHIP ☐ PROPRIETORSHIP ☐ DIVISION/SUBSIDIARY NAME OF PARENT COMPANY _____		
STATE ZIP PHONE	HOW LONG IN BUSINESS _____		

COMPANY PRINCIPALS RESPONSIBLE FOR BUSINESS TRANSACTIONS

NAME :	TITLE:	ADDRESS:	PHONE:
NAME:	TITLE:	ADDRESS:	PHONE:
NAME:	TITLE:	ADDRESS:	PHONE:

BANK REFERENCES

NAME OF BANK	NAME TO CONTACT
BRANCH	ADDRESS
CHECKING ACCOUNT NO.	TELEPHONE NUMBER

TRADE REFERENCES

FIRM NAME	CONTACT NAME	TELEPHONE NUMBER	ACCOUNT OPEN SINCE

CONFIRMATION OF INFORMATION ACCURACY AND RELEASE OF AUTHORITY TO VERIFY

I hereby certify that the information in this credit application is correct. The information included in this credit application is for use by the above firm in determining the amount and conditions of credit to be extended. I understand that this firm may also utilize the other sources of credit which it considers necessary in making this determination. Further I hereby authorize the bank and trade references listed in this credit application to release the information necessary to assist this firm in establishing a line of credit.

X
SIGNATURE   TITLE   DATE

POLICY STATEMENT: INITIAL ORDER FROM NEW ACCOUNTS WILL NOT BE PROCESSED
UNLESS ACCOMPANIED BY THE ABOVE REQUESTED INFORMATION.
TERMS: NET 30 DAYS FROM DATE OF INVOICE UNLESS OTHERWISE STATED.

A-8 Credit application.

CREDIT MEMO

CONTRACT NUMBER: _____

DATE: _____

SHIPPER NUMBER:	DATE SHIPPED
PURCHASE ORDER NUMBER:	PACK SLIP NUMBER
VOUCHER NUMBER:	AUTHORIZED BY:

COMPANY'S NAME _____

PURCHASE ORDER:	SHIPPER:
INVOICE NUMBER:	PACK SLIP NUMBER:
REJECTION NUMBER:	VIA:

Item	Quantity	Part No. Name and Description	Unit Price	Total Price

A-9 Credit memo.

A FRIENDLY REMINDER

No doubt you have overlooked payment, but if you have mailed your payment, please accept our thanks. If you have not mailed your payment, please take a moment to complete this form and return it along with your check. Thank You.

No.	
Date 1st Notice	

Account No.		Amount Due	
NAME			
ADDRESS			
CITY	STATE		ZIP CODE

Due Date	

Customer Report:

☐ PAYMENT ENCLOSED

☐ PAYMENT ALREADY MAILED

Date _____ No. _____

PAYMENT PAST DUE

Second Notice: It there is a reason for not paying this due amount please let us know. Your account is seriously overdue. Please complete this form and mail with your check today. Your credit is important.

No.	
Date 1st Notice	
Date 2nd Notice	

Account No.		Amount Due	
NAME			
ADDRESS			
CITY	STATE		ZIP CODE

Due Date	

Customer Report:

☐ PAYMENT ENCLOSED

☐ PAYMENT ALREADY MAILED

Date _____ No. _____

FINAL NOTICE !

After repeated requests to convince you to pay, we must now notify you that if we do not receive your payment in the next ten days from this notice, we will start collection proceedings to ensure recovery. We urge you to send your check now.

No.	
Date 1st Notice	
Date 2nd Notice	
Date	

Account No.		Amount Due	
NAME			
ADDRESS			
CITY	STATE		ZIP CODE

Due Date	

Customer Report:

☐ PAYMENT ENCLOSED

☐ PAYMENT ALREADY MAILED

Date _____ No. _____

A-10 Credit reminders.

DEBIT MEMORANDUM

Date:	
Debit No:	
Purchase Order Number:	
Account Number:	

VENDOR'S

INVOICE DATE	INVOICE NO.	PACKING NO.

Attention: CREDIT MANAGER

TO DEBIT YOUR ACCOUNT AS FOLLOWS:

☐ ERROR IN PRICE BILLED:

You billed $ _____ each

Purchase Order reads $ _____ each

Difference $ _____ @ No. of pieces _____ $ _____

☐ SETUP CHARGE - BILLED IN ERROR:

NOTE: *The above amount will not be paid until authorized by our buyer, and that any correspondance on the matter should be directed to* _____ *, Purchasing Department, When authorization has been approved, you must re-bill the Debit Memo amount.*

☐ ERROR IN QUALITY BILLED:

You billed _____

We received _____

Difference _____

Unit Price _____ $ _____

☐ OTHER:

Taxes, Purchase Order states: non taxable	$	_____
Freight charge, Purchase Order states: FOB	$	_____

We Debit $ _____

Signed _____

ACCOUNTS PAYABLE

A-11 Debit memorandum.

Position Applied For	Type of Employment		Date
	Full Time ☐ Summer ☐		
	Part Time ☐ Temporary ☐		

Name of Applicant   (please indicate how you wish to be addressed)

Surname	First Name	Initial (s)

Address   (No., Street, City, State, Zip Code)

Social Security Number	Telephone Number (Home) Business

Previous Address In the United States

Some positions in the company require that staff be bonded.

Are you bondable?   YES ☐   NO ☐
Have you ever been bonded?   YES ☐   NO ☐

Are you legally entitled to work in th e United States? ☐ YES ☐ NO	Are you willing to relocate? ☐ YES ☐ NO

Do you have a valid driver's license? ☐ YES ☐ NO   Class

Education

Secondary School attended and location.	Highest grade successfully completed.	Year Graduated

University attended and location.	No. of years completed	Year graduated	Degrees

Major subjects of specialization.

Community College attended and location.	No. of years completed	Year graduated	Degrees

Major subjects of spelcialization.

Other Educational Training/Courses.

Office/Secretarial Applications

Skill/Aptitude	Years of Experience	Words per minute	List secretarial training courses completed and any other training which maybe helpful in considering your application.
Typing			
Shorthand			

A-12 Employment application.

EMPLOYMENT HISTORY (List present or most recent positions first)

1. Name of Employer	Address	No.	Street	City
Type of Business	Department		Your Position	
Duties				

Name and Position of Immediate Supervisor

Date Employed (Day, Mo, Yr)	Date Left (Day, Mo, Yr)	Starting Salary	Final Salary

Reason for leaving.

2. Name of Employer	Address	No.	Street	City
Type of Business	Department		Your Position	
Duties				

Name and Position of Immediate Supervisor

Date Employed (Day, Mo, Yr)	Date Left (Day, Mo, Yr)	Starting Salary	Final Salary

Reason for leaving

3. Name of Employer	Address	No.	Street	City
Type of Business	Department		Your Position	
Duties				

Name and Position of Immediate Supervisor

Date Employed (Day, Mo, Yr)	Date Left (Day, Mo, Yr)	Starting Salary	Final Salary

Reason for leaving

MAY WE ASK YOUR PRESENT EMPLOYER FOR A REFERENCE ☐ YES ☐ NO

REFERENCES (Please do not list relatives or former employers)

Name	Occupation	Address

Whom do you know in this company?

EMPLOYMENT APPLICATION Page 2.

A-12 Continued.

Scholarships

Activities/Interests (Student, Professional, Community, etc.)

Publication, patents and thesis subjects

Languages (spoken, written, read) Note fluency

Other interests or hobbies

Special talents

| Medical | Do you agree to take a medical exam at company expense related to the essential requirements of the position. | ☐ YES | ☐ NO |

We appreciate your interest in seeking employment with us - please feel free to make any additional remarks in the space providedremarks in the space provided below or attach any additional information that would be helpful in evaluating your qualifications.

Additional Remarks

Please Read Carefully

I hereby certify that to the best of my knowledge and belief the answers given by me to the foregoing questions and all statements made by me in the application are correct.

If employed, I agree that all material created and produced whether in written, graphic or broadcasting form, all inventions new or changes in processes developed during my employment are the exclusive property of the company to use and/or sell and that subsequent to my employment with this company I will not disclose, use or reveal any confidential information related to the company without first obtaining written consent from an officer of the company.

I hereby apply for employment upon the basis and understanding that such employment may be termnated at any time upon notice given to me personally or sent to my last known address.

I consent to   **ABC CateringService**   obtaining such personal and job-related information as required in connection with this application.
for employment

_____   _____

Date   Signature of applicant

This application form complies with all Human Rights Legislation.

EMPLOYMENT APPLICATION Page 3.

A-12 Continued.

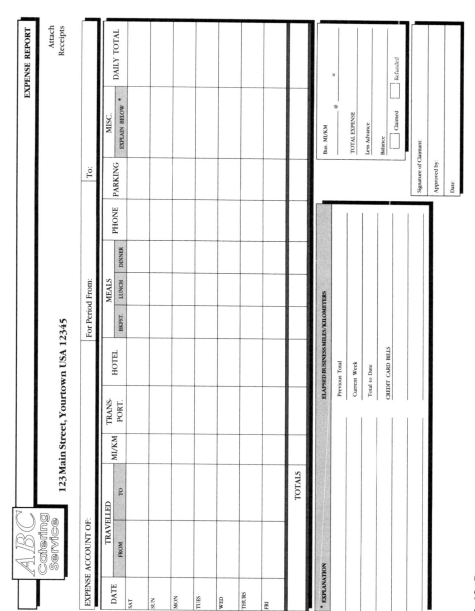

A-13 Expense report.

ABC Catering Service

Inventory

123 Main Street, Yourtown USA 12345

Date	
Page	of

Department :

Location :

Item#	Qty	Description	Price	Total
			TOTAL	

Priced By:	Called By:
Checked By:	Entered By:

A-14 Inventory worksheet.

DATE:

Comments:

Statement of Account

Date	Invoice Number	Description	Amount	Total
Amount Due Now			**Amount Remitted**	

Thank you for your prompt attention

In reviewing your account, we have determined that the above invoices have not been paid and are now past due. We would be most grateful for your prompt attention and remittance. If you have any questions or problems with this billing, please contact us immediately. If your remittance has already been sent out, please disregard this notice.

A-19 Payment past due.

PERFORMANCE REPORT

EMPLOYEE: DATE:

EVALUATE EMPLOYEE FROM 1-5 AND COMMENT IN SPACE PROVIDED

Team Player		
Meets Deadlines		
Organizational Skills		
Communication Skills		

Employer's Comments

Agreed Objectives

Date of Next Evaluation:

A-20 Performance report.

Date:

Code	Description	Unit Cost

A-21 Price list.

PROPOSAL

NUMBER

DATE

Proposal Submitted to:

NAME

ADDRESS

CITY   STATE   ZIP CODE

Job Site Information:

JOB NAME

JOB LOCATION

JOB PHONE

We hereby submit specifications and estimates for:

We hereby propose to furnish material and labor - complete in accordance with the above specifications for

_____ dollars $ _____

Payment to be made as follows:

All matter is guaranteed to be as specified. All work to be completed in a workmanlike manner according to standard practices. Any alternation or deviation from above specifications involving extra costs will be executed only upon written orders, and will become an extra charge over and above the estimate. All agreements contingent upon strikes, accidents, or delays beyond Our Company. Owner is to carry necessary insurance. Our Company workers are fully covered by Workman's Compensation Insurance.

Authorized Signature

X_____

Note: This proposal may be withdrawn by us if not accepted within _____ days

Acceptance of Proposal. The above prices and specifications are satisfactory and hereby accepted. You are authorized to do the work as specified. Payment will be made as outlined above.

X_____
Signature

X_____
Signature

_____
Date of Acceptance

A-22 Proposal.

PURCHASE ORDER

Purchased From:

Ship To:

Requisition By:

P.O. Number:

Date:

Ship Via:

F.O.B.:

Issued By:

Date Issued:

Quantity	Code	Description	Unit Cost	Total
			TOTAL	

Terms and Conditions

_____ _____
DATE   AUTHORIZED SIGNATURE

A-23 Purchase order.

TIME PERIOD FROM: TO:

P.O.#	Date	Issued To	For	Contact	Total

A-24 Purchase order log.

Date:

Quote #

Client: _____

_____

_____

_____

Materials

Quantity	Description	Cost Per Unit	Total
		Total Cost:	

Labor

	Hours	Description	Cost Per Hour	Total
REGULAR				
OVERTIME				
			Total Cost:	

GRAND TOTAL

_____   _____

Authorized Signature   Date

A-25 Quotation form.

Purchase Order No.:	Work Order No.:	Received From:
Invoice No.:	Invoice Amount:	Received At:

Shipped By:		
	PREPAID ☐ COLLECT ☐	CHARGES $_____ CHARGES $_____

Report all damages (including damage to cardboard boxes and crates) and shortages on all copies of the delivering carrier's freight bill and have the delivery person sign his/her name and date on all freight bill copies. Send the freight bill to the Purchasing Department with the Receiving Report. (Include Expense Report for collect payments.)

P.O. ITEM	QTY.	STOCK NUMBER	UNIT of MEAS.	DESCRIPTION	COND.

Comments (Explain damages, shortages, substitutions etc.)

Action to be taken

Received by:	Date:
Reported by:	Date:

COMPLETE ORDER ☐
PARTIAL SHIPMENT ☐

A-26 Receiving report.

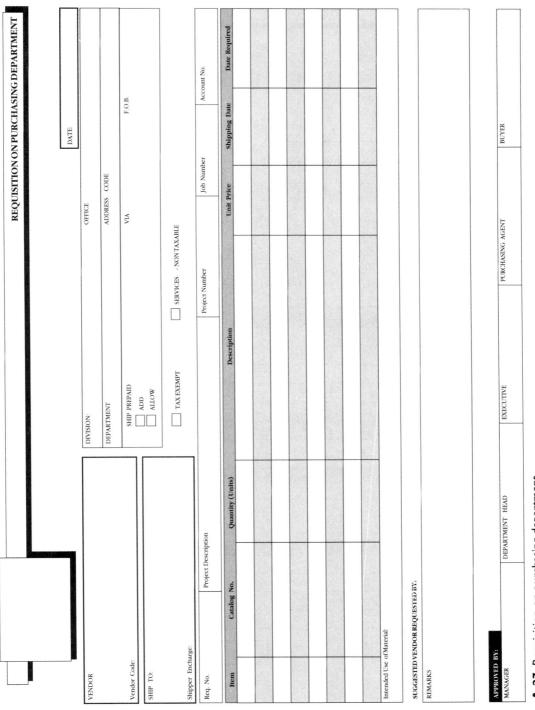

A-27 Requisition on purchasing department.

DATE:

TERRITORY:

SALES AND PROFIT	FORECAST	ACTUAL
Gross Sales		
Gross Profit		
% Gross Profit		
Net Profit		
% Net Profit to Gross Sales		

SELLING COST		
Salary		
Commision		
Auto Expense		
Travel Expense		
Telephone Expense		
Entertainment Expense		
Other Expense		

ACTIVITY		
Total Days Worked		
Number of Calls Made		
Average Number of Calls per Day		

ACCOUNT INFORMATION		
Number of New Accounts		
Number Of Accounts Lost		
Number of Accounts at End of Period		
Number of Potential Accounts		

Prepared by: _____

A-28 Salesperson's analysis.

TELEPHONE CALL RECORD

TIME PERIOD FROM: _____ TO: _____

Date	Caller	Call To	Company and Location	Code	Phone #	Charges

NOTES OR COMMENTS:

A-29 Telephone call record.

TIME SHEET

PERIOD END	MONTH	DAY	YEAR	PERSONNEL #	NAME	DIV

Description of Work	TIME DISTRIBUTION FOR PERIOD																Total Hours
	1	2	3	4	5	6	7	8	9	10	11	12	13	14	15	
	16	17	18	19	20	21	22	23	24	25	26	27	28	29	30	31	
Holiday																	
Personal Illness - Approved																	
Overtime																	
Total Hours																	

FOR INTERNAL USE ONLY

List of Expenses and Dollar Value (attach receipts)			
Description	$	Description	$
Total Expenses			

Overtime Approved By	Time Report Audited

PAGE   OF

A-30 Time sheet.

TRAVEL RESERVATION WORKSHEET

| Made By: |
| Travel Agent: |
| Accepted: |
| On: |

Employee Name:	Department:
Trip Origin:	Destination:
Departure Date:	Return Date:
Flight Reservation:	Class:

AIRLINE	FLIGHT	DATE	FROM	TO	TIME	
					DEP.	
					ARR.	
					DEP.	
					ARR.	
					DEP.	
					ARR.	
					DEP.	
					ARR.	
					DEP.	
					ARR.	
					DEP.	
					ARR.	

HOTEL ACCOMMODATIONS:

CAR RENTAL:

SPECIAL INSTRUCTIONS:

REASON FOR TRIP:

RESERVATIONS APPROVED BY: _____ DATE: _____
EMPLOYEE

_____
SUPERVISOR

A-31 Travel reservation worksheet.

LOCATION /ORG. UNIT			DATE
NAME	HOURS	CLASSIFICATION	DESCRIPTION OF WORK

REMARKS

The undersigned employee certifies that the above and foregoing is the actual, correct number of hours worked by him/her on the day stated, and that he/she has not been told or instructed by anyone having authority over him/her to incorrectly state the number of hours actually worked.

Employee's Signature _____

Supervisor's Signature _____

A-32 Weekly time report.

WORK ORDER

CUSTOMER ORDER NUMBER

NAME	LOCATION
ADDRESS	TELEPHONE NUMBER
CITY STATE ZIP	DATE OF ORDER

JOB NUMBER	JOB NAME	JOB LOCATION

DATE STARTED	TERMS	ORDER TAKEN BY

FOODS

Quantity	Description	Price	Amount
		TOTAL MATERIALS	

LABOR

Hours	Labor	Rate	Amount
		TOTAL LABOR	

Description of work done.

	SUB TOTAL
	TAX %
	TOTAL

WORK ORDER BY

I hereby acknowledge the satisfactory completion of work done.

A-33 Work order.

Index

About the author

Judy Richards has broad experience in business, teaching, and writing. Co-owner of a successful service business, Judy also instructs others on communication skills through a community college program. *Catering: Start and Run a Money-Making Business* is her third book. A native of Camas, Washington, Judy earned her masters degree from Iowa State University. She now lives in Reedsport, Oregon.